BUILDING CATHOLIC CHARACTER

BUILDING CATHOLIC CHARACTER

Developing Christian Life Skills

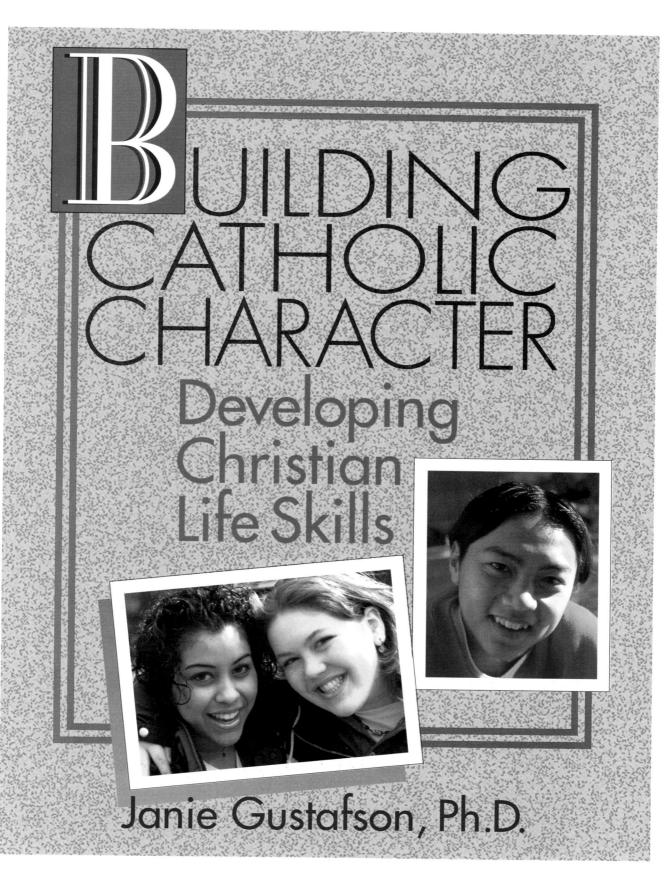

Janie Gustafson, Ph.D.

AVE MARIA PRESS   Notre Dame, Indiana 46556

Imprimatur: The Most Reverend Thomas J. O'Brien
                  Bishop of Phoenix

Given at Phoenix, AZ on 29 April 1998

The *Imprimatur* is an official declaration that a book is free of doctrinal or moral error. No implication is contained therein that those who have granted the *Imprimatur* endorse its contents, opinions, or statements expressed.

International Standard Book Number: 0-87793-642-0

Project Editor: Michael Amodei

Cover and text design by Katherine Robinson Coleman.

Cover photography by Skjold Photographs.

PHOTO CREDITS

Catholic News Service; 76, 144, 149, 150, 170, 176, 188.
National Baseball Hall of Fame Library, Cooperstown, NY; 161, 162.
Courtesy of University of Notre Dame Photographic; 121-122.
Arturo Mari 176.
Maggie Robinson; 136.
Skjold Photographs; cover, 3, 7, 10, 16, 17, 21, 26, 29, 31, 43-45, 59, 64, 66, 74, 87, 89, 91, 93, 99, 106, 108, 111, 112, 127, 141, 153, 158, 159, 165, 179, 181, 186, 207, 211, 217.
Wide World Photos; 225.
Wiechec; 144.
Jim Whitmer; 73, 203, 217.
Bill Wittman; 22, 192.

Printed and bound in the United States of America.

Contents

Dear Student,

Studying religion is very different from other academic disciplines. True, there are facts to learn and tests to take. Unlike other academic subjects, however, religion must be lived. It forms the backbone and substance of who we are—our very identity and character.

To succeed in this course will mean more than getting a good grade on a report card. Instead, it will mean how well you apply the contents of this course to your own thoughts, words, and actions. Your will not reach this goal easily or all at once. In fact, long after this course is over, applying its lessons will continue to be a challenge of your entire life.

Beginning a challenging adventure like this can be very exciting. It can also be rather frightening. You can't predict what lies ahead and what exactly will happen. You don't know how much or what kind of pain and suffering you will encounter along the way. It is important to remember that the name the prophet applied to Jesus of Nazareth was *Emmanuel,* which means *"God-is-with-us."* God is with you at all times and in all ways.

If you give this course your best efforts day by day, you will learn more about yourself. You will learn more about God. You will be able to see yourself as God sees you, with the eyes of love and pride for your goodness and worth.

A Chinese philosopher Lao Tzu once wrote, "A journey of a thousand miles begins with a single step." If you're reading and willing, take that first step now—knowing that Jesus and a large company of fellow Christians walk with you.

Janie Gustafson

PART 1

Human and Christian

Who are you?

What does it mean to be human?

What does it mean to be Christian?

Who Are You?

Knowing who you are is basic to being **human** and being **Christian.** In fact, self-knowledge is the foundation for everything you will think, feel, say, and do throughout life. Self-knowledge means understanding that the "divine image" is present in you and every other person (*Catechism of the Catholic Church*, 1702). God, your Creator, lives and works in you. By free will you are capable of finding perfection for yourself "in seeking and loving what is true and good" (CCC, 1704).

When you were a child, your identity was shaped mostly by your parents and teachers. You followed the lead of others. Now, as an adolescent, through prayer and reflection, you can begin to discover your true identity. You are mature enough to start taking responsibility for your own destiny. You can choose who you want to be, both now and in the future.

Consider the following tale from India:

The Lion-Sheep[1]

A lioness in search of prey came upon a flock of sheep, and as she jumped at one of them, she gave birth to a cub and died on the spot. The young lion was brought up in the flock, ate grass, and bleated like a sheep; it never knew that it was a lion. One day a lion came across this flock and was astonished to see in it a huge lion eating grass and bleating like a sheep. At his sight the flock fled and the lion-sheep with them. But the lion watched his opportunity and one day found the lion-sheep asleep. He woke him up and said, "You are a lion." The other said, "No," and began to bleat like a sheep. But the stranger lion took him to a lake and asked him to look in the water at his own image and see if it did not resemble him, the stranger lion. He looked and acknowledged that it did. Then the stranger lion began to roar and asked him to do the same. The lion-sheep tried his voice and was soon roaring as grandly as the other. And he was a sheep no longer.

Being Human

What does it mean to be human? Depending on whom you ask, you'll get a variety of answers.

For instance, if you ask a scientist, you'll get an answer something like this: A human being *(homo sapiens)* is a member of the animal kingdom. Humans are vertebrates (we have a spinal chord), warm-blooded (we maintain a constant body temperature), and mammals (females feed their live-born young with milk from their breasts, or mammary glands).

Although human beings are part of the animal kingdom, people have always known that they are different, apart from, and higher than animals. Think about it:

Animals are content with food, warmth, sex, and sleep. As humans, we share these basic needs, but we have many more needs as well. For example, we need friends and families. We need to understand the

---

1 Swami Vivekananda, *The Complete Works of Vivekananda*, Vol. I. (Mayavati: Advaita Ashrama, 1950), pp. 324–5.

world around us and to feel that we are understood by others. We need to shape the world and change it, re-creating it in ways that make our lives better. We need to achieve and feel that we are successful. We need to dream and believe that we have the power to make our dreams come true. Most importantly, we need to have a sense of meaning and purpose, that our lives are destined for a life beyond this world.

Animals are content with their lot. They live from day to day, in the present moment. Humans, however, are aware of the past, the present, and the future.

Relationships in the animal kingdom are based on the rule of "survival of the fittest." Only the strong, the healthy, survive. In the wilds, you won't find a leopard who is blind or a giraffe who is missing a leg. Such "weaklings" cannot fend for themselves. They soon die or are killed by other animals.

Humans, however, are capable of feeling compassion, kindness, and respect. Many humans feel a sense of responsibility to take care of other humans who are sick or who are mentally or physically handicapped.

Being Christian

Animals don't question their existence or their purpose in life. They simply exist. Humans, however, have the capacity to reflect, to reason, and to ask "Why?" Unlike animals, we have an immortal soul that lives on past death. We have a spiritual dimension, the capacity to relate to God.

What does it mean to be Christian? The following two chapters will help you answer this question.

LET'S TALK

1. What is your favorite animal? Why? In what ways would you want to be like that animal?

2. What are certain human characteristics given to specific animals (e.g., "sly as a fox")? Why do you think these traits are applied to animals?

3. What needs do you have that are beyond the needs of an animal?

4. What are some questions you have about life?

5. What do you think it means to have a spiritual dimension?

1. Your Spiritual Side

CHAPTER GOALS

In this chapter, you will:

- ◆ Discover that being fully human means recognizing and developing your spiritual side—searching for and finding meaning according to God's plan for your life.

- ◆ Understand the meaning of "good character" and begin to see how character affects a person's beliefs, attitudes, and actions.

- ◆ Explore ways you can grow spiritually.

All humans have a **spiritual** dimension, an inner restlessness, searching, and yearning for something more. Have you ever had your search for meaning, purpose, and personal identity expressed in a song you like? In this text, you will read some song lyrics related to specific themes. You will be asked to share other lyrics from your own favorite music. To begin, consider how the following lyrics of a Billy Joel song represent the search for something more:

> In the middle of the night, I go walking in my sleep, through the jungle of doubt, to a river so deep. I know I'm searching for something, something so undefined that it can only be seen by the eyes of the blind, in the middle of the night.[1]

The Search for Meaning

In order to be fully human, every person has to undertake a spiritual journey. This journey is a life-long quest, a searching for the answers to life's mysteries and ultimate meaning.

Thousands of years ago, people differed from you in the clothes they wore, their modes of transportation, and their lack of technology. The questions they asked about life's meaning, however, were very similar to the questions you are probably asking right now.

The ancient Israelites were slaves in Egypt. They yearned for something more. Daily, they searched for a clearer sense of their own identity. They knew there was more to being human than just their day-to-day work for Pharaoh. They also had a strong sense that the answers they sought were somehow connected to a personal relationship with God.

The answers did not come easily or quickly for the Israelites. Read the following scripture passages that tell about the Israelite's spiritual journey. Compare these passages to Billy Joel's song. How do the lyrics connect to the Israelite's experience?

LET'S TALK

1. What do you think the song lyrics mean?

2. What is something you are searching for in life?

Song Lyrics	Scripture Passage
In the middle of the night I go walking in my sleep. . .	Exodus 12:31–42

---

1 Billy Joel, "River of Dreams." Copyright © 1993 Impulsive Music. All rights controlled and administered by EMI April Music, Inc. All rights reserved.

Song Lyrics	Scripture Passage
to a river so deep	Exodus 13:17–22; 14:10–22
I hope it doesn't take the rest of my life until I find what I've been looking for	Numbers 14:26–38
through the jungle of doubt to a river so deep. . .	Numbers 33:50–54
to the promised land	Joshua 3:1–17

NOTABLE QUOTABLES

"The search for meaning is intrinsic to human nature. As thinking creatures, we want to understand why we find ourselves on this road and where the journey is taking us."

—William Bennett, *The Moral Compass*

"With God, nothing is empty of meaning."

—St. Irenaeus

For Your Eyes Only

1. In your spiritual journey thus far, what have been your "mountains of faith"? your "valleys of fear"? your "jungles of doubt"?

2. At this point in your life, describe your "promised land."

3. How do you think you will find this "promised land"?

DO THIS!

Write the lyrics of a song that has meaning for you. Explain why it reflects your search for meaning and purpose.

Having a Soul

Nobody knows what the immortal soul is or where it is located in the human body. And yet, Catholics believe the soul is the essence of who each person is, the innermost aspect and that which is of greatest value (*CCC*, 363). The soul is what enables you to believe in certain ideals, to have dreams and goals, to live by certain values, and to reach out to others in love. The soul is what enables you to ask questions such as "Who am I?" "Why am I here?" "What should I do with my life?" "What is my destiny?" and "What does life mean?" Furthermore, the soul is what gives you a certain **character.**

What is character? A printing press operator will tell you that a "character" is any letter or mark that is printed on a page. For an author every person in a story who is involved in a struggle or problem is a "character." There are good characters, there are bad characters, and there are characters who are in between.

A third definition of character is "a distinctive quality or trait that is etched into something permanently." It is all the attributes or features that make up a human being, that allow us to be accountable for ourselves and enable us to act responsibly toward God and others.

Character is not the same as personality. Two people with happy-go-lucky personalities, for example, can have totally different characters. Character is also very different from your emotions or moods, which can change from day to day or hour by hour.

Rather, character is something stable, something that is always there. Your character affects everything you think, feel, and do. It gives you a specific outlook on life. It colors your attitudes and emotions. It affects the words you say and the actions you engage in.

A person of good character lives by good values. He or she is usually considered to be someone to admire and imitate. A person of bad character tends to choose **vice** instead of **virtue, sin** instead of lawfulness. He or she is usually seen as someone to avoid.

Christians believe that the more good character we have, the more human we become. Having good character is also associated with relating better with others and with being happy. How would you describe your own character?

Different Characters

Recent U.S. Census figures report that there are approximately 41 million 10–18-year-olds living in this country. While these young people have many things in common, each one has a different character. The following real-life stories provide a sampling of some of the various characters of today's teenagers. Read about each one. Discuss the questions that follow.

Two Arizona Teens [2]

A 13-year-old girl did all the right things yesterday when a man broke into her home while she was alone. The girl said she woke up when the man "rang the doorbell over and over again" at about 10:30 a.m. at her house. When she didn't answer the door, she saw the man go around to the side of the house. She ran into her bedroom, locking the door behind her, and called 911 on the cordless phone next to her bed. When she heard glass breaking in the kitchen, she went into the bathroom, locked the door, and began describing what was going on to the 911 operator.

By then, six police officers were on their way to the house.

The girl said she could hear the burglar "opening and shutting drawers" and going into different rooms. She kept talking to the 911 dispatcher, describing what she could hear. Then she heard the man "bumping hard" against the bathroom door.

She also heard police yell: "You're surrounded! Give up!"

Carlos M., 18, was arrested. Police found a stereo, a videocassette recorder, and a camera stacked up and ready to be taken out of the house. Carlos M. was charged with first-degree burglary and theft and was being held last night on a $50,000 bond in the county jail.

California Teen [3]

In Los Angeles, a 15-year-old boy killed his employers at an ice-cream store after they mildly criticized his tardiness. As the husband and wife drove him home one night, the teen pulled a sawed-off shotgun from his book bag, shot them both in the head, and stole the day's receipts.

LET'S TALK

1. What traits do you associate with good character?

2. Give an example of the best character and the worst character in a book you read, video game you played, or TV show you saw recently. Discuss the reasons for your choices.

3. What does it mean to say that a person acted "out of character"?

NOTABLE QUOTABLES

"What am I? I am myself a word spoken by God. Can God speak a word that has no meaning?"

—Thomas Merton, *Contemplative Prayer*

"It is the peculiarity of humans, in comparison with the rest of the animal world, that they alone possess a perception of good and evil, of the just and the unjust."

—Aristotle

Teen From Texas[4]

When Logan Johnson stopped his car while delivering pizza in North Dallas, he may have saved two lives—one of them his own. Around 8 p.m. on a Wednesday night, Johnson, then 17, spotted a car rolling into a pond. He ran to the water and plunged in. Johnson pulled open a rear door. As the car sank, he dragged the driver—the Rev. John Kershaw, 65, who had lost consciousness while driving—over the back seat and to the shore.

At the time of the rescue, Johnson's own life was floundering. He had dropped out of high school, had family troubles, and was on antidepressants. But saving a life gave Johnson a new outlook on his own life. He returned to school, enrolled in the Marine Reserves, and now plans to go to college. "You can't explain how it feels to save someone's life," Johnson said. "I value friends, family, school, everything, a lot more than I did. Five minutes turned it all around."

North Carolina Teen[5]

On a June night in 1996, a 13-year-old white girl was charged with setting fire to an old wooden sanctuary on the grounds of a black church the previous week in Charlotte. Investigators refused to provide the identity or motive of the girl, although one said she "was a very troubled teenager" who confessed to setting the fire.

Investigators said they believed she had acted alone, used material she found in the 93-year-old white clapboard building, and had not been involved in other church fires. The girl will be tried in juvenile court.

In a small group, discuss the following questions. Copy each grid in your notebook, filling in the group's answers. Be prepared to share your group's thoughts with the class.

1. Based on each teen's actions, what do you think is each one's most important value or priority in life? How do you think each teen would define what it means to be human?

	Top Value	Being Human
AZ Female		
AZ Male		
CA Teen		
TX Teen		
NC Teen		

2. How are character and humanness connected?

4 Lyric Wallwork Winik, "'I Just Reacted—I Don't Know How,'" *Parade Magazine* (June 2, 1996), p. 6.
5 *The New York Times* (June 11, 1996).

Good Character and Heroism

Not every person with good character turns out to be a hero. But heroes almost always have some degree of good character. The following Mexican folk tale will give you some insights into how good character and heroism are connected.

A True Hero

PART 1: Once there was a very old man in Guadalajara who was about to die. He wanted to leave a diamond, the only wealth he had, to one of his three sons. But he could not decide which one should get it. He called the three sons into his room and told them:

"My sons, I am not a rich man. The only thing I have that is worth much is this diamond. It has been in our family for generations, and I would not want it to be sold. Because it cannot be sold or divided, I can give it to only one of you. I will give the diamond to the one who accomplishes the greatest good in a week's time. Go now. Return in a week to tell me what you have done."

PART 2: A week passed and the sons returned. They found their father even weaker than before and unable to leave his bed. He asked each son to tell what he had done. "My father," said the first son, "I made a list of all my property, divided it in half, and gave one half to the poor people in this city."

"Father," said the second son, "when I was returning home from work one day, I saw a little girl caught in the Rio Grande River. I can hardly swim, but I jumped into the river. I almost drowned, but I pulled the girl out and saved her life."

"Father, a wonderful thing happened to me," said the third son. "One morning I saw a man wrapped in a blanket, sleeping at the edge of a cliff. If he moved at all in his sleep, he would certainly fall over the cliff, thousands of feet down into the valley below! I came quietly closer, because I didn't want to frighten him. And guess who the man was? Sancho, my worst enemy! He has threatened many times to kill me if he had a chance.

"I moved as close as I could to the man. I put my arms gently around him. Suddenly his eyes opened and he looked into mine. I saw that he was afraid, so I told him not to be afraid and I rolled him away from the cliff.

"He told me that he had come that way the night before. It was so dark and he was too tired to continue. So he walked off the path and went to sleep. He had no idea where he was. If he had walked any farther or turned in his sleep, he would have been killed. Sancho said, 'You saved my life—friend—after I threatened to kill you!'

"We went into one another's arms and swore to be friends forever. We wept and understood that each of us found a friend, although we had been enemies before."

LET'S TALK

If someone asked you to accomplish the greatest good in a week's time, what would you do? Be realistic!

LET'S TALK

If you were the old man about to die, to which son would you give your diamond? Why?

15

Scripture

LET'S TALK

According to the story, the strongest trait of good character is a willingness to love an enemy. Do you agree or disagree?

1. Compare the following passages to each son's actions:
◆ First son—Matthew 19:16–22
◆ Second son—Mark 5:21–24, 35–43
◆ Third son—Matthew 5:43–48

2. What does each passage tell us about the character traits Christians are to have?

PART 3: This is what the old man decided:

He said to the first son, "Ah, that is good, but not good enough. Everyone should help the poor as much as possible."

He said to the second son, "That is good, too. Everyone should be willing to risk their own life to save a child."

Then he said to the third son, "This is a beautiful story and an example of someone becoming a hero by a good action. Very few will risk their lives to help the enemy. You are a truly great man. This diamond is yours."[6]

A Day-by-Day Challenge

Developing good character and becoming more human is not something that happens overnight. The process is made up of many daily choices and the consequences of those choices.

Some of these choices are related to those of the sons in the story:

◆ to give to the poor. St. John Chrysostom wrote: "Not to enable the poor to share in our goods is to steal from them and deprive them of life. The goods we possess are not ours, but theirs."

◆ to lay one's life down for another. Jesus' command to love when taken to its greatest extreme is to give up one's life for another person. Sometimes this involves heroic life-saving actions. Mostly it involves smaller daily actions that are given as pure gift from one person to another.

6 Adapted from "The Noblest Deed" from Grant Lyons, *Tales the People Tell in Mexico* (New York: Julian Messner, a division of Simon & Schuster, 1972).

Another way to gauge your character development is by how well you develop your spiritual side. Some people develop their spirituality by spending time in natural settings—a garden, the beach, a hiking trail, a quiet meadow. Others grow spiritually by reading the Bible. Some people like to write their spiritual reflections and questions in a private journal.

The Catholic church describes seven special ways to grow spiritually. These ways are called the **spiritual works of mercy.** They are as follows:

1. *Counsel the doubtful.* Do you have a friend who is confused? who is having a problem with parents, with school, or with another friend? Spending time listening to your friend is an important way to offer support and encouragement. Your words may help your friend see his or her way clear through a difficult situation.

2. *Instruct the ignorant.* Think of all the things you have learned since you were a child. Have you ever thought about sharing your knowledge as a religious education volunteer in your parish? What about teaching English to a new immigrant? reading stories to sick children in the hospital? helping a younger child with a piano lesson? Sharing your knowledge with someone else can add meaning to that person's life and to your own.

3. *Admonish the sinner.* Have you ever been with a friend when he or she did something wrong? Perhaps he shoplifted or she lipped off to her younger sister. You didn't say anything, however, because you were afraid you would be ridiculed or lose your friend. As the saying goes, "silence gives consent." By not saying anything, you're giving your friend the impression that you approve of his or her behavior. True friends, however, are honest with one another. They help one another become their best selves.

4. *Comfort the sorrowful.* Do you know the meaning of the term "fair-weather friend"? This kind of friend is someone who is around when you are happy, but disappears when things are going badly and you are sad or hurting. One way to let others know that you truly care for them and that they are worthwhile is to spend time with them when things are not so great. Letting someone cry or talk about a problem in front of you without worrying about being ridiculed can provide that person with an important sense of hope and being valued.

5. *Forgive injuries.* At your age, you have likely been hurt physically, emotionally, or spiritually at least once. If the person who hurts you wants your forgiveness, it is important to give it. No one is perfect. Accepting the person back as a friend can be the start of even greater understanding between the two of you.

6. *Bear wrongs patiently.* It's hard not to get angry and want to retaliate when you feel you've been treated unfairly. Keeping your "cool" in such a situation can be an inspiration to others. Refraining from destructive words and behaviors is the meaning of this work of mercy. Your action or inaction can encourage others to be strong and courageous in their own situations of unfairness.

7. *Pray for the living and the dead.* It's never too late for a person to change for the better. Your prayers can have a powerful effect for good. Remember, Jesus pointed out that great faith can move mountains. God always listens to and answers those who are sincere.

Prayer

LEADER: God has given us a wonderful gift by giving us human life. Let us spend a few moments now reflecting on what it means to be human, to be spiritual, and to have a good character.

READER: Psalm 8

ALL: Loving Creator, we thank you for giving us minds to think with, for filling us with knowledge and intelligence. We thank you for giving us the ability to dream and to set goals for ourselves. We thank you for giving us hearts that enable us to feel love and concern for others. Continue to put your light in us. Teach us how to become more human and heroic in all our actions. Amen.

Further Activities

1. Search through recent newspapers and magazines to find examples of people who show that they have good character, that they are truly being human. Report your findings to the class.

2. Prepare a report on one of the following people. How did the person show heroic character?

◆ St. Maria Goretti   ◆ Jackie Robinson
◆ Helen Keller   ◆ Abraham Lincoln
◆ Lou Gehrig   ◆ Oscar Romero
◆ Harriet Tubman

3. Keep a journal with ideas for how you can develop your spiritual side. Include ideas like the following: (1) pray (both alone and with others); (2) become involved in the arts (e.g., dance, painting, sculpture, etc.); (3) participate in Sunday and weekday liturgies; (4) celebrate the sacrament of reconciliation.

4. Write a poem, compose a song, draw a picture, or create something artistic (collage, sculpture, or craft) that expresses what you think it means to be fully human.

At Home

Compliment a family member on his or her good character.

2. Christian Character

CHAPTER GOALS

In this chapter, you will:

- See that Christian character requires developing a loving, personal relationship with the Trinity.
- Realize that Christian character is grounded in faith in Jesus and hope in his message about God's kingdom.
- Discover how the Holy Spirit is within you, helping you reach out in love to others.

According to a recent poll conducted by *U.S. News & World Report*, 95% of all Americans say they believe in God or a universal spirit. The poll also reported these findings:

- 68% are members of a church,
- 60% attend religious services regularly,
- 80% believe the Bible is the inspired word of God, and
- 33% believe God is always with them during a crisis.

Such statistics, however, do not tell the whole story. Even though a majority of the nation claims to be religious, there remain a great number of heinous crimes committed that oppose good moral character and the beliefs of most religions. Just think about the number of violent crimes committed each year in our country, or consider these three real-life stories:

- A 14-year-old student at York High School in Dupage County, IL, stabbed three students after being teased about his Satanic beliefs. Two of the victims were hospitalized. The boy reportedly carved an upside-down cross on his arm after being arrested.
- Two girls, ages 12 and 13, carried out a Satanic murder-suicide pact in Montgomery County, Maryland. Both girls had told school friends they wanted to die so they could "meet Satan."
- A 19-year-old young man who had practiced Satanism for at least four years was charged with killing his 38-year-old mother. Police and medical reports show that she had been stabbed 40 times. Her throat had also been slit.[1]

F.Y.I.

There are more churches per people in the United States than in any other nation on earth. There is one church for about every 900 Americans.

In each of these instances, teenagers rejected Christianity and other mainstream religions. They turned, instead, to **Satanism**—the worship of the devil. They engaged in a lifestyle of perversion, in which they upheld evil and ridiculed moral goodness.

Why?

Why do some teens turn to Satanism? Some teens are angry at the teachings of traditional churches; they turn to devil worship as an act of defiance against parents and authority. Some teens feel that God has not

---

1 Elizabeth Karlsberg, "Satanism: The Scary Truth," *Teen Magazine* (June, 1993), p. 24.

answered their prayers; they need to participate in some type of symbolic ritual action that is "effective." Others feel bored and lonely; they need to belong somewhere and have friends. Still others feel overstressed and powerless about their lives; they think that Satan will give them the power they seek.

Here is one teen's experience:

"I was never very popular . . . kind of kept to myself most of the time," says David (not his real name). "One day at lunch, this guy came up to me. He seemed pretty cool, like he had it all together. He invited me to a party, and I decided to go.

"They were playing this weird music, and people were drinking and doing drugs. They all seemed to be having a good time. It wasn't until this guy took me into a room—painted black, with candles everywhere and these posters of skulls with wings and stuff, that I realized these people were into something different. Even though it kind of freaked me out, I felt like, hey, these people want me to be a part of them. It felt really good.

"Pretty soon, I was going to cemeteries with them, doing rituals. We'd dig up graves, cut up animals and hang them from trees. Some of the people would drink blood. I never got into that, but my grades started dropping, and I got into drugs.

"Eventually, my parents went ballistic. They said I couldn't hang out with these people anymore. Then they forced me to see a therapist. I'd go, but at first I'd just tell a bunch of lies. Then, I don't know how, but the therapist made me see how messed up I was and how my life wasn't better because of Satanism. My life was just a big lie." [2]

Scripture

Read and discuss each of the following scripture passages. What do Christians believe about Satan? How are Christians to act with regard to Satan's temptations?

◆ Matthew 4:1–11
◆ John 8:42–44
◆ Matthew 12:22–28
◆ Luke 13:10–17
◆ Romans 16:17–20

Becoming Christian

Although you are continuing to develop in many ways, being human is who you *already* are. You don't *become* human. You are created human from the moment of your conception. Christian character, however, is another story. Christian character is an identity you can choose to accept or to reject. In order to *be* Christian, you first have to *become* Christian.

The process of becoming Christian involves developing a loving, personal relationship with God, with other members of the Christian community, and with the world. It means following the teachings of Jesus, God's own Son, and being open to the inspirations of the Holy

---

2 Elizabeth Karlsberg, "Satanism: The Scary Truth," *Teen Magazine* (June, 1993), p. 25.

LET'S TALK

1. What "values" do the teens in these stories seem to have?

2. Why do you think some teens turn to Satanism, rather than the worship of God?

3. Do you know of any teens involved in Satanism? How big of a problem is it in your town or city?

LET'S TALK

1. What do you think David really wants out of life? Why did he get involved in Satanism?

2. Do you think Satanism really delivers the power and happiness it promises? Explain.

Spirit through the teachings of the pope and bishops, the successors to the apostles, and through the living example of the people of faith who are part of your life. Becoming Christian is a life-long journey of **conversion**—a turning away from sin and evil and a turning toward the way of Jesus.

F.Y.I.

Every year, on or near Holy Thursday, the bishop blesses the oils that will be used in every parish of his diocese. The three different kinds of oils that are blessed are chrism (used at baptism, confirmation, and holy orders), oil of the sick (used at anointing of the sick), and oil of catechumens (used to bless those preparing for baptism).

In order to understand more fully what Christian conversion means, it helps to look more closely at the sacrament of **baptism**. Through this ritual action, people mark the first "official" step to becoming members of the church.

Presently, the Catholic church has two ways to receive new members: the Rite of Baptism of Infants and Children, and the Rite of Christian Initiation of Adults **(RCIA)**. Both rites celebrate the same reality—the gift of God's grace in allowing us to die to evil and to rise to a new life in which we assume Christ's own character. Both baptismal rites contain the following parts:

1. *Liturgy of the Word with prayers of intercession.* Because Catholics believe that the Bible is the inspired word of God that gives us life, one or two scripture readings (especially one from the gospels) are read aloud. The priest or deacon then gives a short homily. All those assembled pray for the needs of the community (the prayers of intercession) and ask the **saints** to be with those being baptized (the litany of saints).

2. *Prayer of Exorcism.* An **exorcism** is a rite in which evil spirits are driven out of a person or place by the authority of God and with the prayer of the Church. In the prayer of exorcism, the church prays that those being baptized will be delivered from original sin and all personal sins. (In the RCIA, rites of exorcism take place during Lent.) The prayer is followed by an anointing with the **oil of catechumens**. This oil is a symbol of the wisdom, strength, and protection from evil that Christ brings to all Christians.

3. *Blessing of water, renunciation of sin, and profession of faith.* The priest or deacon blesses the water and then invites the baptismal candidate (or, in the case of a baby, the godparents and parents) to promise to reject Satan and to profess faith in all that Christians believe. This profession of faith is based on the Apostles' Creed.

4. *Baptism with water.* The actual baptism may be performed in one of two ways—by **immersion** of the whole body or of the head

For Your Eyes Only

When were you baptized?
Where were you baptized?
Who are your godparents?

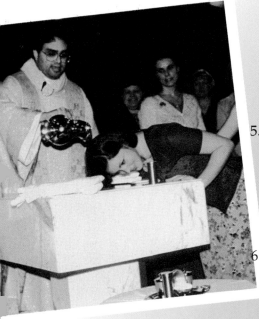

only, or by **infusion,** the pouring of water over the person's head. As this action is taking place, the priest or deacon calls the person by name and says, "I baptize you in the name of the Father, and of the Son, and of the Holy Spirit." The ritual action recalls the Israelites' journey from slavery to freedom through the Reed Sea, as well as Jesus' death and resurrection to new life. The ritual words recall the belief that God has called each of us by name to be his own. (See Isaiah 43:1–3.) They also fulfill Jesus' command to baptize all nations in the name of the Trinity. (See Matthew 28:16–20.)

5. *Anointing with chrism.* **Chrism** is a blessed oil (olive or vegetable oil mixed with balm) that is used only at the sacraments of baptism, confirmation, and holy orders. This ritual action shows that the person has been marked with a new, "indelible" character, something that can never be erased. The oil is a sign that the newly baptized person shares in the priesthood of Christ and is a member of the People of God, the church.

6. *Clothing with a white garment and receiving the lighted candle.* Clothing the newly baptized person in a white garment symbolizes that he or she has "put on" Christ and will work to grow in Christian character. (See Romans 13:12–14.) The lighted candle symbolizes the person's promise to follow Jesus, the light of the world who casts out all evil and darkness. (See John 8:12.)

7. *Prayer over the ears and mouth.* This ritual action reminds us of the time Jesus cured a deaf-mute by saying the word *ephphetha,* which means "Be opened." (See Mark 7:31–37.) The priest or deacon touches the person's ears and mouth, praying that he or she will be open to hearing and living God's word throughout life. (In the RCIA, this rite occurs during Lent.)

8. *Conclusion.* The community celebrates the newly baptized "son or daughter of God" by praying together the Lord's Prayer, in which everyone present recognizes God as a loving Father. Finally, there is a prayer of blessing for the new Christian.

The Basics of Christianity

Baptism celebrates the fundamental belief that we are children of God, made in God's image. As the Book of Genesis tells us, "God created humankind in his image, in the image of God he created them; male and female he created them" (1:27). To understand the nature of Christian character, then, it is important to explore what we mean by *God.*

Christians, following centuries of Jewish tradition, believe there is only one God who always existed and who always will exist. Unlike the Jews, Christians believe that God is a **Trinity**—three Persons in one God. God is Father, Son, and Holy Spirit. The mystery of the Holy Trinity is the central mystery of the Christian faith and of life itself (CCC, 234).

Christians are baptized in the name of the Father, Jesus, and the Holy Spirit. Whenever we make the Sign of the Cross or pray the

DO THIS!

Attend a baptism in your own parish. Report to the class about how the actions and symbols of the rite affected you and symbolize what you, as a Christian, believe.

Doxology ("Glory be. . ."), we profess our belief that:

◆ We are loved by God who is Creator;

◆ We belong to the body of Christ, the Christian community; and

◆ We are temples of the Holy Spirit.

These beliefs are not based on abstract theory; instead, they stem from our own experience and the experiences of Christians who have lived before us. They represent the three distinct ways that Catholics have come to know and relate to God's presence in their lives. The doctrine of the Trinity, officially declared at the Council of Nicea and the Council of Constantinople, both in the fourth century, was experienced from the time of Jesus' own baptism when the presence of Father, Son, and Holy Spirit were witnessed and testified to. (See Mark 1:9-11.)

God as Father

One of the most startling teachings of Jesus is that God is our "Abba," or "Daddy." God is not an impersonal force that rules the universe with no care for us as individuals. Instead, God is extremely personal, intimate, caring, and loving. God not only created us but continues to sustain us and breathe life into us. God is our good Parent, who "gives us this day our daily bread," who "leads us not into temptation," and who "delivers us from evil."

A Christian, then, sees himself or herself as a child of God the Father. Christians remain continually open and receptive to God's self-revelation. God has made himself known in stages throughout history. In this final stage, God has spoken to us through his Son. In Jesus, God has "said" everything. Christians learn to see with the "eyes of faith"; to see how Jesus sees, to understand that Jesus and the Father are one. Christians discover God's presence in all things and search for God's will in all situations. Christians believe in a loving God who knows our individual needs and provides us with all we need for our salvation.

Scripture

One of the ways Christians discover God's self-revelation is in the Bible. Read the following passages. In a small group, discuss what each one tells you about God the Father.

◆ Matthew 6:1–8   ◆ Luke 10:21–22

◆ Luke 12:22–31   ◆ Matthew 20:1–16

◆ Matthew 7:7–11   ◆ Luke 15:11–32

Having Faith

"**Faith**," according to the letter to the Hebrews, "is the realization of what is hoped for and evidence of things not seen." With faith, we trust that God knows us and loves us. Faith in a loving and caring God affects our sense of dignity and purpose. We exist to know God. We exist to love God. We come to understand that God intends a unique purpose for our lives.

LET'S TALK

Name and describe a human parent who models God the Father for you.

The Late Bloomer[3]

A cactus stood all alone in the desert, wondering why it was stuck in the middle of nowhere.

"I do nothing but stand here all day," it sighed. "What use am I? I'm the ugliest plant in the desert. My spines are thin and prickly. My leaves are rubbery and tough. My skin is thick and bumpy. I can't offer shade or juicy fruit to any passing traveler. I don't see that I'm any use at all."

All the cactus did was stand in the sun day after day, growing taller and fatter. Its spines grew longer and its leaves tougher, and it swelled here and there until it was lumpy and lopsided all over. It truly was strange-looking.

"I wish I could do something useful," it sighed.

NOTABLE QUOTABLE

"Faith is the courage that conquers doubt, not by removing it, but by taking it as an element into itself."

—Paul Tillich, *The Eternal Now*

For Your Eyes Only

According to the *Catechism of the Catholic Church*: "By calling God 'Father,' the language of faith indicates two main things: that God is the first origin of everything and transcendent authority; and that he is at the same time goodness and loving care for all his children" (#239).

1. What are some parts of creation that speak to you of God as Creator?

2. God is the perfect parent. List some qualities that you perceive are essential to perfect parenthood.

By day the hawks circled high overhead. "What can I do with my life?" the cactus called. Whether they heard or not, the hawks sailed away.

At night the moon floated into the sky and cast its pale glow on the desert floor. "What good can I do with my life?" the cactus called. The moon only stared coldly as it mounted its course.

A lizard crawled by, leaving a little trail in the sand with its tail. "What worthy deed can I do?" the cactus called.

"You?" the lizard laughed, pausing a moment. "Worthy deed? Why, you can't do anything! The hawks circle way overhead, tracing delicate patterns for us all to admire. The moon hangs high like a lantern at night, so we can see our ways home to our loved ones. Even I, the lowly lizard, have something to do. I decorate the sands with these beautiful brush strokes as I pull my tail along. But you? You do nothing but get uglier every day."

And so it went on, year after year. At last the cactus grew old, and it knew its time was short.

"Oh, Lord," it cried out., "I've wondered so long, and I've tried so hard. Forgive me if I've failed to find something worthy to do. I fear that now it's too late."

But just then the cactus felt a strange stirring and unfolding, and it

---

3 Adapted from William Bennett, *The Moral Compass* (New York: Simon & Schuster, 1995), pp. 718–19.

felt a new surge of joy that erased all despair. At its very tip, like a sudden crown, a glorious flower opened in bloom. Never had the desert known such a blossom. Its fragrance perfumed the air far and wide and brought happiness to all passing by. The butterflies paused to admire its beauty, and that night even the moon smiled when it rose to find such a treasure.

The cactus heard a voice. "You have waited long," the Lord said. "The heart that seeks to do good reflects my glory, and will always bring something worthwhile to the world, something in which all can rejoice—even if for only a moment."

Because we believe that we are made in God's image, our Christian faith brings us to several other realizations. First, to be truly happy, we must find oneness or communion with God. Only God can fill us up and make us satisfied. Second, even though we don't understand why we were born or why we have to suffer in certain ways, God knows what is best for us. There is a purpose for everything. We have a reason for being here. Our lives have meaning.

God as Son

Christians believe that Jesus is both human and divine. Jesus is the second Person of the Trinity, existing with God forever. As we profess in the Nicene Creed at Sunday Mass, Jesus is one with the Father, "begotten, not made, true God from true God." Jesus is God himself (CCC, 454).

At the same time, Christians believe that Jesus was fully human, like us in every way except sin. He sweated, had aches and pains, grew tired, felt hungry, and got appropriately angry. His death on the cross was not an "improvisation." He really suffered and died, offering himself to the Father in atonement for the sins of the world.

Through his life and his death, Jesus taught us the meaning of having genuine love for others. As the three Persons of the Trinity act in communion with one another, we too share in this **community** in each of these instances:

◆ whenever a man and woman truly love one another in a committed marriage (see Matthew 19:3–6),

◆ when two or more people gather to pray (see Matthew 18:19–20),

◆ when friends share food with one another (see John 6:1–14),

◆ when people console a friend who is grieving (see John 11:1–45), and

◆ when people help the poor, the homeless, or the sick (see Matthew 25:31–40).

Moreover, Jesus taught us what it means to love God "with all your heart, and with all your soul, and with all your mind" (Matthew 22:37)—to surrender completely in trust and obedience to God's will. (Matthew 26:36–46.) He taught us what it means to love "our neighbors as ourselves" (Matthew 22:39)—to lay down one's life for one's friends (John 15:12–13).

NOTABLE QUOTABLES

"Our hearts are restless, O God, until they rest in You."

—St. Augustine

"I have been made for heaven and heaven for me."

—St. Joseph Cafasso

LET'S TALK

Describe a time when other people revealed God's presence to you in each of the following situations:

◆ in a committed marriage.

◆ in praying with others.

◆ in eating a meal with friends.

◆ in consoling someone who is grieving.

◆ in welcoming a stranger.

For Your Eyes Only

1. What is your first memory of Jesus?

2. What is your favorite gospel story?

Developing a Christian character means trying to live like Jesus: growing in holiness, participating in the Christian community, and caring about, praying for, and acting on behalf of the welfare of others.

Having Hope

In all his actions and teachings, Jesus gave people **hope.** His basic message was this: "The kingdom of heaven, the reign of God, is here among you." (See Matthew 4:17.) This kingdom is not a specific place we can find on a map. Rather, the **kingdom of God** is the presence of God in our lives. The kingdom was initiated by Jesus through living examples of justice, peace, love, joy, and mercy. The kingdom of God is fully realized in eternity.

How do you imagine the eternal kingdom of God?

NOTABLE QUOTABLE

"Hope warms the heart. Humans cannot exist without a future. To concentrate on the present only is inhuman. We need a dream. The tension between our dream and our present becomes a life-giving force; from such a force new worlds are born."

—Ladislaus Orsy, *The Lord of Confusion*

Scripture

If you could design a world of perfect relationships, what would it be like? Read the following descriptions of God's kingdom. Discuss and summarize their meaning. Based on your findings, design a newspaper ad for God's kingdom to "sell" others on the idea. Be as specific as possible and be prepared to share your group's vision with the class.

◆ Matthew 13:3–9, 18–23   ◆ Matthew 13:45–46
◆ Matthew 13:24–30, 36–43 ◆ Matthew 13:47–50
◆ Matthew 13:31–32   ◆ Matthew 18:23–35
◆ Matthew 13:33   ◆ Matthew 25:1–13
◆ Matthew 13:44   ◆ Mark 4:26–29

Jesus, Our Hope

To prove that God's kingdom—perfect relationships with others—is possible, Jesus brought people hope in tangible, visual ways. He cured the sick, enabled the lame to walk, gave speech to the mute, empowered the blind to see, helped the deaf hear, freed people from demons, and raised the dead. He gave people hope that life could be different, somehow better.

Christians today share this same hope. We trust that our efforts to get along with others are helping to make God's kingdom a reality. We trust that God's kingdom will one day come in fullness. Because we have hope, we can approach all relationships with a positive attitude. Even when things go wrong, we can persevere and never give up. Furthermore, we can approach life with joy and laughter because "with God, all things are possible" (Matthew 19:26).

God as Holy Spirit

Unlike the second Person of the Trinity who took human form, we cannot see the Holy Spirit with our eyes. However, we can sense the very real presence of this third Person of the Trinity in other ways. Here are some analogies:

◆ You can't see wind, but you can feel it on your skin and see its effects on your hair, clothes, and other objects. You *know* the wind is there.

◆ You put out birdseed for the wild doves. You watch for a long time at the window, but never see any doves. The next morning, the food you put out is gone and near it are bird droppings. From these signs, you *know* the doves have been there.

◆ Suppose you are a firefighter. You enter a house that is filled with smoke, but you don't know for sure where the fire is. You touch a door to the next room and feel that it is hot. You *know* the fire is there behind the door.

These experiences so closely resemble our experience of the third person of the Trinity, that the Holy Spirit is often described as the wind, a dove, or fire. We *know* God's Spirit is active in us by the effects the Spirit produces in us. These effects, which are called the **fruits of the Spirit,** are "love, joy, peace, patience, kindness, generosity, faithfulness, gentleness, and self-control" (Galatians 5:23). We actually *feel* these effects of the dimension of God who is within.

Scripture

Read the following passages that describe God's Spirit. Discuss what the passages mean. Then, as a group, write your own description of what the Holy Spirit is like.

◆ Matthew 3:11   ◆ Mark 1:12   ◆ John 1:32–33   ◆ Acts 2:2–3
◆ Luke 3:22   ◆ Matthew 3:16   ◆ John 3:8

True Christian Spirit

The best sign of the Holy Spirit is **love**. The Father and Son love each other with an eternal, perfect love. This love between Father and Son is the third Person of the Trinity, the Holy Spirit. Hence, the Holy Spirit is often described as a "Spirit of Love." With the Spirit's help, we can be open to the Father's unconditional love for us, and we can love the Father in return "with our whole hearts, minds, and souls." The Spirit teaches us to pray, even when we can't find the right words. Because of the Spirit, we know what it means to have and be a friend. The Spirit helps us reach out in love to others—being patient, kind, understanding, and forgiving.

Indeed, love—which along with faith and hope is a **theological virtue**—is a vital aspect of true Christian character. As Jesus tells us, when we die God will not judge us according to our textbook knowledge of the catechism or our ability to score well on religion tests. Instead, God will judge us according to how well we have loved others. (See Matthew 7:12–23.) Living in the Spirit of love is what separates a real Christian from those who merely profess faith in Jesus.

For Your Eyes Only

1. What is one thing you hope for?

2. Agree or disagree: Without Jesus there is no hope.

DO THIS!

In a dictionary, look up the definition of each fruit of the Spirit listed in the text. Explain the meaning of each fruit. How might a typical teenager experience each fruit of the Spirit in a specific decision or situation?

For Your Eyes Only

Invent another analogy that expresses the presence of the Holy Spirit using winds, birds, fire, or another image you think fits.

Consider the basic question of the famous story *The Hunchback of Notre Dame:* "Who is the monster and who is the man?" As you recall the story, rethink it in the form, "Who is the Christian and who is not?"

The Hunchback of Notre Dame

In fifteenth-century Paris, the town is divided between "respectable" Christians and gypsies. The gypsies are looked down upon because, according to tradition, they refused to give hospitality to the Holy Family when Jesus, Mary, and Joseph fled to Egypt to escape Herod's persecution. Now it is the gypsies who must wander the earth as outcasts—poor, unwelcomed, and homeless.

Judge Claude Frollo is an ardent Christian who believes it is his duty to rid the world of sinners—who, in his view, are the gypsies. He kills Quasimodo's parents and is about to kill him, too, when the rector of the Cathedral of Notre Dame stops him.

Frollo hates Quasimodo, not only because he is a gypsy but also because he is deformed. He has a distorted face and is hunchbacked. To appease the priest and maintain the appearance of righteousness, Frollo raises Quasimodo as his own, locking him up in the cathedral bell tower.

One day, on the Feast of Fools, Quasimodo mixes with the people of Paris. They laugh at him because of his looks and begin to throw things at him, but Esmeralda, a gypsy girl, comes to his rescue and befriends him. She treats him as a person, not as an object to be hated or ridiculed.

Esmeralda is a truly loving person. Even though she must seek sanctuary in the cathedral to escape the wrath of Frollo, she does not pray for her own needs. Nor does she pray for wealth, fame, glory, or material possessions. Instead, she asks God to help all the poor and hungry. Because of Esmeralda, Quasi knows what love is for the first time in his life.

LET'S TALK

1. Who are the outcasts in today's society? Why are these people considered outcasts?
2. Name some people in today's world who—through their words, attitudes, and actions—reveal God's Spirit of love.

Mission Impossible

Finding the words to describe the mystery of the Trinity with complete accuracy is an impossible mission. It simply can't be done. As St. Augustine once wrote, trying to understand God is like trying to scoop the entire ocean into a small bucket. St. Catherine of Siena agrees. For her, the Trinity is "a deep sea. The more I enter You, the more I discover, and the more I discover, the more I seek You."

Having the right words to describe God is not nearly as important as the willingness to become more like God. St. Paul describes this as the desire to "put on" Jesus Christ. (See Romans 13:14.) Although God does not really have character like humans have character, God does have certain attributes or characteristics that we, as Christians, strive to make our own. Six **attributes of God** that we will focus on in the rest of this course are *goodness, power, wisdom, love, mercy,* and *justice.* In the following chapters, you will be exploring the meaning of these divine attributes and their importance in the development of your own good character.

Prayer

LEADER: The Trinity is the central Christian mystery. All that we have and all that we are is because of this loving God. In gratitude and praise, we now come together in prayer, beginning as always "In the name of the Father, and of the Son, and of the Holy Spirit."

ALL: Amen.

READER 1: Ephesians 4:1–6

READER 2: Ephesians 5:1–2

READER 3: Ephesians 5:8–10

ALL: Most loving Trinity, we believe in your creative and sustaining presence. Strengthen our faith, hope, and love as we continue to relate to you in the persons of Father, Son, and Holy Spirit and to one another. Make your home in us, now and forever. Amen.

Further Activities

1. Read the Nicene Creed on page 235. Use the *Catechism of the Catholic Church* to research the meaning of each creedal statement. Write a summary of each statement.

2. Make a list of the five most important beliefs in your life. Then, in one or two paragraphs, explain why these beliefs are most important to you, and why.

For Your Eyes Only

I promise to devote time to my relationship with God this week by . . .

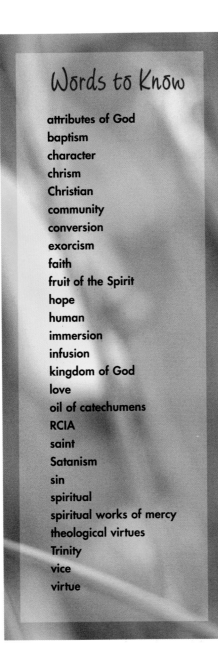

Words to Know

attributes of God
baptism
character
chrism
Christian
community
conversion
exorcism
faith
fruit of the Spirit
hope
human
immersion
infusion
kingdom of God
love
oil of catechumens
RCIA
saint
Satanism
sin
spiritual
spiritual works of mercy
theological virtues
Trinity
vice
virtue

3. Learn how to communicate the Lord's Prayer, the Glory Be, and the Apostles' Creed in sign language. Teach these prayers to hearing-impaired students, or a classroom of primary age students.

4. Develop a model for the Trinity that can aid you in witnessing and explaining this central Christian mystery of faith to others.

At Home

Ask a parent or guardian to share with you how he or she has experienced faith, hope, and love in his or her life. Together, discuss what you each hope for the future.

Part 1 Review

1. What are five ways in which humans differ from animals?

2. What is character? What does it mean to have good character?

3. How are good character and humanness connected?

4. How are good character and heroism connected?

5. How does character affect a person's beliefs? attitudes? ability to love?

6. What are two ways you can help yourself develop good character?

7. What are the spiritual works of mercy?

8. What does *becoming Christian* mean? How is it a process of conversion?

9. Name the eight parts of the sacrament of baptism and what they mean.

10. How does the Christian concept of God differ from the Jewish concept of God?

11. For Christians, what does it mean to "see with the eyes of faith"?

12. Name the theological virtues. How does each one help us relate to God?

13. What is the kingdom of God?

14. What are the fruits of the Spirit?

15. What is the central Christian mystery?

15. What are six attributes of God?

GOODNESS

What is goodness?

How is healthy self-esteem related to good character?

In what ways are integrity and honesty important aspects of good character?

What Is Goodness?

As Christians, we believe that all people are made in God's image. We also believe that **goodness** is a vital part of who God is. What exactly is goodness?

Webster's dictionary defines *goodness* as "the quality or state of being good." Obviously, this definition is not very helpful. In order to understand the meaning of *goodness*, we first have to know what is meant by the word *good*. What does *good* mean in each of the following sentences?

1. Your friend is very good-natured.
2. He is a good-looking man.
3. Jesus died on Good Friday.
4. It is important to set a good example.
5. Very few people can really afford to live the good life.
6. Good luck on your job interview.
7. She devoted her life to good works in the community.
8. He sacrificed his own wants for the common good.
9. Good weather is forecast for tomorrow.
10. All I want is a good night's sleep.

Depending on how it is used, "good" can have many different meanings. When we refer to goodness, it is understood that we are referring to a virtue that is positive and valuable.

DO THIS!

Write a letter to someone who doesn't know of God's goodness. Try to explain to this person how God is good. Read your letter to a partner.

How God Is Good

When we say that God is good, we mean that God is morally virtuous, right, commendable, honorable, and reliable. Furthermore, God is *perfectly* good—good in every aspect. In this case, the dictionary does provides us with insight: To be *perfect* means to be "entirely without fault or defect." It means being complete, whole, excellent in quality, and flawless. If God were an Olympic athlete, the judges would give God a perfect score in every category for every event! That's how good God is.

To find out more, read and discuss the following scripture passages that describe God's goodness:

◆ Psalm 23   ◆ Psalm 143:10–12
◆ Psalm 34:8   ◆ John 10:11–14
◆ Psalm 118:1   ◆ James 1:17

NOTABLE QUOTABLES

"God is the beginning, the middle, and the end of every good."

—St. Mark the Ascetic

"What is good in itself glorifies God because it reflects God."

—Flannery O'Connor

Signs of God's Goodness

There is an old saying, "Goodness is as goodness does." What this saying means is that someone's true goodness can be seen in his or her actions. The same is true of God. As the *Catechism of the Catholic Church* tells us, "God is infinitely good and all his works are good" (385). The world God created—the mountains, oceans, plants, animals, people—is good. (See Genesis 1.) In all of creation, "God displays not only His . . . goodness, . . . but also His . . . truth" (214).

Two Aspects of Goodness

Because God is perfectly good, God alone has perfect self-knowledge and perfect self-acceptance. God is neither proud, arrogant, and boastful, nor is God falsely modest or humble. Because God is perfect goodness, only God can truly say, "I am who I am" (Exodus 3:14) and wholly love that identity. Thus, the first aspect of God's goodness that Christians try to imitate is healthy self-esteem.

The second aspect of God's goodness that Christians try to imitate is honesty. Each Sunday in the Nicene Creed, we profess our belief that God is the one true God. In the Bible (sometimes known as "the good book"), we hear the good news that Jesus is the true vine (John 15:1). He is "the way, the truth, and the life" (John 14:6). Likewise, the Holy Spirit is the spirit of truth (John 14:17) who will guide us to all truth.

As you will explore further in the next two chapters, we must be honest about who we are if we want to arrive at healthy self-esteem. Furthermore, we must be truthful in our dealings with others if we are to become good and Godlike.

NOTABLE QUOTABLE

"Good character consists of knowing the good, desiring the good, and doing the good—habits of the mind, habits of the heart, and habits of action."

—Thomas Lickona, *Educating for Character*

34

3. Healthy Self-Esteem

CHAPTER GOALS

In this chapter, you will:

◆ See that healthy self-esteem is based on a person's goodness, not on possessions, looks, popularity, or power.

◆ Discover how healthy self-esteem differs from pride, one of the seven capital sins, and false humility.

◆ Explore ways to foster healthy self-esteem in yourself and in others.

Have you ever noticed that when you get good at a particular skill (playing basketball, sewing clothes, drawing, reading music, learning how to use a computer), you automatically feel better about yourself? Well, the same is true with moral goodness. Whenever you choose to act in a virtuous way rather than in a bad way (such as choosing to do your homework rather than copying a friend's work) or whenever you help others instead of being selfish, your perception of yourself goes up. This type of perception is called **self-esteem.**

If you have healthy self-esteem, you have a sense of contentment about who you are as a human being. You consciously appreciate your own worth and importance. In other words, you have a good reputation with yourself. You like yourself.

Unfortunately, many teenagers do not have healthy self-esteem. They lack confidence. Some doubt themselves; others actually hate themselves. Some teens feel worthless and empty; they think their lives have no meaning or purpose. Still other teenagers have such a poor self-image that they think they are unlovable. They also think their situation will never change for the better.

The statistics are sobering: The 1995 *Statistical Abstract for the United States* reports that in 1992 alone, 10.8 out of every 100,000 fifteen- to nineteen-year-olds committed suicide. Indeed, suicide is among the top three killers of teens today. In our country, a teenager commits suicide every 90 minutes. While more girls than boys attempt to kill themselves, more boys actually succeed in completing the act.

There are many reasons why these teens choose to end their lives. Certainly, the popular media—such as television shows, movies, and some music is an influential factor in a number of these deaths. Other teen suicides are the result of "suicide pacts" with friends. Still others are "copycat" actions of previous suicides in the news or committed by friends and family members. Though the reasons for suicides are rarely clear, teen suicides are somehow related to low self-esteem.

LET'S TALK

What are some reasons many teenagers have low self-esteem?

F.Y.I.

There are more than 200 suicide prevention centers throughout the United States. Most major cities have a suicide prevention hot line that is listed in the telephone directory.

Self-Esteem and Body Image

There is a media myth that: "You're only good if you're tall, thin, and beautiful." Many teens have low self-esteem because they don't measure up to society's standards of the "perfect" body. Consider the following real-life example:

She's Too Fat[1]

"She's too fat to make the Olympic gymnastics team."

It was a simple, offhand remark, made by a judge at a 1990 gymnastics competition. But it was enough to send world-ranked gymnast Christy Henrich, age 18—4 feet 10 inches tall and only 93 pounds—on a diet and into a downward spiral that resulted in her July, 1994, death from anorexia nervosa. By the time she died, she weighed just 47 pounds.

Unfortunately, many teens (and adults) mistakenly equate goodness with being good-looking. Social researchers have shown that attractive people get better jobs and are considered nicer, smarter, and sexier than their plain counterparts. In other words, a person's character is often equated with his or her outward appearance. If a person looks good, we think he or she is morally good, too.

A letter dealing with this issue appeared in a recent issue of *Teen Magazine.*

Ask Jack[2]

Dear Jack:

Why do guys only like the beautiful girls? I have this friend who spends a lot of time with me, and I've started to really like him. But he treats me like one of the guys. How do I get him to see that I could be a great girlfriend? I'm not that pretty or popular. Do you think that's why he doesn't like me?

In Love, California.

Dear In Love:

This question works both ways. Guys are just as concerned with their image at school as girls are. Why do girls like the good-looking, popular guys most of the time? It seems like people need to get past looks and popularity and pay more attention to people as people. Maybe this guy doesn't know how you feel about him. Subtly let him know that you're interested in being more than friends. Or, consider telling him straight out that you like him.

---

1 Adapted from Anne Conover Heller and Maura Rhodes, "Is your daughter at risk for an eating disorder?" *McCalls* (November, 1994), p. 94.
2 "Ask Jack," *Teen Magazine* (April, 1995), p. 18.

For Your Eyes Only

How highly do you esteem yourself right now? Think about the following areas of your life. Give yourself a grade (A to F) for each one.

◆ Academics
◆ Athletics
◆ Physical looks
◆ Clothing
◆ Friends
◆ Sexuality
◆ Relationship with parents
◆ Talents and skills
◆ Ability to make good decisions
◆ Compassion
◆ Ability to forgive, including self

DO THIS!

Write ad copy describing the "perfect" male or female from (1) society's perspective and (2) from Jesus' perspective.

For Your Eyes Only

Write the initials of five friends. Next to each initial write the person's primary strength. How many of the primary strengths you listed have to do with good looks?

LET'S TALK

1. Describe the ideal looking girl or boy. Share your description with a partner. How are they similar? different?

2. How would you respond to In Love, California?

3. How much do you think body-image affects teen success regarding (a) school, (b) social situations, and (c) healthy self-esteem? Explain.

All That Glitters

When you were a kid, did you ever find a sparkling rock that you thought was real gold? If so, then you probably remember how excited you got at the thought of striking it rich! You probably also remember how disappointed you felt when you found out the rock was simply "fool's gold," or pyrite.

The experience of being fooled by appearances is so common that a saying developed, "All that glitters is not gold." The truth of this saying also applies to people: Good-looks do not tell the whole story.

Consider the story line of a recent movie:

The Truth About Cats and Dogs

Abby is a veterinarian who has a radio talk-show about animals and how to relate to them. She is short, a little overweight, and is rather plain-looking. Although she's smart, bright, and witty, she has low self-esteem. She hasn't had a boyfriend in three years. She doesn't think she's pretty enough to have a serious relationship with a man.

Abby's neighbor, Noelle, is a tall, thin, blonde model who can stop traffic without even trying. Men instantly gravitate toward her because of her looks. Ironically, she, too, has low self-esteem. Her current boyfriend takes her for granted and sometimes physically abuses her.

Abby and Noelle get to know each other because they live in the same building. Abby supports Noelle as a person and helps her separate from her abusive boyfriend. Eventually, Abby and Noelle become friends.

Meanwhile, Brian is a shy, handsome photographer who is trying to shoot a roller-blade commercial. He has put the roller blades on a dog while filming the commercial and he can't get them off. He calls Abby's radio show for help. Brian is impressed with Abby's advice and is attracted to her voice. He wants to meet her, but Abby is afraid he will be put off by her looks. So she describes herself as Noelle—tall, thin, and gorgeous.

Brian starts to date Noelle, but finds she's not the same in person as she is over the phone. Brian calls Abby, thinking she is Noelle, and they talk for seven hours.

Abby falls in love with Brian, but Brian is in love with Noelle, thinking she is Abby. Noelle is tempted to keep Brian for herself, but then sees how much that would hurt her friendship with Abby. In the end, Noelle, Abby, and Brian all learn the same lesson: being good means much more than good looks. It's what's inside that counts.

As Good as Gold

Healthy self-esteem has several important aspects. First, healthy self-esteem is based on a person's essential moral goodness, not on possessions, looks, popularity, or power—things that have nothing to do with good character. Moral goodness is, of itself, attractive and likable. The more you try to lead a morally good life, the more reasons you have for liking yourself and the more reasons others will have to like you, too.

Second, healthy self-esteem is not here one minute and gone the next. It is an underlying sense of well-being and acceptance that stays with you in the various situations throughout life. Healthy self-esteem enables you to try to be your best even in new experiences.

Third, healthy self-esteem is not based on what other people think of you. For example, others may think you are ugly, stupid, clumsy, or fat. If you have healthy self-esteem, however, you can value your own worth regardless of what others say. You know yourself better than they do.

Indeed, healthy self-esteem is based on accurate self-knowledge. A basic part of that knowledge is the Christian belief that God made the world and all creatures in it good. At your core, you are a good person because that is the way God made you. Even if no one else in the world thinks you are wonderful, God does. Because God loves you, you are "as good as gold." You have dignity, worth, and lasting value.

If you really know that you are good and loved by God, you will also grow in the ability to like and love yourself. Loving yourself is the first step toward genuinely loving others because you can see the good in them, too. Jesus affirmed this when he told his followers to "love your neighbor as *yourself*" (Matthew 22:39) and "treat others as you would want them to treat you" (Matthew 7:12). Many psychologists today agree. They say that you can't really love others until you first love yourself.

Scripture

In a small group, read one of the following passages. Discuss what it says to you about healthy self-esteem. Be prepared to summarize the passage and share your insights with the class.

◆Matthew 4:1–11 ◆Luke 9:46–48
◆Luke 1:46–55 ◆Philippians 2:1–11

Self-Esteem vs. Pride

Having healthy self-esteem and self-love is not easy. Aristotle was aware of this reality when he said that virtue, or good character, lies in the middle between two extremes. What did Aristotle mean? Well, imagine yourself trying to walk across a rope stretched tightly between two pedestals.

In order to stay on the rope (the narrow path of virtue, goodness, and healthy self-esteem), you need to keep a steady balance. If you love yourself too highly—if you are proud, boastful, and self-centered—you will tilt too much to one side and fall off the rope. Likewise, if you love yourself too poorly—if you have false humility or self-hatred and neglect your basic needs—you will tilt too far to the other side and fall off the rope in that direction. To understand the virtue of healthy self-esteem more fully, it is important to explore the nature of pride and its opposite virtue, humility.

The Catholic church names **pride** as one of the seven **capital sins.**

Capital sins are the root of all other sins that people choose to commit. People who are sinfully proud exaggerate their self-importance. They are vain, conceited, over-confident, and self-indulgent. People with extreme pride consider themselves to be God's equal.

Indeed, people who are sinfully proud are usually egotistical. They are self-centered, basically selfish, and think only of their own needs. If you were on a sinking ship and there was room for only one more person in the lifeboat, the egotist would make sure he or she got on the lifeboat and wouldn't think twice about leaving you to drown!

Furthermore, an egotistical person tends to take credit for everything good that happens. An egotist on a sport's team, for example, puts personal statistics and glory ahead of team effort.

People who are sinfully proud also tend to brag a lot. They boast much of the time about their accomplishments. The message is clear: "I'm the greatest, and you should think so, too." Sometimes, proud people brag by being name-droppers. ("My dad's company handles the finances for *fill in the name of a current star*.") Or they make sure everyone knows that they wear designer clothes and shoes, attend the hottest concerts, and have the best parties. In short, they tend to think they are better than everyone else.

A person of good character knows that such pride is foolish. He or she is not "thrown off-balance" by self-flattery or the praise of others. The following story illustrates this lesson.

NOTABLE QUOTABLE

"The secret of my success is that at an early age I discovered I was not God."

—Oliver Wendell Holmes, Jr. (1841–1935), U.S. Supreme Court Justice

LET'S TALK

1. What are some other examples of sinful pride? (No names, please!)

2. What is the difference between healthy pride in oneself (self-esteem) and sinful pride? Use examples to explain.

3. How is the sin of pride related to other types of sins (e.g., lying and cheating)? Give an example.

King Canute on the Seashore[3]

Long ago, England was ruled by a king named Canute. Like many leaders and men of power, Canute was surrounded by people who were always praising him. Every time he walked into a room, the flattery began. One day he was walking by the seashore; his officers and courtiers were with him, praising him as usual. Canute decided to teach them a lesson.

"So you say I am the greatest man in the world?" he asked.

"O king," they cried, "there never has been anyone as mighty as you, and there never will be anyone so great ever again!"

"And you say all things obey me?" Canute asked.

"Absolutely!" they said. "The world bows before you and gives you honor."

"In that case," the king answered, "bring me my chair. Put it right at the water's edge."

They scrambled to carry his royal chair over the sands. The king sat down and surveyed the ocean before him. "I notice the tide is coming in. Do you think it will stop for me?"

His officers were puzzled, but they did not dare say no. "Give the order, O great king, and it will obey," one of them assured him.

3 Shortened and adapted from James Baldwin. Quoted in William Bennett, *The Book of Virtues* (New York: Simon & Schuster, 1993), pp. 67–68.

"Very well," cried Canute. "Sea, I command you to come no further! Waves, stop your rolling! Surf, stop your pounding! Do not dare touch my feet!" He waited a moment, quietly, and a tiny wave rushed up the sand and lapped at his feet.

"How dare you!" Canute shouted. "Ocean, turn back now! I have ordered you to retreat before me, and now you must obey! Go back!" In answer, another wave swept forward and curled around the king's feet. The tide came in, just as it always did. The water rose higher and higher. It came up around the king's chair and wet not only his feet but also his robe. His officers stood about him, alarmed.

"Well, my friends," Canute said, "it seems I do not have quite so much power as you would have me believe. Perhaps you have learned something today. Perhaps you will remember there is only one King who is all-powerful, and it is He who rules the sea and holds the ocean in the hollow of His hand. I suggest you reserve your praises for Him."

The royal officers and courtiers hung their heads and looked foolish. Canute took off his crown soon afterward and never wore it again.

NOTABLE QUOTABLE

"The gate of heaven is very low; only the humble can enter it."

—St. Elizabeth Seton

LET'S TALK

1. Define the word *humble*.
2. Tell about a time you were praised excessively like King Canute.
3. Who do you know, either personally or from the news, who shows the same humility as King Canute?

Humility

Healthy self-esteem includes having **humility**. The word *humility* comes from "humus," the same word for earth, or ground. The concept of humility stems from the story in the Book of Genesis in which God creates humans from the earth's soil. (See Genesis 2:4–7.) To be humble means to know your proper place in society. You acknowledge your submissiveness to those greater than you and your dependence on others. You are not arrogant or haughty; you are not a "know-it-all." You do not consider yourself God's equal.

Humility is not only an important virtue of healthy self-esteem; it is also an important part of the Christian concept of goodness. Christians believe that God who is all-good created the world good. God also created humans good. We know from experience, however, that the world is not perfect. Neither are we. Evil and suffering exist everywhere. How is this possible? How can a God who is good allow evil and suffering to exist? How can good people commit horrendous sins against society and one another?

The answers to these questions *are* not easy to understand. The world and the people in it are basically good, but they are not perfect. Goodness is not the same as being complete or perfect. The *Catechism of the Catholic Church* explains it this way:

Creation has its own goodness and proper perfection, but it did not spring forth complete from the hands of the Creator. The universe was created "in a state of journeying" toward an ultimate perfection yet to be attained, to which God has destined it. (302)

In giving us the gift of life, God also gave us the gift of freedom. Goodness is not something we have to be; it is something we can choose. We have the free will to choose virtue or to choose vice. The constant temptation within us to choose vice is related to **original sin**. The term refers to the story in which the first humans, Adam and Eve, sinned for the first time. (See Genesis 3.) Original sin is not an actual sinful action that we commit personally; rather, it is a state into which we are born. The more we choose to do good and to grow in good character, the easier it becomes to be virtuous. Original sin has less influence on us. The opposite is true also: the more we choose evil, the harder it becomes to develop good character. The "pull" of original sin becomes stronger. As the *Catechism* puts it: "All subsequent sin would be disobedience toward God and lack of trust in his goodness" (397).

The Poor in Spirit

True humility involves another balancing act. It means accepting both your strengths (your good points) and your imperfections (your bad points). It means accepting yourself as imperfect, but nevertheless good.

Jesus called people with true humility "the poor in spirit." Such people know they are not God and that they depend on God. Such people also love goodness and try their best to do good. That is why Jesus further says, "Blessed are the poor in spirit, for theirs is the kingdom of heaven" (Matthew 5:3). Truly humble people are happy because they know that God loves them despite their imperfections.

Healthy self-knowledge and faith in God are the basis of our belief in salvation. Even though the human race is not perfect and has sinned, God continues to love us. In fact, God loved us so much, he sent his Son, Jesus, to share our humanness and to redeem us. Christians believe that Jesus—through his life, death on a cross, and resurrection—has saved us from sin and death.

What does redemption mean in terms of your own self-esteem? It means this: No mistake you make will ever be great enough for God to reject you. No matter how bad your situation is, God's goodness is always stronger than the evil. God can always bring good out of bad. (See Romans 8:28.)

Good people sometimes act in bad ways, but this does not mean they cannot change or be redeemed. Even if you have done something terrible, there is no reason to despair. God, as loving Father, understanding Savior, and indwelling Spirit will always be with you. If you want it and will cooperate, God will always help you get back up on the tightrope of virtue that leads to good character.

Many teenagers, when confronted with the realization of one weakness or imperfection, tend to think that *everything* about them is bad. If they have made a mistake, they think they will always be branded by that mistake, that they can never get past it. Christian faith, however, can help us get a more accurate perception of God's love and confidence in us. If we truly believe in God's goodness, we must also believe in our own basic goodness. We can then be less harsh and critical with ourselves. We can "lighten up" because we truly know and believe the good news of Jesus, the gospel message of God's eternal love.

Scripture

Read one of the following accounts of the passion, death, and resurrection of Jesus. Then, in a small group, discuss the questions.

◆ Matthew 26:1–28:20   ◆ Luke 22:7–24:12

◆ Mark 14:12–16:20   ◆ John 13:1–38; 18:1–20:18

1. What are some examples of God's love for us during the events of the Last Supper and Jesus' passion?

2. Jesus was crucified with two thieves. Both of these men sinned, and yet the church calls one of them "the good thief." Why?

3. St. Paul wrote that without Jesus' resurrection, our entire faith is empty. (See 1 Corinthians 15:14.) What do you think Paul meant by this?

Scripture

Both Judas and Peter were good people who betrayed Jesus. They both made terrible mistakes. Read the following passages. Then discuss the questions.

◆ Judas (Matthew 26:14–25; 47–50; 27:3–10)

◆ Peter (Matthew 26:31–35; 69–75; John 21:1–19)

1. How was Judas's betrayal of Jesus different from Peter's betrayal of Jesus?

2. The Catholic church once defined suicide as a **mortal sin**. The church did not allow people who had committed suicide to have a Catholic funeral or to be buried in a Catholic cemetery. The 1983 revised Code of Canon Law does not mention those who have committed suicide among those who are to be forbidden church funeral rites. Why do you think the church changed its position?

3. What are some examples from your own life in which God was able to bring good out of a bad situation?

How Goodness Transforms Us

As Christians, we believe that Jesus is the light of the world who conquers every darkness (John 9:5). The goodness of Jesus conquers and transforms evil. The more we develop a personal relationship with Jesus, the more his light transforms our darkness (our natural tendency to choose evil). We become strengthened in our goodness; we develop even more traits of good character.

When we are in touch with the goodness and love of God, we are transformed in the way we see and esteem ourselves. We no longer magnify our imperfections and flaws; instead, we celebrate the goodness that is ours. The more we develop good character in ourselves, the more clear our perception of others also becomes. We can more easily recognize the real value in others, their basic goodness. Instead of judging others by their outward appearance, we can see how some people

For Your Eyes Only

What does the resurrection of Jesus mean to you personally, in terms of the way you see yourself and your future?

DO THIS!

Write a letter from God to you that details what God finds attractive about you.

are truly "as good as gold." When we recognize a person's good character, he or she becomes more beautiful to us. A person's beauty is more than skin deep. No matter how the years of aging change a person's body, he or she remains lovable. That is why many couples married for forty, fifty, or sixty years can look at their spouses and honestly say that he or she is "more beautiful than the day we met."

F.Y.I.

A mortal sin is a very serious sin that inflicts a "mortal" or deadly wound on one's relationship with God and others. In essence, the relationship is killed. In contrast, a **venial sin** is a less serious sin that hurts or weakens one's relationship with God and others.

Ways to Grow in Self-Esteem

Healthy self-esteem is not something that just happens. It takes work and practice. Here are some things that you can do to foster in yourself a sense of healthy self-esteem:

1. Accept yourself as you really are—both your strengths and your weaknesses. Know that you don't have to be perfect all the time to be a good person or to be loved by God.

2. Trust yourself. Develop a Christian conscience. Follow what your conscience tells you is the right thing to do.

3. Set realistic expectations, dreams, and goals for yourself. If your dreams are impossible to reach, you'll just feel bad about yourself. On the other hand, don't expect too little of yourself. That's false humility!

4. Explore new thoughts, behavior, and possibilities. Don't be afraid to try a new sport or hobby just because you've never done it before. You may learn something about yourself you never knew before!

5. Forgive yourself and others. People with healthy self-esteem learn from their mistakes. They also don't let resentment toward others prevent them from moving on with their life and their goals.

6. Express your feelings in ways that do not hurt others. Don't keep everything bottled up inside! Psychologists tell us that depression is often simply anger turned inward.

7. Be creative. Learn to express your own goodness in a variety of ways that are pleasing not only to yourself but also to others.

8. Spend time with God in prayer. Listen to what God has to say about your own goodness and worth.

9. Appreciate your body. Keep yourself healthy, clean, and looking as good as possible. Exercise, eat a balanced diet, and get enough sleep. Be your best self, but don't try to change everything about you or be someone you're not.

10. Appreciate your mind. Think positive thoughts that build self-esteem and goodness. Choose to reject thoughts in which you blame yourself for everything that's wrong with the world or continually put yourself down.

11. Take responsibility for your own decisions and actions. Don't blame others for your mistakes! Likewise, don't take credit for something good you didn't do. Recognize the balance between freedom and responsibility.

12. Value goodness and both affirm and develop it in yourself.

Ways to Build Self-Esteem in Others

People with healthy self-esteem reach out to others and help them recognize their own value and goodness. Read the following scripture passages. How did Jesus help others grow in healthy self-esteem?

◆ Matthew 9:9–13   ◆ John 4:1–30
◆ Luke 5:17–26   ◆ John 8:1–11
◆ Luke 7:36–50

How can you, as a teenager, follow the example of Jesus and help build self-esteem in others? Here are some ideas:

1. Spend time with a younger brother, sister, or child. Provide an environment of physical support and safety so that he or she can try something new and build self-confidence.

2. Whenever you are with someone else, give that person your full attention. Learn to listen respectfully.

3. Demonstrate acceptance and support for a friend, especially when he or she is going through a difficult time.

4. Encourage healthy achievement in others. Help others excel at what they do best.

5. Appreciate the benefits of a multicultural society. Develop friends of other races and help them appreciate the good parts of their heritage.

6. Negotiate conflicts. Trying to work out a problem with another person shows that you respect him or her and consider him or her to be worth the effort.

7. Tutor classmates or elementary students during lunch or after school. Instill in them a sense of accomplishment and confidence. Encourage them to struggle and succeed on their own.

8. Volunteer to work with younger boys and girls through a scouting program, summer camp situation, after-school recreation program, etc. Teaching them new skills and helping them learn good sportsmanship will help bolster their self-esteem.

9. Humbly serve the needs of others. Look around your neighborhood, school, or city, and see who needs your help. Do what you can—either alone or with others—to help others restore their sense of pride and self-respect.

10. Be a good role model. Help others discover and capitalize on their strengths and uniqueness because of your own faith in God's love for you.

11. Pray for the needs of others, especially for an improvement in their self-esteem.

12. Model forgiveness to someone who has hurt you. The lesson this teaches will be a lasting one.

NOTABLE QUOTABLE

"Persons with healthy self-esteem choose to serve others out of their sense of personal fullness and their joy of being alive. In the process of serving, we deepen and reinforce our own self-esteem."

—California State Department of Education,
Toward a State of Esteem: The Final Report of the California Task Force to Promote Self-Esteem and Personal and Social Responsibility

Prayer

LEADER: God knows us even better than we know ourselves. God always sees the goodness in us and reaches out to us in love. Let us spend some time now reflecting on the great love God has for us. Let us thank God for making us who we are.

READER: Psalm 139:1–18

ALL: Thank you, God, for the goodness you have placed in each of us. Help us develop this goodness every day of our lives, in all our actions and relationships. Strengthen our belief in your everlasting love for us. Make good come of our mistakes and sins. Teach us to know and accept ourselves as you know and accept us. Amen.

Further Activities

1. Analyze a recent movie or video you have seen. What type of message does this movie or video give viewers about body image and good character? Do you think this message is healthy or unhealthy in terms of self-esteem? Explain.

2. Write a children's story with an "appearance-impaired" character who is the hero or heroine and with a good-looking character as the villain.

3. Write a letter of affirmation to someone you know who needs cheering up. Mail the letter or personally deliver it to the person.

At Home

Spend time with a parent or family member, playing a game or working together on a household project. Pay attention to what the person is saying and affirm his or her goodness.

4. Integrity and Honesty

An important aspect of goodness is honesty. Christians believe that God equates with truthfulness. If we want to become more Godlike and good, we must seek the truth at all times and in all our relationships. Once we know what the truth is, we have a duty to stand up for it.

As the dictionary explains, honesty is "the refusal to lie, steal, or deceive in any way." Even more, **honesty** means being sincere and straightforward—both in our words and our behavior. Whenever we choose to act on the values we hold true, we are said to be acting with **integrity**. Acting with integrity, then, involves two steps. First, it means being honest about our values and beliefs. And second, it means being faithful to those values and beliefs.

When you were younger, it probably seemed that the commandments, "You shall not steal" and "You shall not bear false witness against your neighbor" were very clear. Respecting the property of others and telling the truth were good; stealing and lying were wrong, period. Now that you are older, you are probably starting to realize how the truth can be distorted.

Indeed, many people are confused about what the truth really is. Many adults find it difficult to be people of integrity and honesty. Strong pressures in today's society—money, power, career advancement, fame—can tempt normally good people to cheat, steal, and tell lies. Unfortunately, dishonesty has become so commonplace that many young people no longer think it is wrong. They even think that people who are honest are just plain stupid. Honesty doesn't seem "to pay," and cheaters seem to get ahead.

Despite the prevalence of dishonesty in today's world, Christians continue to believe that good character involves honesty. We continue to try to live by the saying, "Honesty is the best policy." We try to follow the words of Jesus, "If you live continue in my word, you are truly my disciples; and you will know the truth, and the truth will make you free" (John 8:31–32).

CHAPTER GOALS

In this chapter, you will:

◆ See how shoplifting, stealing, and cheating are all forms of dishonesty.

◆ Discover why people of integrity try not to lie, gossip, or slander others.

◆ Appreciate the importance of sincerity and genuineness and learn how the sacrament of reconciliation can help you grow in integrity.

DO THIS!

Search recent newspapers and magazines for an example of dishonesty in one of the following areas: politics, business, the military, college, high school, personal relationships. Be prepared to share your example with the class.

NOTABLE QUOTABLE

"When you seek truth, you seek God whether you know it or not."

—St. Edith Stein

Shoplifting and Stealing

One prevalent type of dishonesty is **stealing**—taking property that belongs to someone else. As any police officer will tell you, the law defines many different types of stealing. For example, **larceny** is the unlawful taking of personal property that belongs to someone else. **Grand larceny** is the stealing of property over a certain value. (This value varies from state to state.) **Burglary** is stealing that takes place while breaking and entering a home or building. **Forgery** is stealing that occurs by signing someone else's name to a check or by counterfeiting a document. **Embezzlement** is the stealing of someone else's property or money that has been entrusted to your care. **Fraud** involves intentional deceit or trickery to get a person to part with something of value.

While it may seem that these examples of dishonesty are extreme, statistics show that teenagers are not immune to such forms of stealing. According to the 1995 *Statistical Abstract of the United States*, of all the people arrested in 1993, teenagers constituted the following percentages:

◆ 44.6% of those arrested for motor vehicle theft,

◆ 34% of those arrested for larceny,

◆ 27% of those arrested for possession of stolen property,

◆ 15.3% of those arrested for burglary,

◆ 7.3% of those arrested for forgery,

◆ 5.6% of those arrested for embezzlement, and

◆ 4.8% of those arrested for fraud.

More commonly, teenagers—for various reasons and motives—are involved in **shoplifting** (stealing displayed items from a store) and **swarming** (entering a store in a large group and blatantly stealing everything possible). Some teenagers steal for the thrill of it. Others do it as a result of a dare or peer pressure. Still others tell themselves that such forms of stealing "don't matter," that no one gets hurt because the stores are covered by insurance.

Scripture

Read the following passages to find out what Jesus had to say about people who steal. In a small group, discuss what these passages mean for teenagers today.

◆ Luke 16:1–9   ◆ Mark 11:15–18

◆ John 10:7–10   ◆ Luke 19:1–10

Cheating

Cheating is another type of dishonesty that is very common in today's society. In 1993, *Change* magazine conducted a survey of U.S. college students from 31 different campuses. The results were as follows.

During tests or examinations:

◆ 52% copied from another student,

◆ 37% helped another student cheat, and

◆ 27% used crib notes.

On written work:

◆ 54% copied material without footnoting,

◆ 26% plagiarized,

◆ 29% falsified a bibliography,

◆ 14% turned in work done by someone else, and

◆ 49% collaborated on assignments requiring individual work.

A 1993–1994 survey of students in *Who's Who Among High School Students* reveals that cheating is even more common in high school. Here is what the students said in the survey:

◆ 70% had cheated at one time or another,

◆ 67% copied another student's work,

◆ 40% cheated on a test or quiz, and

◆ 25% used plot summaries to avoid reading an assigned book.

LET'S TALK

1. What are some reasons students have for cheating?

2. Why is cheating really a form of stealing?

3. In your opinion, how widespread is cheating at your school? What, if anything, do you think can be done to improve the situation?

4. How do you think cheating affects society as a whole? For example, would you want a doctor who had cheated her way through medical school to perform surgery on you?

F.Y.I.

In a recent national poll, 40% of U.S. teenagers said they would cheat if they knew they could get away with it.

More About Cheating

Many students cheat because they often get away with it. But what happens when they get caught? Consider the following true-life story:

The Big Cheat [1]

People in the audience that March night remember the gush of emotion. Scrappy, blue-collar Steinmetz High School had scored an incredible come-from-behind victory over Whitney Young, the city's most exclusive public high school, in the Illinois Academic Decathlon competition, a wide-ranging test of brains and knowledge.

As the winners were announced, the nine members of the Steinmetz team seemed overwhelmed by their success. Tears welled in the eyes of their beloved coach. The team had achieved the highest score ever by more than 2,000 points.

For Your Eyes Only

1. Would you be tempted to cheat if you knew you would get away with it?

2. Would you actually cheat if you knew you would get away with it?

---

1 Adapted from "The Big Cheat," *Chicago* (September, 1995), p. 74.

Just after the contest, members of the Steinmetz team smiled their way through a blizzard of congratulatory newspaper and TV interviews. Columnists toasted their achievement, and the Illinois Academic Decathlon Association offered coaching assistance to help them prepare for the national finals. Even when questions about Steinmetz's success emerged, the team members were so convincing that many people refused to doubt their triumph.

The cover-up finally collapsed because of a few eruptions of conscience and relentless pressure from school authorities, but at press time only six of the nine team members had confessed to cheating. And the coach had disappeared.

What happened as a result of the cheating? The victory was revoked. Whitney Young, the second-place team went on to the nationals and placed second. None of the Steinmetz team members was denied admission to college; however, a Chicago philanthropic organization revoked the $1,000 scholarship it had awarded to one student prior to the scandal.

And what of the beloved coach? In June, he sent Steinmetz an invoice for $1,716, representing the second half of his coaching stipend. His time sheet documents 150 hours—27 of them for the week of the state competition. But a check will not be in the mail. "We paid our coach to teach the decathlon team how to win in an ethical manner, not how to cheat," says the school board's lawyer. "If we'd hired him to teach them how to cheat, we'd give him a bonus."

LET'S TALK

1. How do you think the cheating scandal affected the other students of Steinmetz?
2. Why do you think the students cheated? Why do you think their coach helped them cheat?
3. Do you think the punishment in this case was fair? How would you have treated the coach and the students?
4. How do you think the cheating scandal will affect future decathlon competitions?

DO THIS!

In a small group, prepare a skit based on the following situation: Your history teacher assigns a term paper you know you can "borrow" from your older brother. To add to the pressure, if you don't spend more time on physics, you may not get that A or B you need to keep your GPA high enough to get a college scholarship. Write dialogue for three characters in the skit: you, True Blue (the virtue of honesty), and E. Z. Street (the sin of dishonesty). When you have finished, present your skit to the class.

Lying

Another type of dishonesty that is prevalent in today's world is **lying**. The *Catechism of the Catholic Church* tells us that "lying consists in saying what is false with the intention of deceiving the neighbor who has the right to the truth" (2508). Lying, then, has three aspects: what you say, your intention to deceive, and the other person's right to know the truth.

Basically, there are five different categories of lies—false excuses, shifting blame, taking undue credit, image touch-ups, and omission. Let's take a closer look at each kind of lie.

1. *False excuses.* Suppose someone asks you out on a date or to a party. You're available that night, but you don't want to go with this particular person. Because you don't want to hurt the person's feelings,

you make up a false excuse. You say you have to baby-sit or that you're going camping that weekend with your family.

Trying to be nice is one reason some teens resort to lying. And yet, nine times out of ten, the lie backfires and the person gets hurt worse when he or she finally learns the truth. The person not only feels rejected; he or she also feels foolish for having believed your lie.

Ask Julie[2]

Dear Julie:

A guy friend of mine is starting to have romantic feelings for me! He writes me lovey-dovey poems and tells me how beautiful I am. I only like him as a friend. How can I get him to take the hint?

Flustered, Toronto

Dear Flustered:

They say that some of the best romances start out as friendships, but that only works when you both want something more. If you care enough about your friendship, do this guy a favor and tell him that you only care for him as a friend. Don't sugarcoat the truth by saying that you're afraid that if you become a couple you'd lose him as a friend. And don't start treating him like dirt in hopes of scaring him off. Wouldn't you want him to be honest with you if the shoe were on the other foot?

2. *Shifting blame.* This type of lie usually occurs when you've done something wrong and get caught. For example, the teacher wants you to hand in your homework, and you didn't do it. Instead of accepting responsibility for your failure, you say "That is due today? Didn't you say we'd have until Friday? You didn't say it was due today!" You might not have been completely certain when the assignment was due. However, honestly, there were any number of people you could have checked with to figure it out.

NOTABLE QUOTABLE

"I cannot tell a lie. I did it (cut down the cherry tree) with my hatchet."
—Attributed to George Washington as a child

3. *Taking undue credit.* In this type of lie, you take personal credit for someone else's idea or work. Written forms of this lie include the omission of footnotes and **plagiarism**—direct copying of someone else's work. Here are two examples of verbal forms of this lie. The first is an example of a **sin of omission**—not saying something that needs to be said; the second is an example of a **sin of commission**—actually saying something untrue.

---

2 *Teen Magazine* (April, 1995), p. 20.

NOTABLE QUOTABLE

"Oh, what a tangled web we weave, When first we practice to deceive!"
—Sir Walter Scott

DO THIS!

Discuss how a Christian might respond to Flustered's letter. Then read Julie's response. Do you agree or disagree with her response? Why?

For Your Eyes Only

When was the last time a teacher or parent confronted you about something you did wrong? How did you respond to the confrontation?

Example 1

Your mom asks you to wash and wax the family's second car while she runs some errands. While she's gone, a friend comes over and helps you clean the car. The friend leaves before your mom gets back. She praises you for the good job you did and gives you an extra $5 in spending money. You don't tell her that your friend helped.

Example 2

You have an afternoon job at a department store. Your boss asks you to straighten the shelves. You start to do it, but then are called to work the cash register. You ask another employee to straighten the shelves. Later, in private, your boss praises you for the creative and appealing way you arranged the merchandise. Even though you didn't do the rearranging, you accept the praise and a small raise and a promotion, as well.

4. *Image touch-ups.* In this type of lie, people try to make themselves look better than they are. For example, you lie about your weight or height on your driver's license. You say you are older than you are in order to get into a nightclub. You say you are younger than you are in order to get into an amusement park for a lower price. You exaggerate your qualifications on a job application—stretching the truth about your actual experiences.

5. *Omitting the truth.* Some people don't consider omitting the truth a lie, because they're not actually *telling* a lie. But by remaining silent or by leaving out certain information, they are leading others to believe something that is not true. For example, claiming to have 20/20 eyesight may be true—for one eye. Your other eye may have only 20/60 eyesight. Leaving this additional information off an application or other form is really a form of dishonesty.

The Truth About Lying

Some lies are big; they have major consequences. Other lies are small ("little white lies") and have fewer consequences. What is important to remember is that any lie, no matter how little, affects a person's character. Once you start lying, it's hard to stop. One lie tends to breed other lies. Furthermore, if you get into the habit of lying about little things, you're more likely to lie about the big things, too.

Indeed, being a person of integrity and honesty means telling the truth *all the time*. Telling the truth is sometimes difficult as the following situations point out. Read and reflect on each situation. How could you respond appropriately in each situation and yet still be honest?

Situation 1

Your parents give you permission to go to the library. On your way, you run into a friend and you stop and chat—for two hours. When you get home, your parents ask you how the studying went. You know they'll get mad if you tell them you never went to the library.

LET'S TALK

1. What would be the honest response for Example 1 and Example 2?

2. Tell about a time someone you know lied as an image touch-up.

3. Name some more examples when a person might omit the truth in order to gain personal advantage.

You didn't do anything wrong with your friend, so why tell them where you really were and make trouble for yourself?

Situation 2

You know there's going to be a fight after school and that someone is going to get hurt badly or even killed. When the principal asks you if you know anything about it, you're not sure what to say. You don't want to "rat" on anyone. You're also afraid of retaliation if you say anything.

Situation 3

Your best friend asks what you think of her new haircut. You don't like it, but you know she's really sensitive about her looks and you don't want to hurt her feelings.

Let's look closer at the three situations:

Situation 1: So far, you have not intentionally deceived your parents. You intended to go to the library; you just never made it there. Although it may be difficult, it is important to explain to your parents what happened. If they get angry, perhaps you can promise to phone them in the future if your plans unexpectedly change. (Such a response on your part not only shows that you are an honest person; it shows maturity and responsibility in handling problems.)

Situation 2: In this case, telling the principal is not only the honest thing to do; it is the most courageous and loving action you can take. By saying something ahead of time, you may be able to stop the fight and even save a life.

Situation 3: The Golden Rule says that we should treat others as we ourselves would want them to treat us. As the *Catechism* states, this rule "helps one discern, in concrete situations whether or not it would be appropriate to reveal the truth to someone who asks for it" (2510). Perhaps the best way to respond in this situation is to assure your friend that it's not your opinion that is important, but hers. Also assure her that you like her for herself and not because of her hairstyle.

As you can see, being truthful is not always easy. Nevertheless Jesus tells his followers, "Say 'yes' when you mean 'yes' and 'no' when you mean 'no'" (Matthew 5:37). In the long run, honesty *is* the best policy.

Gossip and Slander

The commandment, "You shall not bear false witness against your neighbor," means more than not lying. It also means that we are not to talk about people behind their backs or to spread untrue rumors about them. To **gossip** means to reveal private or sensational facts about others. What you say may be entirely true, but it's really none of your business and it's not the business of those whom you are telling. **Slander**, on the other hand, means deliberately spreading a false story about someone, with the intention of hurting his or her reputation.

LET'S TALK

Tell about a time you faced a situation similar to one of the situations described above.

NOTABLE QUOTABLE

"Tell the truth at all times and in all places. It is better to have a reputation for truthfulness than one for wit, wisdom, or brilliancy."

—*Correct Manners: A Complete Handbook of Etiquette* (late-nineteenth century)

It is obvious why slander is dishonest; it is a lie. It is not as easy, however, to understand why gossip is wrong. Perhaps the following story will help:

The Tongue and How To Use It [3]

A young lady once went to the good man, Saint Philip Neri, to confess her sins. He knew one of her faults only too well. She was not a bad-hearted girl, but she often talked of her neighbors and spoke idle tales about them. These tales were told again by others, and much harm was done, and no good.

Saint Philip said: "My daughter, you do wrong to speak ill of others, and I order you to perform penance. You must buy a fowl in the market. Then walk out of the town, and as you go along the road pull the feathers from the bird and scatter them. Do not stop until you have plucked every feather. When you have done this, come back and tell me."

She said to herself that this was a very singular punishment to suffer. But she made no objection. She bought the fowl, walked out, and plucked the feathers as she had been bidden. Then she went to Saint Philip and reported what she had done.

"My daughter," said the Saint, "you have carried out the first part of the penance. Now there is a second part. You must now go back the way you came and pick up all the feathers."

"But, father, this cannot be done. By this time the wind has blown them all ways. I might pick up some, but I could not possibly gather up all."

"Quite true, my daughter. And is it not so with the unwise words that you let fall? Have you not often dropped idle tales from your lips, and have they not gone this way and that, carried from mouth to mouth until they are quite beyond you? Could you possibly follow them and recall them if you wanted to do so?"

Hypocrisy

Not gossiping or spreading slander about others is a form of honesty based on self-respect and respect for others. Such respect is the basis of another aspect of honesty—being genuine and sincere. People with integrity represent themselves truthfully to others. They do not go around presenting themselves as someone else, like an actor who pretends to be a character on stage. They do not lead people on, appearing to be more interested than they really are.

People who are not sincere or genuine are known as **hypocrites**. Hypocrites are impostors, fakes. Their dishonesty can cause others a great deal of pain.

A song performed by Madonna, "Take a Bow," tells of a person who fakes feelings for another. One line goes: "Do you mean what you say

3 Retold by F. J. Gould in William Bennett, *The Moral Compass* (New York: Simon & Schuster, 1995), p. 149.

when there's no one around watching you, watching me?"[4]

How is being fake or a hypocrite a sign of dishonesty? Always keep in mind the many ways hypocrisy can hurt you and another and prevent you from becoming the person God intends for you to be.

Scripture

Read and discuss the following scripture passages. What does each passage have to say about hypocrisy and genuineness? How do these passages relate to relationships in today's world?

◆ Matthew 7:1–5   ◆ Matthew 24:43–51
◆ Matthew 22:15–22   ◆ Luke 13:10–17
◆ Matthew 23:1–33

For Your Eyes Only

Have you ever been hurt by the hypocrisy of someone else? What happened?

The Christian Challenge

As the previous chapter discussed, we do not live in a perfect world; nor are we humans perfect. Nevertheless, the truth Christians believe in is this: The God of truth loves us even in our imperfection, Jesus is the truthful way to oneness with God, and the Holy Spirit fills us with knowledge of all that is truthful.

4 Babyface and Madonna, "Take a Bow." Copyright © 1994 Sony Songs Inc., ECAF Music, WB Music Corp., and Webo Girl Publishing Inc. All rights on behalf of Song Songs Inc. and ECAF Music administered by Sony Music Publishing, 8 Music Square West, Nashville, TN 37203. All rights on behalf of Webo Girl Publishing Inc. administered by WB Music Corp.

Part of living and acting as a Christian in today's world means accepting the challenge to "[speak] the truth in love, [and] grow up in every way into him who is the head, into Christ" (Ephesians 4:15). Daily, we musk keep trying to "clothe [ourselves] with the new self, created according to the likeness of God in true righteousness and holiness" (Ephesians 4:24).

Meeting this challenge is not easy, but its rewards are worth the effort, as the story line of the following movie emphasizes:

Stand and Deliver

Jaime Escalante, a computer teacher, is hired to teach math at Garfield High School in East Los Angeles. The area has a high crime rate, which Escalante discovers firsthand when his car is broken into and the radio is stolen.

Most teachers at Garfield expect very little of their students who, for the most part, have Spanish surnames and live in the barrio. The students are stereotyped as slow, lazy, and without much of a future. The situation seems hopeless.

As Escalante learns, his students are under enormous pressure. Anita's family wants her to drop out of school and work full time as a waitress in the family restaurant. Angel has to take care of his sick grandmother and, because of his tough image, doesn't want to be seen with books. Pancho, who has a hard time with math, would rather spend his time fixing cars.

Escalante realizes that the only way his students will be able to break out of their cycle of failure is to teach them algebra and calculus—skills that will enable them to get into college, learn how to program computers, and eventually get good jobs. He teaches summer school and constantly encourages the students to believe in the truth that it is possible to achieve whatever it is they desire if they work hard and are honest. "Wouldn't you rather be designing cars than pumping gas into them?" Escalante goads the students. "All you see is the immediate turn. You don't see the road ahead."

The students persevere and finally take the advance placement test. Eighteen students pass the test, but the testing board thinks the students cheated. After all, they are Hispanic students from an inner city school. They couldn't possibly be that smart.

The students stand by their word: They have not cheated. Still the testing board refuses to believe them. Despite the humiliating way they have been treated, the students stand up for the truth of their accomplishment. They "prove" their integrity by retaking the test and passing it again. Finally, the testing board has to admit the students have been honest.

That was in 1982. The hard work of those students not only paid off for them; it also inspired other students to believe in the same truth about themselves: They could succeed if they worked hard

NOTABLE QUOTABLE

"All truth comes from the Holy Spirit."

—St. Thomas Aquinas

LET'S TALK

1. What was the truth that Jaime Escalante believed in?

2. Once the students believed in the same truth, what did they do to be faithful to it?

3. If someone accused you of cheating on an important test and you hadn't cheated, would you retake the test? Why or why not?

and were honest. Five years later nearly 100 Garfield students passed the college calculus advance placement test. The tradition of academic excellence at the school continues to this day.

An Ongoing Struggle

Being honest and maintaining integrity is an ongoing struggle. Honesty is not something you achieve one day and then, for the rest of your life, you are an honest person. Being honest involves making many choices day by day. Sometimes we fail. For Catholics, the sacrament of **reconciliation** can help to get us back on the right track.

The sacrament of penance or reconciliation is all about being honest with yourself, with God, and with other members of the Christian community. The examination of conscience is an opportunity to be honest with yourself. It helps you see how faithful and unfaithful you have been to the commandments, to church teaching, and to what you know to be right and wrong. There are other ways to have your sins forgiven besides going to confession. But the church teaches that you must go to confession if you have committed a mortal sin. It is also wise to confess lesser sins in the sacrament. Doing so helps you to take a personal inventory of your life and gives you a chance to speak to a priest about these areas of concern and receive absolution for your sins through him. Together, the two of you can get a clearer view of the truth. Finally, God's forgiving grace helps you once again to "love not in word or speech, but in truth and action." (See 1 John 3:18–19.)

Prayer

LEADER: St. Paul advised the Ephesians to "stand fast . . . and fasten the belt of truth around your waist" (6:14). Let us now pray for the grace to stand fast to our values as Christians and for the courage to be honest.

READER 1: Psalm 25:4–7

READER 2: Psalm 25:20–21

READER 3: Psalm 119: 29–30

ALL: Jesus, help us always to remember that you are "the way, the truth, and the life." Help us remain steadfast in the truth and be faithful to it in all our actions. Help us to be honest, sincere, and genuine in all our relationships. This we ask in union with your Holy Spirit of truth. Amen.

Further Activities

1. In some states, stolen property of $250 or more is a felony. Anything under $250 is a misdemeanor, unless the property has been stolen directly off a person. Find out what your state's laws are regarding the different types of stealing and prepare a report for the class.

2. Summarize a recent TV show or movie you have seen. Then analyze the characters for their integrity and honesty. What "message" does the TV show or movie give viewers about the value of truthfulness?

For Your Eyes Only

Reflect on the importance of the sacrament of reconciliation for your life. How can the sacrament help you know the truth about yourself and thus "make you free" to "love in truth and action."

NOTABLE QUOTABLE

"Teens with integrity don't do things that would make them ashamed of themselves. They have pride in themselves."

—Janell Holas, Glendive, MT high school student

Tell why you agree or disagree with this message.

3. In a group, read one of the following stories (or another story approved by your teacher). Then, in a skit, song, or rap poem, tell how the person or main character valued or came to value honesty.

◆ "The Young Storekeeper," by Horatio Alger in *Abraham Lincoln: The Backwoods Boy.*

◆ *Pinocchio* by Carlo Lorenzini.

◆ *A Man for All Seasons* by Robert Bolt.

◆ "A Voyage to the Houyhnhnms," by Jonathan Swift in *Gulliver's Travels.*

4. Prepare a reconciliation service for the class on the theme of honesty and integrity.

At Home

Make a daily effort to be honest in your dealings with family members. Keep a journal detailing what you do.

Part 2 Review

1. What is goodness? How is God good?

2. Explain how moral goodness differs from body image (being good-looking).

3. What are three important aspects of healthy self-esteem?

4. How does healthy self-esteem differ from the sin of pride?

5. What is humility? How does it differ from false humility?

6. If God created people good, why aren't people perfect?

7. What does it mean to be "poor in spirit"?

8. What are three ways you can help yourself grow in healthy self-esteem?

9. What are two ways you can build self-esteem in others?

10. What does it mean to be honest?

11. What are eight types of stealing?

12. Why is cheating wrong?

13. What are five different types of lies?

14. What is the difference between a sin of omission and a sin of commission? Why are both sins examples of dishonesty?

15. Is it always appropriate to reveal the truth to someone who asks for it? What does the *Catechism* say?

16. What is the difference between gossip and slander?

17. What is hypocrisy? Give an example.

18. How can the sacrament of reconciliation help you gain a clearer understanding of truth?

For Your Eyes Only

Pretend someone has questioned your integrity. Are there any accusations the person could make against you based in truth?

Words to Know

burglary
capital sins
cheating
embezzlement
forgery
fraud
goodness
gossip
grand larceny
honesty
humility
hypocrite
integrity
larceny
lying
mortal sin
original sin
plagiarism
pride
Reconciliation
self-esteem
shoplifting
sin of commission
sin of omission
slander
stealing
swarming
venial sin

POWER

What is power?

How can you imitate God's power in your dealings with other people?

How can you imitate God's power in your dealings with material things and the natural world?

What Is Power?

Christians acknowledge that God is "all-powerful." What does that mean? A dictionary definition tells us power is "the ability to act or produce an effect." To have **power** means to have authority, control, or influence over others—both people and things. Power is force, energy, strength, and might.

Both Christians and Jews believe that God is omnipotent, or all-powerful. Both religious traditions believe that all power on earth belongs to God (Psalm 62:12) and that God is the almighty—"the Alpha and the Omega, the one who is and who was and who is to come, the almighty" (Revelation 1:8, NAB). God can do all things, and no purpose of God's can be thwarted (Job 42:2). Furthermore, God's power is universal; it extends throughout the cosmos.

LET'S TALK

1. Review the Nicene Creed (see page 235). Discuss what Christians mean by saying that God is the "Father Almighty."

2. How have you seen evidence of God's power in your life? in the world of nature?

Jesus, God's Power

Christians differ from Jews by believing that God showed his power by raising Jesus from the dead (Ephesians 1:20). Indeed, for Christians, Jesus himself is "the power of God" (1 Corinthians 1:24). As both the Apostles' Creed and the Nicene Creed state, Jesus was conceived "by the power of the Holy Spirit."

Throughout his life on earth, Jesus demonstrated the power of God by working miracles or *dynameis* (powers), works of power. Through Jesus, we glimpse the extent of God's power. God has the power to heal and to cast out demons; God has power over nature and over death itself.

NOTABLE QUOTABLE

"The Incarnation is the entrance of the power of God into the world in the person of Jesus Christ."

—John McKenzie, *Dictionary of the Bible*

Scripture

In a small group, read and summarize the passages found in one of the following groupings. Answer for yourself what each passage tells you about God's power. How is this same power of God present in today's world? Plan a presentation that explains the meaning of the passages in your group.

Group 1:
- Matthew 8:2–4
- Matthew 8:5–13
- Matthew 8:14–15
- Matthew 9:2–8
- Matthew 9:20–22
- Matthew 9:27–31

Group 2:
- Matthew 12:9–13
- Matthew 15:21–28
- Matthew 20:29–34
- Mark 7:31–37
- Mark 8:22–26
- Luke 13:10–17

Group 3:
- Luke 14:1–6
- Luke 17:11–19
- Luke 22:49–51
- John 4:46–53
- John 5:1–9
- John 9:1–7

Group 4:
- Luke 8:26–39
- Luke 4:33–37
- Matthew 9:32–34
- Matthew 12:22
- Matthew 17:14–21
- Mark 1:21–28

Group 5:
- Matthew 9:18–19
- Matthew 9:23–26
- Matthew 14:13–21
- Matthew 14:22–32
- Luke 7:11–17
- John 11:1–44

Group 6:
- Matthew 8:23–27
- Matthew 15: 32–39
- Matthew 17:24–27
- Mark 11:20–24
- Luke 5:1–11
- John 2:1–11

DO THIS!

Choose one of the seven gifts of the Holy Spirit. Using the dictionary and a Catholic encyclopedia, research the meaning of this gift. Prepare a class presentation that (1) defines the gift, (2) relates how you have experienced the gift through the example of another, and (3) explains how the gift can be beneficial to teenagers.

The Power of the Holy Spirit

Both Christians and Jews believe that God gives power and strength to people of faith. (See Psalm 68:35.) But Christians further believe that God actually shares his power with us. God empowers us to become children of God, people of good character. (See John 1:12.) Just as the Holy Spirit gave God's own power to the apostles at Pentecost, so we receive God's empowering presence through the sacrament of baptism. This power is strengthened and celebrated within us through the sacraments of **eucharist** and **confirmation**. In all three sacraments, we receive the seven **gifts of the Holy Spirit**—wisdom, knowledge, understanding, right judgment, courage, reverence, and wonder (awe in God's presence). These gifts increase our ability to relate to others with love and with hope. (See Romans 15:13.)

The next two chapters will discuss the power God has given you to establish and maintain right relationships. Chapter 5 deals with the right relationships Christians are called to have with *other people*. Chapter 6 deals with the right relationships Christians are called to have with *material things and the natural world*.

5. Right Relationships With Others

CHAPTER GOALS

In this chapter, you will:

◆ Explore the reasons for disagreements and misunderstandings with parents or guardians and learn ways you can improve communication;

◆ See how sexual abuse and both domestic and dating violence are examples of the misuse of power in relationships;

◆ Discover the power you have to control your bad moods, especially in your relationship with others.

Have you ever experienced a power blackout? If so, then you know what it's like to have no lights, no heat or air conditioning (if you have an electric heater, air conditioner, or fans), no refrigerator, no TV, no VCR, no phone answering machine, and no radio (unless it's battery operated). You can't use your blow drier, computer, printer, dishwasher, washing machine, or microwave. It's no wonder that people often feel helpless when there's no power. They can't do anything about their situation until power is restored. And usually, they have no control over when that will be.

The helpless feeling that comes over many people during a power blackout is similar to the helplessness many teenagers feel about their lives. They feel trapped in their situation at home, at school, or in general. They also feel powerless to change that situation. As a result, an alarming number of teenagers choose to run away from many different kinds of life situations, both figuratively and literally.

A national study conducted in 1994 estimates that between 1/2 to 2 million runaway pre-teens and teens live on the streets in the United States. Among the reasons young people give for running away are school problems, mental health problems, drug abuse/alcoholism, sexual or physical abuse by a parent, violence by other family members, a parent who is a drug abuser/alcoholic, and long-term family economic problems. By far, most of the reasons involve relationship problems—family or otherwise.

Far from solving problems, running away tends to create even more problems. In the United States, runaway teens are not eligible for welfare. Once the money and the knapsack provisions from home are gone, the runaways have only four basic means of survival—charity (soup kitchens and homeless shelters), **panhandling** and shoplifting, **prostitution** (survival sex), and drug dealing. Nine percent of pre-teens and teens who live on the streets have AIDS or are infected with HIV.

For Your Eyes Only

1. Have you ever run away from home or been tempted to run away? Why?

2. Do you know anyone who has run away? What happened?

F.Y.I.

There are over 800 shelters and 1,000 programs for runaway teens across the United States. These shelters and services provide runaways with a temporary place to stay and counseling for them and their families. Most states limit a runaway's stay in a shelter to two to four weeks.

Relating to Parents

According to *Time* magazine (November 21, 1994), an estimated 1.3 million teenagers run away from home each year because of family problems. Most of these family problems come under one heading—relating to parents.

Problems between parents and teenagers are so common that they are often the subject of TV shows, movies, and popular songs.

Mark Twain's famous quotation below expresses the tendency of teenagers to stake out their identities apart from their parents. This natural and normal phenomenon often is accompanied by many conflicts and tensions. Most of these conflicts do not lead to a teen running away, but they nevertheless bring a fair amount of pain and turmoil to a family.

LET'S TALK

1. What is something you or other teenagers today blame the previous generation for?

2. What expectations and hopes do your parents have for you? Do you feel hostage to those hopes? Explain.

3. What would you do differently than your parents if you were raising a teenager? What would you do the same?

NOTABLE QUOTABLE

"When I was a boy of 14, my father was so ignorant I could hardly stand to have the old man around. But when I got to be 21, I was astonished at how much the old man had learned in seven years."

—Mark Twain

Why Parents and Teens Argue

Most arguments between parents and teens involve a struggle for power. As a small child, you had little or no power at all. You depended on your parents or guardians for everything. Now that you are older, physically bigger, and more intellectually and emotionally capable, the balance of power is shifting. You are becoming more responsible and independent. You want more freedom to make your own decisions.

Most parents, whose job it has been to protect their young children, still want to protect their teenagers. Teenagers, however, resent being treated like children. They assert their independence in a variety of ways. Unfortunately, the tension between parents and teens can become so high that communication deteriorates. Parents seem to speak only in ultimatums: "Don't roughhouse in the living room." "Pick up your clothes." "Get out of bed right now!" "Call me when you get there." "Do your homework first." "Be home by nine." Teenagers, who think their parents don't trust them, often rebel out of frustration. Simple misunderstandings can soon escalate into a constant battle. Parents and teens become enemies; in every encounter, one side must win and one side must lose.

In one form or another most of these battles between parents and teens center around the rate at which the teen becomes independent. A teen asks to stay out late or go to a certain party and parents say "no," in part because they fear their child is growing up too fast, becoming an adult before he or she is really ready. This argument is a classic one, as represented by the following ancient Roman myth:

Phaeton[1]

Phaeton was the son of Apollo, the sun god who drove a fiery chariot across the sky each day. Many times Phaeton had watched the sun riding across the sky, and he had dreamed of what it would be like.

One day, Apollo promised to give Phaeton anything he wanted.

"I want to drive your chariot across the sky and bring light to the world." Phaeton cried at once.

Instantly Apollo realized the foolishness of his promise, and he shook his head in warning. "The first part of the way is steep," he said, "So steep that even when the horses are fresh in the morning, they can hardly make the climb. The middle part of the journey takes me high up in the heavens, and I can scarcely look down without alarm. The last part of the road descends rapidly and requires the most careful driving. Beware, my son, lest I be the donor of a fatal gift. I beg you not to ask this one thing. It may destroy you."

He ended, but his warning did no good, and Phaeton held to his demand. So, having resisted as long as he could, Apollo led the way to where the lofty chariot stood. The boy sprang into the chariot, stood erect, and grasped the reins with delight, pouring out thanks to his reluctant parent. The horses darted forward and sliced through the clouds, into the winds from the east.

It wasn't long before the steeds sensed that the load they drew was lighter than usual. They rushed headlong and left the traveled road. Phaeton began to panic. He had no idea which way to turn the reins, and even if he knew, he had not the strength. When the unhappy Phaeton looked down upon the earth, now spreading in the vast expanse beneath him, he grew pale and his knees shook with terror.

The horses dashed into unknown regions of the sky. The clouds began to smoke, and the mountain tops caught fire. Fields grew parched with heat, plants withered, and harvests went up in flames. Cities perished, with their walls and towers, and whole nations turned to ashes.

Jupiter saw that all the Earth would perish if he did not quickly help. Brandishing a lightning bolt in his hand, he flung it at the charioteer. At once the car exploded, the wheels shattered, and the wreckage scattered across the stars. Phaeton, his hair on fire, fell like a shooting star. He was dead long before he left the sky. A river god received him and cooled his burning frame.

For Your Eyes Only

1. What was the nature of the last disagreement you had with your parent(s)? How did your independence factor in?

2. How would seeing issues through the eyes of your parents help to improve communication between you?

---

1 Adapted from a Roman myth told by Ovid.

Ways to Communicate

Learning how to communicate effectively is an important way to increase your power in your relationships with parents, guardians, teachers—everyone. Like power itself, communication can either be misused or used correctly. Here are some types of communication that show a misuse of power:

1. Wearing down parents/teachers until you get what you want—asking over and over again until they give in.

2. Using a sob story, making a play for sympathy.

3. Dividing and conquering—setting one parent against the other or a parent against a teacher.

4. Threatening a public fight—embarrassing a parent in front of relatives or company unless you get what you want.

5. Procrastinating—saying you'll do your homework later if you get what you want now.

6. Omitting to tell the truth—not telling your parents what really happened.

7. Lying outright. (Numbers 6 and 7 were covered in Chapter 4.)

8. Silent treatment—not telling your parents anything and expecting them to read your mind.

9. Being rude or sarcastic, using put-downs, or lipping off—using flip remarks, hurtful comments, cruel one-liners, and smart-alec comments.

10. Being defensive and refusing to listen—seeing yourself as completely right and your parent(s) as completely wrong.

LET'S TALK

Share an example of a time when you wanted to do something, your parents said "no," and they turned out to be right.

All of these types of communication misuse power. All of these types of communication are really forms of manipulation. They are childish; furthermore, they do not show respect for the other or desire on your part to work through a problem and find a mutually-agreed upon solution.

In contrast, the correct use of power involves respect for others, courteous communication, and a willingness to compromise, or be flexible. Such virtues are implied in the fourth commandment, "Honor your father and your mother." Loving, respectful communication is called for at all stages in the parent-child relationship—when the child is young, when the child is a teenager, and when the child is an adult.

Scripture

What do the following passages say about the "right" way to communicate, or relate, to parents?

◆ Luke 2:41–51   ◆ John 2:1–12   ◆ John 19:25–27

What's Eating Gilbert Grape?

As you probably realize by now, "right" communication with parents is not easy. It is often a process of trial and error, a skill that is acquired only through practice. This trial-and-error process is the subject of the movie, *What's Eating Gilbert Grape?*

In the movie, a teenager named Gilbert feels trapped by his family situation. He is stuck in Endora, Iowa—a town where nothing much happens—working at Lamson's grocery store to support his 500-pound mother, his mentally challenged brother Arnie, and his two self-centered sisters. He longs for the freedom and independence he sees in the campers who come each year for the summer and then leave for parts unknown. But Gilbert has responsibilities and—unlike his older brother who moved away and unlike his father who committed suicide in the basement—he feels duty-bound.

Perhaps in an effort to rebel or to break out of his dull routine, Gilbert has an affair with Mrs. Betty Carver. Gradually, Gilbert realizes this relationship is not right and will never bring him the happiness he seeks. He ends the affair and starts a friendship with Becky, a teenage camper who travels across the country with no responsibilities to hold her back.

Things at home continue to get worse. Gilbert is ashamed of Bonnie, his mother, because of her weight. He is humiliated because the townspeople openly stare and laugh at her when she comes out of her house to rescue Arnie from jail. Gilbert takes out his frustration by hitting Arnie.

Becky loves Gilbert despite what he has done to Arnie. She thinks Bonnie is a brave person and treats her with sincere respect when they meet. Through Becky's eyes, Gilbert grows to appreciate his mother. He discovers that the happiness he seeks will be found—not by escaping, but in loving relationships with his family.

When Bonnie dies, it will take a crane to remove her body from the house and take it to the mortuary. Gilbert does not want this. He knows that everyone, including the morticians, will laugh at her immense size

LET'S TALK

1. What kinds of character is represented by the responses of Gilbert, Gilbert's older brother, and Gilbert's father to family problems?

2. Why do you think Gilbert grows to appreciate his mother, even though she hasn't changed?

3. Why do you think Gilbert no longer feels trapped, even though he remains in Endora?

and make jokes about her. In a gesture of love and respect, Gilbert burns down the house with his mother's body in it. He finds a new sense of freedom in his relationship with Arnie and his two sisters. Now, although he chooses to remain with them in Endora, he no longer feels trapped. He knows he can go anywhere he wants and be a success because he is truly a good person.

NOTABLE QUOTABLE

"Love begins at home, and it is not how much we do but how much love we put into what we do."

—Mother Teresa of Calcutta

Communication That Works

Usually, there is a correlation between your **responsibility** and having a good relationship with your parents. The more responsible you are, the more your parents will trust you and let you be independent. Consider the following real-life example:

Flexibility[2]

Rosie felt that her parents didn't trust her. "They said they only wanted the best for me, but then they always turned around and said, 'No, you're too young.'" She seethed at the curfew, at the leashes on her social activities, at the restrictions on her dating. Even getting a job at a local mall didn't seem to help; her mother insisted on chaperoning her to and from work.

Rosie was not willing to recognize the only thing her parents could see. She was young. She was inexperienced. She didn't have the street smarts to be free of the leash. Her parents were concerned that she would get in over her head if they did not exercise some kind of supervision.

Fortunately, Rosie and her parents were willing to meet each other half-way. Rosie proposed a compromise: If she found a job closer to home and a ride to work with a fellow employee, could she go to work unchaperoned? Her parents agreed. Rosie found the job, got the ride, gave her parents a copy of her schedule, and reassured them that they could call her at work. When the new arrangement proved successful, Rosie and her folks renegotiated their deal. Rosie got a second-hand car. Her mother stopped calling her at work. As she proved herself capable of handling her job, her parents relented in other areas as well. Within a few months, Rosie was handling her social life and staying out late enough to enjoy both dinner *and* a movie.

---

2 Elizabeth Caldwell, *Teenagers!* (San Diego, CA: Silvercat Publications, 1996), pp. 28–29.

LET'S TALK

1. How did Rosie show her parents that she was a responsible person? What effect did this have on them?

2. Have you ever been in a situation similar to Rosie's? What did you do to show that you are responsible? How did your parent(s) react?

For Your Eyes Only

1. Do you ever feel embarrassed by your parent(s) or other family members? When? Why?

2. What is one thing you can do today to improve the communication between you and your parents?

Learning to Communicate Well

Good communication involves a balance of power. Both parties are allowed to express their feelings in a respectful way. Both parties keep trying to work through the conflict until anger or other negative feelings have been resolved. Both parties try to listen to one another and to cooperate. Impossible, you say? Not really. All it takes is practice and the belief that you *do* have the power to make your relationship with parents (and other people) better. Here are some actions you may want to practice the next time you and your parents have a disagreement:

1. Show your parents that you recognize them as people with real concerns. Listen to what they have to say.

2. Acknowledge that you have heard them. Perhaps repeat what they said, using your own words. (Remember to be respectful with your words and your tone of voice!)

3. Calmly state your own opinion or reasons for wanting to do something. If your parents see that you are being calm and logical, they will be more apt to cooperate with you.

4. Make sure you keep any bargains or promises you make with your parents. If they agree to let you go to a party on the condition that you be home at 10 p.m., make sure you're home then. By doing so, you'll prove that you are a person of your word, someone who is responsible and deserving of trust.

When Parents Are Wrong

Many times in an argument, parents will be right simply because they have more experience than you. There are times, however, when parents are wrong. For example, it's not right for a parent to compare you to someone else or to expect you to be someone you're not. It's not O.K. for parents to refuse to listen to you because they're convinced they're right. Nor should they use sarcasm or put-downs to keep you in your place.

Nevertheless, Christians are called to respect all people, even when they are wrong. Since your parents are only human, you should not expect them to be perfect or to behave as "ideal parents" all the time. Even when your parents or guardians are wrong in a disagreement with you, the fourth commandment challenges you to respect them and to keep trying to communicate with them.

Other Problem Relationships

In addition to having problems communicating with their parents, some teenagers are plagued by other relationship problems involving power. Among these "power problems" are sexual abuse, dating violence, and excessive mood swings. Because these problems are serious, we'll deal with each one separately.

NOTABLE QUOTABLE

"To act the right way toward the right person, in due proportion, at the right time, for the right reason, and in the right manner—this is not easy, and not everyone can do it."

—Aristotle

Sexual Abuse

Sexual abuse occurs when someone (usually an adult or someone who is older) kisses, fondles, or has sexual intercourse with you against your wishes. Sexual abuse may happen between a parent and a child, between a relative and a child, between an adult acquaintance or neighbor and a child. Such behavior is not about sex; it is about the misuse of power. The older, stronger person exerts power over the younger, weaker person. He or she happens to do this in a sexual way.

Although sexual abuse is against the law in every state in the U.S., experts estimate that 12% of all girls are abused before reaching the age of 14. Many young people are afraid to tell about the abuse because they have been threatened into silence or because they feel they are to blame for what happened. As a result, the abuse may continue for a long period of time; the young person may have psychological scars for the rest of his or her life.

A *Teen* magazine article (May, 1995) offers some good advice to pre-teens and teens about judging what is right and not right in a relationship. Here is the advice:

1. Your body belongs to you. It's that simple.

2. Good people are capable of doing bad things. It can be confusing if people you love and trust abuse you. But it's still wrong for them to abuse you.

3. The abuse is *never* your fault. It is always the abuser's fault. Nothing you do or don't do ever justifies a reason for someone using your body for sexual pleasure against your will.

4. Always tell someone whom you can trust if you believe that you are being talked to, touched, or handled in a way that you are uncomfortable with, even if you were made to promise you wouldn't. The feelings of shame, repulsion, anger, fear, and guilt don't go away by themselves. They need to be talked out with a trusted adult. If the first adult you tell doesn't listen, find another one you trust, and tell your story again until you find someone who'll listen.

5. What happens to the abuser after you come forward isn't your fault. If an argument ensues, remember that person caused the fight by his/her actions. You didn't cause the fight. If the person leaves, it's because of his/her actions. If that person goes to jail, it's because of his/her actions. Not yours.

6. Never minimize the abuse. Just because the abuse doesn't involve sexual intercourse does not mean you are not being sexually abused.[3]

LET'S TALK

1. Why is sexual abuse about power?

2. Why is it important for someone who has been sexually abused to talk about it with a trusted adult?

Dating Violence

When it comes to right relationships with others, George Washington once said, "Every action in company ought to be with some sign of respect to those present." Violence of any kind—verbal or physical—is wrong because it does not show respect for others. Violence has no place in right family relationships, nor does it belong in a healthy dating relationship.

Domestic violence is any type of violence that occurs between family members or between two people who are involved in a dating relationship. Examples of domestic violence include husbands who beat up wives, parents who beat up children, and boyfriends who beat up girlfriends. Unfortunately, domestic violence is on the rise in the United States. According to the FBI, 29% of all female murder victims in 1993 were slain by a boyfriend or husband.

Despite these statistics, a 1996 study shows that one in every four teens is involved in an abusive relationship. Why does this happen? One reason is that the violence often happens in private. Publicly, the abusive person is charming, lovable, and desirable. The person being abused thinks he or she must be to blame. Secondly, many teens feel that having a boyfriend or girlfriend—even a bad one—is better than not having a date at all.

F.Y.I.

If you are a victim of sexual abuse or know of abuse that is occurring in another family, here are places you can get help:

◆ Child Protective Services Hotline—(800) 330-1822.

◆ National Child Abuse Hotline—(800) 422-4453.

◆ Catholic Social Services—(800) 234-0344.

---

3 Shortened from "What You Should Know about Sexual Abuse," *Teen* (May, 1993), pp. 22-25.

LET'S TALK

1. How much pressure do you feel to have a boyfriend or girlfriend? Where does this pressure come from? Why?

2. Agree or disagree: It is better to have a boyfriend or girlfriend—even a bad one—than to be dating no one? Explain.

Here is one teen's story:

My Boyfriend Hit Me [4]

Rebecca was a 15-year-old honor roll student when she fell in love for the first time. It was March, 1991, her freshman year at Quakertown Community High School in Pennsylvania, and she'd just started dating Dan, a popular junior, 17.

At first, things with Dan were great. But six months after they started dating, he began to show a different side, insisting Rebecca not talk to other guys. As the months passed, he became more controlling, telling Rebecca what to wear and constantly checking up on her. He also became aggressive, roughhousing with her in jest. Although his behavior intimidated Rebecca—Dan was, after all, a 180-pound bodybuilder—she accepted it as normal.

The first time he hurt her, she was late picking him up from wrestling practice. "He was so upset he pushed me on the ground in front of his friends," recalls Rebecca. Later Dan apologized and vowed never to do it again.

Soon, however, he was lashing out at Rebecca whenever she made him angry. "One time, when I smiled at a store clerk, Dan slapped me." On another occasion, at a shopping mall, he punched her in a rage of jealousy.

Each time Dan assaulted her, Rebecca forgave him. "I always felt it was my fault," she says. "I shouldn't have walked that way, dressed that way, talked to that person." She stayed with him for nearly two years.

Now a sophomore at Rollins College in Florida, Rebecca speaks out against dating violence at high schools and colleges.

NOTABLE QUOTABLE

"It is excellent to have a giant's strength, but it is tyrannous to use it like a giant."

—William Shakespeare

For Your Eyes Only

Is there a trusted adult you would turn to if you needed to talk about a serious problem such as sexual abuse? Why would you choose this person?

LET'S TALK

1. How is dating violence a misuse of power?

2. Do boyfriends and girlfriends have a "right" to be jealous? Is jealousy part of healthy love? Explain.

3. Why do you think Dan became more and more violent with Rebecca?

4. Why do you think Rebecca always forgave him and stayed with him for as long as she did?

---

4 Shortened from Marianne Jacobbi, "My boyfriend hit me," *Family Circle* (April 2, 1996), p. 84.

Excessive Mood Swings

Excessive mood swings, which are usually the product of the body's hormone balance or imbalance, are commonplace among many teenagers. Some days, for no known reason, some teens just wake up grouchy, angry, or cranky. They "hate" the world and everyone in it. It's easier to "share" their bad mood with others than to pretend that everything is fine. And so, they go about their day making everyone else just as miserable as they are. They are uncooperative, argumentative, and obstinate.

People who use their bad moods as an excuse to be rude, sarcastic, or mean to others are really being immature. They are also acting like victims, people who are totally helpless about their situation.

On the surface it seems true: No one can help how he or she feels. A mood is a mood. It's real. However, it's also true that mature people, people of good character, can exert a certain amount of control over their moods. They can maintain right, courteous relationships, despite the way they feel. They don't take their negative feelings out on others.

In the story about Rebecca and Dan, Dan had little or no control over his anger. Instead of working to gain power over himself, Dan took out his anger on Rebecca. What Dan didn't realize was that no one can *make* us feel anything. Anger, depression, crankiness—only we have power over our own feelings.

The second thing Dan did not realize is that we always have a choice about how we are going to respond to our moods. **Reactive responses** are like knee-jerk reactions. We don't really think. If we feel anger, we just lash out. **Proactive responses**, on the other hand, show maturity and good character. We recognize our bad mood, and we realize that we can choose how to deal with it. We have the power not to let it ruin our day or our ongoing relationships. The bad mood does not control us; we control it.

Psychologists say that it *is* possible to pull yourself out of a bad mood. Here are some suggestions how:

1. **Be honest with yourself.** Recognize the fact that most bad moods don't "just happen." Maybe you're feeling down because you've got the flu or a bad cold. Maybe you're disappointed that you didn't get selected for the football team or the cheerleading squad. Maybe you're really feeling lonely because your best friend is out of town. Perhaps you're feeling like a failure because you didn't meet a goal you had set for yourself (which may have been an unrealistic goal to begin with).

For Your Eyes Only

What would do if you found yourself in a violent dating situation?

For Your Eyes Only

1. How do you usually act toward others when you are in a bad mood?

2. Describe a time when someone took his or her bad mood out on you.

People of maturity take time to be honest with themselves. They explore what's really causing the bad mood. Once they know the cause, they can regain a sense of power over the mood; they can start to figure out how to respond or even how to remedy the situation.

2. **Try to get some perspective.** If you're having a bad day or are in a bad mood, remember the times when you felt better, more optimistic. Instead of concentrating on the negative aspects of your life, think about the positives. This type of thinking can help you regain a sense of balance. It can also counteract negativity and the temptation to despair.

3. **Spend time with others.** Instead of hiding in your room and isolating yourself in your bad mood, make a special effort to reach out to others. Call a friend, go to the store, invite a friend over. Don't necessarily talk about your problems. Find out what's happening with others. Their good mood just might rub off on you!

4. **Laugh.** Play with your pet dog or cat; watch a comedy on TV; read a book of jokes. The physical act of laughing can actually make you start to feel better.

5. **Help someone else or do something nice.** Run an errand for your mom. Do some volunteer work at a preschool, homeless shelter, hospital, library, or soup kitchen. Helping others often helps the helpers. They start to feel better about themselves and their situations.

6. **Get physical.** Clean out the garage, the basement, your bedroom, and/or your closet. Move the furniture around in your bedroom. Wash the car or lift weights. In fact, do *anything* that gets your heart beat up and makes you breathe harder. Pretty soon, your body's own chemistry will kick in, and you'll find yourself feeling better.

7. **Do something creative.** Make a present for a friend. Fool around on the piano or guitar. Get out your markers or paints and draw something that expresses you.

8. **Spend time with nature.** Look at the stars at night. Listen to the ocean's waves. Walk through a meadow or forest. Hike on a mountain trail. Getting outside can help you realize there's more to reality than you and your bad mood.

9. **Empower yourself.** You may not be able to change others, but you can change yourself and your attitude toward your situation. Think positive!

10. **Pray for guidance.** Remember that the Holy Spirit is always with you, helping and guiding you. God has shared his own power with you. The more frequently you take charge of your feelings and actions, the easier it will be to relate to others in healthy ways, despite your mood.

Prayer ❧

One way I will try this week to improve my relationship with my parents is . . .

LEADER: O God, you showed us how you want us to relate to others through the interactions of Jesus with his parents, his apostles, and his persecutors. Empower us to follow the example of your Son, for this we now pray.

READER 1: Ephesians 6:1–4

READER 2: Ephesians 3:14–21

ALL: Almighty Father, you are the source of our power and abilities. Help us use the gifts of your Spirit to enrich our relationships with others. Help us gain control over our moods and our actions, and show us how to communicate clearly in ways that respect others. We ask this through your son, Jesus. Amen.

Further Activities ❧

1. Find out more about one of the following parent-teen relationships. What were the conflicts in the relationship? Were they resolved? Report your findings to the class.

   ◆ St. Monica and her son, St. Augustine.

   ◆ St. Francis of Assisi and his father, Peter Bernadone.

2. Research the life of one of the following people. How did the person help runaway teens?

   ◆ Father Flanagan, founder of Boy's Town, in Nebraska.

   ◆ Cal and Mimi Farley, founders of Boy's Ranch and Girlstown, U.S.A., both in Texas.

   ◆ St. John Bosco.

3. Call the regular phone number (not the hotline) of an agency that helps with domestic abuse. Ask for information about the agency to be mailed to you. Report on the information to the class. Also, inquire about volunteer opportunities at the agency.

4. Plan and participate in a communion service for elderly people at a nursing home who are unable to attend Mass in the parish.

5. Speak to a group of junior high students about the importance of maintaining good communication with and listening to their parents.

At Home ❧

Attend a weekday Mass or prayer service with one of your parents. Then take a walk and catch up on the events of each of your lives.

St. Monica and her son, St. Augustine.

6. Right Relationships With Things and Nature

CHAPTER GOALS

In this chapter, you will:

♦ Explore the materialism and consumerism of American society, as well as their negative effects;

♦ Discover your call to good stewardship, to cherish and protect the earth and its resources;

♦ See how some teens are using their God-given power to protect the earth and brainstorm practical ways you can develop a right relationship with things and nature.

As Christians, we believe we not only have the power to improve our relationships with others; we also believe we have the power to establish and maintain right relationships with material things and the natural world. Unfortunately, many teens (and adults, as well) are "clueless" when it comes to knowing what exactly is a right relationship with material things.

In the movie *Clueless*, a rich teenager named Cher worships the latest in fashion fads; she believes that happiness can be found in the accumulation of possessions. So she makes sure she has everything that's "in"—designer clothes, computer programs, pager, cellular phone, makeup, hairstyle, CDs, and Jeep (even though she's not quite old enough to get a driver's license).

Gradually, she realizes that something is missing in her life, but she doesn't quite comprehend what it is. She goes shopping, she tries to get her driver's license, and she tries to get the attention of a good-looking boy named Christian. Slowly, Cher realizes that the happiness she seeks will be found in helping others and doing good deeds.

She plays matchmaker for the debate coach, Mr. Hall, and her guidance counselor, Ms. Geist. In her next project, she gives Tai, a new student, a complete makeover. The result is a gorgeous Tai who becomes the most popular girl in school; too late Cher realizes she has created a monster—someone who worships material possessions even more than she does. Tai is no longer her friend, but her rival as the No. 1 Material Girl on campus.

When Cher compares herself with her step-brother Josh, a college student who is interested in environmental law, she realizes she comes up short. "I'm not good enough," she complains. "I need to make over my soul."

Now Cher has a new agenda—to win over Josh. By collecting food and clothes for disaster relief victims, she sets out to show Josh that she is a truly good person. She's definitely moving toward the Christian concept of having a right relationship with things, but the movie leaves us with many unanswered questions. We're not sure if Cher's "conversion" to **environmentalism** is genuine or is merely another fad. Is it just a "cosmetic" makeover, or is it something that will last? Has she really gotten the "bigger picture" regarding Christian values, or is she still clueless?

Teen Power

When it comes to spending money, American economists and business experts agree: Teens have a great deal of buying power. Consider the following facts:

◆ According to a study conducted by Simmons Market Research Bureau for a recent year, teenagers bought 25% of America's movie tickets. In the same year, teenagers bought 27% of all videos (a total of $6.6 billion) and spent $1.5 billion on designer jeans.

◆ In 1993, U.S. teenagers spent $57 billion of their own money on high-tech sneakers, designer jeans, video games, varsity jackets, soda and food, beepers, stereos, TVs, and cosmetics. [Note: Cosmetics are not just bought by females! According to the Federal Food, Drug, and Cosmetic Act, a *cosmetic* is any article (other than soap) "intended to be applied to the human body for cleansing, beautifying, promoting attractiveness, or altering the appearance without affecting the body's structure or functions." Examples of cosmetics that teens buy include the following items: skin care creams, lotions, and powders; perfume, cologne, and toilet water; makeup (lipstick, foundation, blush, mascara); nail polish, polish remover, and cuticle softener; hair coloring preparations; deodorants; shaving cream, aftershave lotion, and skin conditioners; shampoos; bath oils and bubble bath; mouthwash and toothpaste.]

◆ In 1995, U.S. teenagers collected $102 billion from jobs, allowances, gifts of cash, savings bonds, and other investments. Over the same 12 months, teen consumers spent $67 billion of their own money on material possessions.

◆ Economists and business executives want the spending trend to continue. "Buying things contributes to the American economy," they argue. "When consumers buy, stores stay in business and workers keep their jobs." In their eyes, it is "un-American" to live simply or to do without. What's important is the immediate gratification that comes from "buying now."

LET'S TALK

1. How do teenagers today share Cher's original materialistic outlook on life? Give specific examples. (No names, please.)

2. Do you think Cher's "conversion" is genuine or cosmetic? Explain.

F.Y.I.

In 1995, the average 16-year-old had a weekly paycheck of $51 and an allowance of $33.

—*Money*
(December, 1995).

DO THIS!

1. Study the ads in magazines of interest to teenagers. Focus on one of the following topics: cosmetics, clothing, cars, shoes. What is the advertisement selling (besides the product)? How does the advertisement claim the teen's life will be better if the product is purchased?

2. For one week keep track of how much money you spend and on what. At the end of the week, tally the results. Discuss what the results say about your buying power and values. Compare your findings with those of others in your class.

Basic Attitudes Toward Money

What you perceive as a "right" relationship with material things and the natural world is closely connected to your attitude toward money.

Some people, like the prodigal son in Luke 15:11–32, are spendthrifts. Money burns a hole in their pockets. They tend to spend everything they have, and then some. Other people, like the rich man in Luke 12:16–21, are misers. They love their money so much that they don't want to spend any of it. Both extremes—the prodigal and the miser—worship something other than God. The prodigal worships wasting money in order to have a "good time." The miser, like the Israelites who worshipped a golden calf in the desert, simply worships money. (See Exodus 32.)

People who are caught up with **materialism** and **consumerism** tend to worship the accumulation of possessions or the actual act of buying. They believe that owning and/or using an increasing number of goods and services is the surest route to personal happiness, social status, and national success. The following statements tend to reflect their thinking:

◆ Buy now, pay later.

◆ It costs more, but you're worth it.

◆ Life is short, so spend the money and just do it.

◆ If it doesn't have the right brand name, it isn't good enough.

◆ If you don't have it, then you're not good enough.

◆ You are who you are by the stuff you've got.

Such people feel that they are *entitled* to use the world, both material and natural, for their own benefit and gain. This is a misinformed and incorrect interpretation of Genesis 1:28–30, in which God gives humans dominion over all the plants and animals on earth.

LET'S TALK

1. How would you rate your present attitude toward money? Are you more the miser or the prodigal? Why do you think you have this attitude?

2. Which of the following is most important to you? Explain why.

◆ Improving the world your children will inherit.

◆ Having a better lifestyle than your parents or guardians.

◆ Saving for college.

◆ Having designer jeans, sneakers, and other possessions in order to "fit in" with other teens.

◆ Earning a lot of money.

The Sin of Greed

Very often, materialism and consumerism are motivated by the sin of greed. Greed is the excessive desire for money and material possessions. Greedy people are never satisfied with what they already have. They always want more. Consider the lesson from the following nineteenth-century Russian fable by Ivan Kylov:

Fortune and the Beggar[1]

One day a ragged beggar was creeping along from house to house. He carried an old wallet in his hand and was asking at every door for a few cents to buy something to eat. As he was grumbling at his lot, he kept wondering why it was that folks who had so much money were never satisfied but were always wanting more. "People never seem to be satisfied unless they can gain the whole world," the beggar said. "As for me, if I had only enough to eat and to wear I would not want anything more."

Just at that moment Fortune came down the street. She saw the beggar and stopped. She said to him: "Listen! I have long wished to help you. Hold your wallet, and I will pour this gold into it. But I will pour only on this condition: All that falls into the wallet shall be pure gold, but every piece that falls upon the ground shall become dust. Do you understand?"

"Oh, yes, I understand," said the beggar.

"Then have a care," said Fortune. "Your wallet is old, so do not load it too heavily."

The beggar was so glad that he could hardly wait. He quickly opened his wallet, and a stream of yellow coins was poured into it. The wallet soon began to grow heavy.

"Is that enough?" asked Fortune.

"Not yet."

"Isn't it cracking?"

"Never fear."

The beggar's hands began to tremble. Ah, if the golden stream would only pour forever!

"You are the richest man in the world now!"

"Just a little more," said the beggar.

"There, it's full. The wallet will burst."

"But it will hold a little more, just a little more!"

Another piece was added, and the wallet split. The treasure fell upon the ground and turned to dust. Fortune vanished. The beggar had now nothing but his empty wallet, and it was torn from top to bottom. He was as poor as before.

NOTABLE QUOTABLE

"Who except God can give you contentment? Has the world ever been able to satisfy the heart?"

—St. Gerard Majella

---

1 Shortened and adapted from Ivan Krylov. Quoted from William Bennett, *The Moral Compass* (New York Simon & Schuster, 1995), pp. 169–170.

LET'S TALK

1. Why do you think many people are not satisfied with what they already have?

2. A significant number of people who become overnight millionaires by winning a lottery later have to declare bankruptcy. Why do you think this happens so frequently?

The Effects of Materialism

Greed is not the only sin associated with materialism. There are others as well: crime, the continuation of poverty, the over-accumulation of trash, toxic pollution, and depletion of the earth's resources. Let's examine some of these societal problems.

Crime

Excessively wanting material possessions leads some people to steal in order to get them. It leads others to gamble away what money they have in search of instant riches.

Here are just a few statistics:

In 1994, New Orleans enacted a curfew law that banned people under age 17 from being on the streets from dusk to dawn. In the first year the curfew was in effect, youth crime fell 27%, armed robberies by juveniles dropped 33%, and auto thefts fell 42%.

In 1993, teenagers constituted 7.6% of all people arrested for gambling.

An incorrect view of materials relates to other crimes, such as **arson** and **vandalism,** that show a disrespect for the property of others. According to the 1995 *Statistical Abstract of the United States*, 49.3% of the people arrested in 1993 for arson were juveniles. Of all the people arrested for vandalism that year, 45.6% were under 18 years of age.

The Continuation of Poverty

It's one thing to want and to be able to afford a pair of athletic shoes that cost over $150 or designer jeans that cost nearly $60. It's quite another thing to realize how the American lifestyle of materialism affects people in other countries. First of all, the American lifestyle is possible because people in other countries are poor and so have no choice but to work for low wages when all that is offered. Secondly, our continued lifestyle of materialism keeps people in other countries poor. Because they "have not," we can continue to "have." To learn more about this point, read and discuss the following two newspaper items:

LET'S TALK

1. How prevalent is vandalism (graffiti, the destruction of property, etc.) in your neighborhood? at your school? in your town or city?

2. How are arson and vandalism related to materialism?

F.Y.I.

In 1993, 20% of the world's people earned 64% of world income.

—Sierra Club

Honduran Teen [2]

Washington, DC—A Honduran girl spoke yesterday of beatings and intimidation at a production plant that previously made pants for the Wal-Mart clothing line carrying the name of celebrity Kathie Lee Gifford.

"If I could talk with Kathie Lee, I would ask her to help us, to end all the maltreatment, so that they would step yelling at us and hitting us," Wendy Diaz, 15, said at a Capitol Hill news conference.

The girl, who said she began working at the Global Fashion plant in Honduras at age 13, was brought to the United States by civil rights groups. She was introduced at the news conference by lawmakers trying to get American clothing retailers voluntarily to assure consumers their products don't come from **sweatshops** or plants using child labor.

Mrs. Gifford said she severed her ties with the Honduran factory last fall after learning of the working conditions. Wal-Mart has since ended its contract with the Honduran company that paid workers, mostly young people, 31 cents an hour to make the Kathie Lee clothing line.

Indonesian Workers [3]

Portland, OR—Michael Jordan has made millions of dollars for playing basketball. He also rakes in millions above and beyond that for endorsements.

Across the Pacific, in factories where Nike, one company he helped make famous, manufactures its shoes, the workers often get pennies for an hour's work.

The monthly wage of the average Nike worker in Indonesia is roughly equal to the U.S. price of a pair of Air Jordans ($115 in 1996). In Indonesia, the minimum wage is $56 per month, or about 25 cents an hour based on a 55-hour work week. Nike says that while some of its employees may be paid the minimum wage, the average salary it pays its Indonesian workers is $117 per month, or 53 cents an hour.

Joel Joseph, chairman of the Made in USA Foundation, said Nike is the chief culprit among the many manufacturers, including other shoe companies, who take advantage of poverty-stricken lands to make gigantic profits.

---

2 "Honduran teen pleads for end to sweatshop misery," *Associated Press* (May 30, 1996).
3 "His Airness drawn into sweatshop debate," *Associated Press* (June 7, 1996).

LET'S TALK

1. Realistically, would you be willing to pay more for designer jeans or athletic shoes so that workers could be paid higher wages? Do you think other teens would be willing to pay more?

2. What are some possible solutions to the situations involving the exploitation of workers described in the preceding examples?

The Accumulation of Trash

Did you know that astronauts traveling in space can see piles of waste and smoke from garbage incinerators when they look down at earth? Garbage goes hand-in-hand with materialism. When people consume a lot, there is a lot of waste, or trash. Materialistic thinking has little regard for the value of things. The philosophy is: "Use it and then discard it. Buy something else." With this kind of thinking, it's easy to take things, money, (and people) for granted.

In 1993, each person in the United States generated 4.4 pounds of garbage per day. Over 62% of this garbage (41% of which was paper) ended up in landfills. According to the Environmental Protection Agency (EPA), that added up to 162 million tons of landfilled municipal solid waste by the end of the year. Most of the remaining garbage was burned in incinerators.

One of the problems with garbage—even **biodegradable** garbage—is where to put it. In some parts of the country, landfills are full. People are now considering the possibility of dumping their garbage in the ocean or in landfills in Third World countries.

DO THIS!

Search through the clothes and shoes in your closet or drawers. Where are your clothes and shoes made? Check the labels to find out. Write down the information and be prepared to share it with the class.

NOTABLE QUOTABLE

"If all people would take only according to their needs and would leave the surplus to the needy, no one would be rich, no one would be poor, and no one would be in misery."

—St. Basil

DO THIS!

1. Weigh the garbage your family throws out each day. At the end of a week, bring your results to class. Add up the class weight for garbage. Spend the next week increasing your efforts at recycling waste. Add up your garbage again and compare the weight totals.

2. Find out what happens to the garbage in your area. Where are the nearest landfills and trash incinerators? How much garbage is collected? How much of this garbage is burned? Is space for garbage a problem in your area?

Toxic Pollution

While many people see garbage itself as a problem, there are even more serious effects of materialism—effects that contribute to **global warming** and **ozone depletion.** Among these effects are toxic waste, ground water pollution, acid rain, and urban smog.

According to the Environmental Protection Agency, there are 38,000 identified hazardous waste sites in the United States. Up until 1997, less than a thousand of these sites had been cleaned up. Many people (unless they happen to live next to a hazardous waste site) think the problem of toxic pollution is "out there," way beyond their realm of responsibility or caring. But the truth is, the average U.S. house or apartment contains 63 hazardous chemicals.

Household hazardous waste (HHW) includes used motor oil, antifreeze, house paints, weed killers, insect sprays, pool chemicals, paint strippers, paint thinners, household cleaners, and old car batteries. Improper disposal of HHW can harm municipal waste water treatment plants, aquifers, waterways, soil, and landfills. Toxic waste can lead to cancer, respiratory illness, and death, both in humans and in animals.

DO THIS!

1. Find out where there are hazardous waste sites in your area. Is there or has there ever been a health problem or pollution problem because of these wastes? Report your findings to the class.
2. Find out what HHWs are in your home. Bring your list to class. Research proper ways to dispose of these HHWs.

Depletion of the Earth's Resources

In order to keep up with the demands of consumerism and materialism, we are fast depleting the earth's fossil fuels, clean air, clean water, metals, and trees. Plants, animals, and/or their habitats are destroyed each year in the name of "economic progress." Here are just a few facts:

DO THIS!

Find out what one of the following groups is doing to help endangered species. Also find out what teens can do to help in conjunction with the efforts of these groups.

◆ Sierra Club
◆ Greenpeace
◆ Audubon Society
◆ Northern Forest Alliance

◆ Every hour, 23.5 square meters of tropical rain forest are destroyed. Slash-and-burn forest clearing condemns countless plant and animal species to **extinction**.
◆ It takes just 10 minutes for a logger to cut down a 1,000-year-old tree. In contrast, a stack of recycled newspapers 47 inches high equals the amount of paper produced from just one tree.
◆ More than 99% of all plant and animal species that ever lived on earth are now extinct.
◆ There are over 900 animals and plants on the **endangered-species** list. Of the animals, only seven have bounced back due to human efforts: the brown pelican, gray whale, arctic peregrine falcon, three birds from the Palau Islands in the western Pacific Ocean, and a milkvetch plant in Utah. (Note: The American alligator has also made a great comeback, but it is still on the list to protect its endangered look-alike, the American crocodile.)

It is easy to look at the facts and think that the environmental impact of materialism is so large that one person cannot make a difference. But the attitude of protecting the earth, of protecting plants and animals from injustice and from extinction, is—as the following story shows—an attitude that begins with individual efforts.

84

The Old Horse [4]

A long time ago, the King of Atri hung a fine large bell in a tower in the marketplace. A long rope that reached almost to the ground was fastened to the bell. The smallest child could ring the bell by pulling upon this rope.

"It is the bell of justice," the king explained to the villagers. "It must never be rung except in case of need. If any one of you is wronged at any time, he may come and ring the bell. And then the judges shall come together at once, and hear his case, and give him justice."

Many years passed by after this. Many times did the bell in the marketplace ring out to call the judges together. Many wrongs were righted, many ill-doers were punished. At last the rope was almost worn out. It became so short that only a tall man could reach it.

"This will never do," said the judges one day. "What if a child should be wronged? The youngster could not ring the bell to let us know."

They gave orders that a new rope should be put upon the bell at once. But since there no such rope in all Atri, they had to send across the mountains for one. It would be many days before it could be brought. Meanwhile, they replaced the worn-out rope with a long grapevine—its leaves and tendrils still upon it—that trailed to the ground.

On the hillside above the village, there lived a miser. Day after day he sat among his moneybags and planned how he might get more gold. And day after day his horse stood in his bare stall, half starved and shivering with cold.

"What is the use of keeping that lazy steed?" the man thought. "Every week it costs me more to keep him than he is worth. I might sell him, but there is not a man that wants him. I cannot even give him away. I will turn him out to shift for himself and pick grass by the roadside. If he starves to death, so much the better."

So the horse was turned out to find what he could among the rocks on the barren hillside. Lame and sick, he strolled along the dusty roads. Boys threw stones at him, dogs barked at him, and in all the world no one pitied him.

One hot afternoon, when no one was upon the street, the horse chanced to wander into the marketplace. He saw the grapevine rope that hung from the bell of justice. The leaves and tendrils upon it were still fresh and green. What a fine dinner they would be! He stretched his thin neck and took one of the tempting

4 Shortened from "The Bell of Atri" by James Baldwin. Quoted in William Bennett, *The Book of Virtues*, pp. 208–211.

morsels in his mouth. It was hard to break it from the vine. He pulled at it, and the great bell above him began to ring.

The judges heard it and came running. "Ha!" cried one, "it is the miser's steed. He has come to call for justice, for his master has treated him most shamefully."

"The horse pleads his cause well," said another.

"And he shall have justice!" said the third.

So the judges called the miser before them.

"This horse has served you well for many years," they said. "He has saved you from many a peril. He has helped you gain your wealth. Therefore we order that one half of all your gold shall be set aside to buy him shelter and food, a green pasture where he may graze, and a warm stall to comfort him in his old age."

The miser hung his head and grieved to lose his gold. But the people shouted with joy, and the horse was led away to his new stall and a dinner such as he had not had in many a day.

For Your Eyes Only

1. How well have you cared for an animal? Have you ever treated an animal cruelly?

2. Rate yourself as a gardener. When do you tend to indoor or outdoor plants?

DO THIS!

Find out what one of the following groups is doing in your local community to improve the lot of plants and animals. Report your findings to the class.

◆ City Parks Department
◆ Humane Society
◆ SPCA (Society for the Prevention of Cruelty to Animals)

Good Stewardship

In contrast to materialistic thinking and consumerism, Christians interpret Genesis 1:28–30 as God's willingness to share power with us. We not only have a right to use plants and animals for our benefit and survival; we also have a Godlike duty to take care of all creatures and natural resources on the earth. We call this duty **stewardship**.

What is good stewardship? Its meaning is contained in the beatitude, "Blessed are the meek, for they shall inherit the earth" (Matthew 5:5). The meek are not served by the earth. Rather, they work together with the earth to serve the needs of all of nature proportionately. For example, when the Aleutian people killed a whale, they used every part of it and asked for forgiveness before they killed it. Native American tribes killed only enough buffalo to meet their needs.

NOTABLE QUOTABLE

"Faith strips the mask from the world and reveals God in everything."
—Venerable Charles de Foucauld

Cherishing the Earth

Another word for good stewardship is the verb *cherish*. As a Catholic writer explains:

> Cherishing is the opposite of consuming, using, and discarding. Lots of things worth cherishing can't be bought: relationships, principles, and self-esteem, to name a few....To appreciate, to value, to save, to realize in each human being—and in each new day—God's grace in our world, to grasp why we who call ourselves Catholic hold that life is sacred—this is the task of a lifetime.[5]

---

5 Nancy Hellion Reading, "The adolescent 'good life': how it affects youth ministry." *The Catholic World* (September-October, 1995), p. 234.

Whenever we cherish and take care of material possessions, plants, animals, and the earth's natural resources, we are acting rightly, as good stewards. Whenever we act selfishly or heedlessly, we misuse our power of stewardship. We risk destroying the earth and the very resources we need for our survival.

Scripture

Read and discuss the following passages. What was Jesus' attitude toward money? toward materialism? about stewardship? How can these passages be applied for Christians today?
- Matthew 6:19–34
- Matthew 16:24–26
- Matthew 19:16–26
- Matthew 25:14–30

The Power to Make Things Better

People of good character are connected to the earth. They use their God-given power to care for the earth and to make sure that its resources are shared, not only with people living today, but with future generations. People of good character realize that every person has a role in preserving the earth and its resources. They also share the hope that all efforts—even those of one person—can help to make things better.

Here are the stories of three teenagers and how they have used their power to be less materialistic and better stewards of the earth.

Help for Manatees [6]

"Manatees are very friendly creatures and they're curious," says 15-year-old Heather McAteer, who has raised big bucks to help save these endangered aquatic mammals. "They'll swim right up to your boat," she adds.

That habit helped land the manatee on the endangered-species list. The U.S. Fish and Wildlife Service estimates that 25% of manatee deaths in this country are caused by collision with boats. Other manatees die when they get trapped in canals or eat fish hooks or litter.

McAteer, a sophomore at Central Catholic High School in Palm Bay, FL, makes clay manatee sculptures and jewelry to raise money for the species. People buy her creations at crafts fairs, Epcot Center, and Disney World. McAteer donates 20% of her gross profits—about $5,000 so far—to the Florida Audubon Society. The Audubon Society uses the money to help fund manatee research and educate the public about boating speed limits and other laws that help protect the animals.

Educating people is what McAteer enjoys most about her business. What's the worst part? Mass production. McAteer estimates that after seven years in business, her manatee sculptures now outnumber the approximately 1,800 animals that remain in the wild.

6 Adapted from Emily Costello, "Endangered species: moneymaker for manatees," *Science World* (April 12, 1996), pp. 16–17.

Sometimes McAteer gets discouraged by people's lack of caring about the manatee. But she says it's important to be persistent. "Our endangered-species list is rapidly growing," McAteer points out. "There is hope, but only if we start now. 'Endangered' means we still have a chance, but 'extinct' is forever."

River Warriors [7]

Suzanne Rhee and forty-two other students got wet and dirty to remove six tons of trash from New Jersey's Hackensack River last August. They cleaned up the river as part of a week-long environmental camp.

Scooping out the soggy trash was not exactly a glamour job. Like one in three rivers, the Hackensack is so polluted that it's unsafe for swimming, fishing, and/or aquatic life.

Three years ago, when the cleanup started, trash was everywhere. But this year, the teens had to hunt for trash. Billy Dietsch, 17, says the teens turned the cleanup into a competition to see who could find the most garbage and unload their boats fastest.

By the end of the six-hour shift, the teens had removed enough trash to fill more than two large dump trucks. They found balloons, plastic bags, cans, bottles, twenty shopping carts, assorted car parts, a garage door, a bike, an armchair, and a kitchen sink!

"Seeing all that trash in the river makes people begin to care about environmental issues," Rhee says. She hopes that when others read that she and her peers care enough to clean it up, "maybe they will think twice before they throw garbage in."

Waste? Not! [8]

After brown-bagging it for years, 16-year-old Zach Udko realized he had probably thrown away hundreds of lunch bags. What a waste, he thought, and came up with a plan. "I made a reusable lunch bag," says Udko. "By using the bag, we can stop wasting paper and help save trees."

"The bag's made of nylon and it's shaped like a paper lunch bag," says the teen, who attends Brentwood School in Los Angeles. "There's a Velcro strip on its flap top, so you can close it and pull it open."

Zach came up with a unique way to sell his invention—and get others to care about the environment. He wrote and produced a musical called *Save Our Planet*, starring himself and nine other

7 Adapted from Sarah Endo and Anita Flanagan, "Water: River Warriors," *Science World* (April 12, 1996), pp. 10–11.
8 Adapted from Lynda Jones, "Trash: Waste? Not!" *Science World* (April 12, 1996), pp. 8–9.

teens. "The play includes a scene about a kid who makes a reusable lunch bag. Since the bag is featured in the play, Udko sells them after each performance for $6.95 each. The cash covers the cost of making more bags."

St. Gregory the Great once offered this advice: "Be not anxious about what you have, but about what you are." The deeds and decisions of these three teens show good stewardship—the challenge of all Christians—and put St. Gregory's words into action.

DO THIS!

Discuss practical ways your class can help promote one of the following messages to other teens:

◆ You don't need to be rich to be happy.

◆ Real success is not measured in material possessions.

◆ The world, with all its plants and animals, is meant to be protected and shared.

◆ Good stewardship (or environmentalism) begins at home.

◆ Consider sponsoring an Earth Day (traditionally in April) at your school, in which your group carries through with its ideas.

Prayer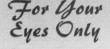

LEADER: Loving Creator of the earth and all its plants, animals, and people, we come before you today to praise your work and to thank you for giving us the power to be stewards of the world. Help us to realize even more fully how precious the earth's resources are and to cherish them always.

READER: Psalm 65: 6–9

ALL: Teach us, Lord, how to be good stewards. Increase our sense of responsibility to take care of your creation and to cherish it through our actions. Help us, in all our attitudes and decisions, to have a right relationship with material possessions and the natural world. We ask this in the name of your Son, Jesus Christ, and through the intercession of the Holy Spirit. Amen.

Further Activities

1. Launch a school-wide recycling campaign. Organize and carry out this campaign for the rest of the school year.

2. Form a team to work regularly with local law enforcement officials to paint over graffiti in your town or city.

3. Build a backyard habitat for birds, butterflies, small mammals, and/or reptiles. (For more information, write to: Backyard Wildlife Habitat Program, National Wildlife Federation, 8925 Leesburg Pike, Vienna, VA 22184-0001.)

4. Find out where a fast-food restaurant near you gets its beef.

For Your Eyes Only

1. One practical way I will show that I cherish the earth's plants and animals this week is:

2. One practical way I will be less materialistic this week is:

(It may be from South America where farmers have cleared rain forests to provide grazing land for cattle). If there is a negative environmental connection, circulate a petition among students at your school and send it to the restaurant, asking it to find a more "environmentally-friendly" meat source.

5. Contact your state's department of Environmental Protection to find out which endangered animals and plants live near you. Organize a walkathon, bake sale, or car wash to educate people and to raise money for the endangered species.

At Home 🌿

Clean out your closets and donate whatever you don't need or no longer use to the St. Vincent de Paul Society. Talk with family members about how your family can live less materialistically.

Words to Know

arson
biodegradable
confirmation
consumerism
domestic violence
endangered species
environmentalism
eucharist
extinction
gifts of the Holy Spirit
global warming
greed
household hazardous waste
(HHW)
materialism
ozone depletion
panhandling
power
prostititution
responsibility
sexual abuse
stewardship
sweatshop
vandalism

Part 3 Review

1. In what ways is God powerful?

2. How did Jesus demonstrate God's power?

3. Name the seven gifts of the Holy Spirit.

4. Why do some teenagers choose to run away and live on the streets? How do they survive on the streets?

5. What is the root of most arguments between parents and teens?

6. What are ten types of communication that show a misuse of power?

7. What are four actions you can take to improve communication with your parent(s) or guardian(s)?

8. Define sexual abuse.

9. What is domestic violence? What is dating violence?

10. What are three ways you can help yourself get out of a bad mood?

11. Define greed.

12. What is the connection between materialism and (A) crime? (B) the continuation of poverty in other countries? (C) the over-accumulation of trash? (D) toxic pollution? (E) the depletion of the earth's resources?

13. What are three examples of household hazardous waste?

14. What is the difference between being endangered and being extinct?

15. What was Jesus' position toward materialism and consumerism?

16. Define stewardship.

17. How is the verb *cherish* related to good stewardship?

18. How do people of good character relate to material things? to the natural world?

PART 4

WISDOM

What is wisdom?

How can you grow in wisdom when making decisions concerning alcohol, drugs, tobacco, and inhalants?

How can you grow in wisdom when it comes to work—household chores, school work, a job, or team competition?

What Is Wisdom?

Wisdom is a type of knowing that involves the ability to discern the truth, as well as the best course of action. Other words for wisdom include insight and good sense. Two virtues associated with wisdom are **prudence** (the ability to be cautious, to weigh the consequences of a decision or action) and **right judgment** (the ability to make the best choice in a certain situation). Wisdom is another one of God's attributes and is the focus of the next two chapters.

Both Christians and Jews believe that God alone has true wisdom. (See Romans 16:27). We see God's wisdom in action whenever we look at all the various types of plants and animals in the world and how they interrelate with one another in ecosystems. (See Proverbs 3:19; 8:27–31; Job 38–39.)

Christians believe that, as God's Son, Jesus is "the wisdom of God" (1 Corinthians 1:24). As a human being, however, Jesus "grew in wisdom" (Luke 2:52). His wisdom as an adult was widely recognized by others. (See Matthew 13:54 and Mark 6:2.)

We can glimpse what divine wisdom is like whenever we encounter people who are wise. Wise people know the appropriate words to say and how to act in various types of social and moral situations. Wise people know how to advance their own success and happiness without hurting others. Wise people respond without undue anxiety whenever opposition, setbacks, mistakes, or failures occur.

Scripture

What do the following passages tell about what it means to be wise? Read the passages and discuss your answers.

◆ Genesis 41　　　　◆ 1 Kings 3　　　　◆ Proverbs 4

LET'S TALK

1. What is meant by the term "street wise?" Who do you know who fits this definition?

2. Describe a person you consider to be most wise.

Divine Wisdom vs. Human Wisdom

Repeatedly the Bible points out that human wisdom is not the same as divine wisdom. As St. Paul explains to the early Christians, Jesus' decision to die on the cross seems utterly foolish. But in God's eyes, according to the overall scheme of God's plan, the crucifixion is true wisdom. (See 1 Corinthians 1:18, 22-25)

Divine wisdom comes from God. It is seen as the very words of God. (See Sirach 24:3-29.) Divine wisdom views life in its entirety. Human wisdom often focuses only on a particular situation or area of life. The following story points out the difference between divine wisdom and human wisdom:

For Your Eyes Only

Often we do not know if we have made a wise decision until a much later time. Describe a decision you made earlier in your life. Tell whether you now think the decision was wise or foolish. Explain why.

NOTABLE QUOTABLE

"Wisdom keeps you from making mistakes, and comes from having made plenty of them."

—Bernard Baruch

The Four Blind Men [1]

Once there were four blind men who went to a circus. The question arose, "What does an elephant look like?" One blind man felt the elephant's leg and said it looked like a tree trunk. Another blind man felt the elephant's tail and said it looked like a rope. A third blind man felt the elephant's tusk and said it looked like a sword. The last blind man felt the elephant's side and said it looked like a wall.

Each of the blind men was wise from his own perspective, but that perspective wasn't big enough to describe the entire elephant. Likewise, human wisdom can be compared to the wisdom of each blind man. It has limits. God's wisdom, however, is like seeing the entire elephant. It has no limits because it takes in the whole picture.

That is why wise people realize they don't know everything. As humans, we must continually grow in wisdom. Such wisdom comes from making mistakes and learning from them. It also comes from practice—the practice of making good decisions and persevering in carrying them out.

As Christians, we believe that God shares his divine wisdom with us. We receive divine wisdom, one of the gifts of the Holy Spirit, at baptism. (See Ephesians 1:8, 17.) We grow in this virtue the more we apply it to our daily decisions. Some decisions, such as deciding whether or not this shirt goes with that pair of pants or whether to have chocolate or vanilla ice cream for dessert, are **amoral**; they have nothing to do with choosing between right and wrong. Other decisions are **moral**; they involve choosing between a right action and a wrong one. When it comes to moral decisions, we prove that we are wise by our right conduct. (See James 3:13–15 and Romans 1:18–21.)

In this section, you will explore how wisdom relates to good character. Chapter 7 discusses wise decisions involving alcohol, tobacco, and drugs. Chapter 8 deals with wise decisions having to do with work.

LET'S TALK

1. Describe two amoral decisions you made today.

2. What are some examples of common moral decisions teenagers face?

3. If you could offer one suggestion for "growing in wisdom" what would it be?

Scripture

How are you called to be wise? Respond to this question in light of the following scripture passages.

◆ Matthew 10:16

◆ Matthew 7:24–27

◆ Matthew 25:1–13

NOTABLE QUOTABLE

"The wiser we get, the more we recognize our own limitations."

—William Bennett, *The Moral Compass*

---

1 "The Blind Men and the Elephant." Quoted in William Bennett, *The Moral Compass*, (New York: Simon & Shuster, 1995), p. 192–193.

7. Making Good Decisions

Very often, we are asked to make a decision on the spur of the moment. Because we feel pressured—either by others or by a time deadline—we don't think about the consequences of our choice. We simply act, and in doing so we may act foolishly. Consider the following true story about a decision one teenager made:

Poor Judgment [1]

One evening George received a phone call from a friend. She was stuck at school and needed a ride home. Even though George was at work when he received the call, he decided to give his friend the ride. He didn't bother to call home to notify his parents about his change of plans.

He also didn't bother to consider whether it was a good idea. It was snowing. It was icy. George's car was not winterized. In fact, it didn't have a heater, a defroster, snow tires, good brakes, or working headlights. Still, George felt the call of responsibility.

By the time he picked up his friend, the storm had made the streets dangerous. The snow plows had been too busy with the interstates and main roads to pay any more than minimal attention to the side streets. George didn't see the divider in the middle of the road until he hit it. The car died right there. An unsympathetic policeman gave George thirty minutes to remove the car from the street if he didn't want it to be towed.

George finally called his parents who picked up the two teens in time to get a stern tongue-lashing from the police. *What kind of parent would let an inexperienced sixteen-year-old driver loose on snowy streets?* The girl friend got home around midnight. George and his parents spent the rest of the night arguing about what George did and what he should have done.

Wisdom and Responsibility

Thankfully, George's decision had only minor negative consequences. But the consequences of his rash choice could have been very serious, even fatal. Truly wise people are responsible. They make the

---

1 Elizabeth Caldwell, *Teenagers!* (San Diego, CA: Silvercat Publications, 1996), pp. 150–151.

CHAPTER GOALS

In this chapter, you will:

◆ See that good decisions involve responsibility—getting all the facts and thinking through the consequences *before* acting;

◆ Learn some facts about alcohol, reckless driving, drugs, tobacco, and inhalants so that you can make wise decisions regarding them;

◆ Discover seven steps to becoming wise when making decisions.

LET'S TALK

1. If you were George, how would you have responded to your friend's call for a ride? Why?

2. Do you think George showed poor judgment? Why?

3. Do you think George's parents were justified in being angry with him? Why?

4. In hindsight, how do you think George should have responded to this situation?

97

effort to think through things *before* acting. Unlike the blind men and the elephant, wise people try to get all the facts, the whole picture, before making a decision or judgment. In other words, they consider the consequences of their choices.

The film *Mr. Holland's Opus* says a lot about the connection between wisdom and responsibility when it comes to making good decisions. Glenn Holland, a musician, wants to be a composer, but he decides to teach music temporarily at a high school in order to support himself and his wife Iris. He thinks it will be an easy job, and he only expects to keep it for four years.

Mr. Holland has a rude awakening when he starts to realize just how difficult it is to teach uninterested students about music appreciation. He makes another decision—to work harder at being a good teacher and to spend extra time working one-on-one with students. Then Glenn faces another change of plans: Iris is pregnant; they need a larger house. Glenn will have to be a teacher much longer than he wants. Although at first he's not happy with this change, Glenn assumes his responsibility as the family breadwinner and agrees to teach summer school in addition to teaching during the regular school year.

Another threat to Glenn's desire to be a composer occurs when he and Iris discover that their son Cole is deaf. Cole will need special schooling, an added expense. Furthermore, Glenn himself will have to spend time learning sign language. Now there is even less time to compose music.

During rehearsals for a senior class review, Glenn works one-on-one with the lead singer, Rowena Morgan. She is young, extremely talented, and wants to become a professional singer. Once again Glenn is faced with a decision: to run away with Rowena to New York and pursue his dream of being a composer, or to remain true to his responsibilities to Iris and Cole. Glenn chooses Iris and Cole instead of Rowena, knowing full well the decision will prevent him from ever becoming a professional composer.

The years pass, and only then is it apparent to Glenn and everyone else that he has made a lifetime of wise decisions. At his retirement party, his former students honor him by playing the composition he has worked on over the years. His greatest opus, however, is not the composition, but his relationships with his wife, his son, and his students.

LET'S TALK

1. What does Glenn's decision to be responsible to his family tell you about his character?
2. What do you think would have happened if Glenn had gone with Rowena to New York?
3. How does viewing the entire teaching career of Glenn help you understand that he made many wise choices?

For Your Eyes Only

When you reach at the end of your life, for what do you want people to remember you? What do you want to be your greatest opus? Why?

Some Important Decisions

As a teenager, you will be faced with many important decisions. Some of these decisions will deal with alcohol, reckless driving, tobacco, drugs, and inhalants. What you choose will reflect both your wisdom and your sense of responsibility. Your choices will not only tell others something about your character; your choices will very likely have a lasting impact on the rest of your life.

To help you make wise choices in each of these areas, it is important to get all the facts. That is the purpose of the next sections of this chapter.

Decisions Regarding Alcohol

In all 50 states and the District of Columbia, the legal age for drinking alcohol is 21. Yet many young people begin drinking years before that. In 1993, most American school children reported that by fourth grade, they were pressured to drink alcohol. During the same year, 18 percent of all 12–17 year olds admitted they had drunk alcohol. According to the 1995 *Statistical Abstract of the United States*, over 21 percent of those arrested for violating liquor laws and about 2.3 percent of those arrested for drunkenness in public were teenagers.

There are many reasons pre-teens and teens start drinking alcohol. One reason is that drinking seems to be a "grown-up" thing to do. Another reason is that alcohol is usually readily available at home. A third reason is the enormous influence of ads for alcohol. Statistics show that the alcohol industry spends $2 billion per year on advertising. Most ads run during televised sporting events. Others are in magazines, on the radio, or on billboards, posters, and buses. Their message is simple: "It's fun to drink. It'll make you popular." The ads also promote the misconception that alcohol use is part of everyday adult life. And many young people believe the message.

Alcohol is seen by some teens as an escape from their problems. While it is true that alcohol can dull pain and produce a temporary high, it is also true that too much alcohol kills brain cells and causes permanent liver damage. **Binge drinking** (drinking five or more drinks in a short period of time) especially can be fatal for pre-teens and teens. Other negative effects of alcohol include hangovers, puffy faces, bad headaches, slipping grades, troubles with family and friends, loss of interest in fun activities, trouble with the police, and auto accidents.

According to the American Council for Drug Education, one-third of all students—before leaving high school—will have a serious problem in school, at home, or with the law because of alcohol use. Consider the following three real-life stories:

F.Y.I.

By age 18, the average American teen will have seen 100,000 TV beer commercials.

LET'S TALK

1. Do you agree that John's decision to drink on the French Club trip was wrong? Explain.

2. Are there any situations where teens can drink alcohol responsibly? Explain.

The French Club Trip [2]

John, an intelligent and ordinarily trustworthy boy, joined four classmates on a dinner outing during the school's French Club trip to Quebec. Because these students had a reputation for responsibility, their teacher gave them special permission to go off alone. With their dinner, the students ordered a bottle of wine. Doing so violated the school's "No drinking on school trips" policy, which was well known to all the students. When the teacher later learned of the violation, she felt personally betrayed by the students' behavior. Upon the students' return to school, the principal gave all five a day of in-school suspension.

When John's father learned what he had done, he was quite upset and sat him down to discuss it. John said, "I honestly didn't see anything wrong with it—I knew we weren't going to get drunk." His father helped John to see that what he and his friends did was wrong for several reasons: It violated the personal trust of their teacher; it broke the school's drinking rule, which the students understood and had in effect agreed to by going on the trip; and it endangered future school trips, which were already known to be in jeopardy because of previous problems with student drinking.

The Graduation Party [3]

When police responded to a call Wednesday night about a large graduation party in Tucson's affluent El Encanto neighborhood, officers did not know what to expect. Upon arriving, they saw a street jammed with cars and a house packed with more than 400 young people, many of them drinking from several beer kegs. It took 56 officers, some of them wearing riot gear, and three police dogs to tame the crowd at the residence.

Partygoers lobbed objects from the roof at the first squad of 14 officers, and close to 70 kids successfully scurried into the night. Eventually, the scene was brought under control and no one was injured. The police made 264 arrests, the most in one night. Of those arrested, about 200 were cited at the midtown party for alcohol violations.

At the party, police also confiscated four loaded guns from four youths 18 and under. Three of the teens were charged with carrying concealed weapons without a permit. The other teen, whose weapon was visible, may still face charges.

A parent who was home during the party, later was charged with 416 Class 1 misdemeanors in connection with her supervision of a May 23 graduation party in the El Encanto neighborhood. Sgt.

---

2 From Thomas Lickona, *Educating for Character* (New York, NY: Bantam Books, 1991), p. 54.

3 Adapted from Anne McBride, "Cops don riot gear, bring in dogs to break up keg party," *The Arizona Daily Star* (May 24, 1996) and Ann McBride, "Woman faces 416 charges tied to underage drinking," *The Arizona Daily Star* (May 30, 1996).

Reuben Nuñez said this is the most charges ever brought in the city against one person.

He said that 138 young people at the party were charged with underage drinking. The parent was charged with three liquor violations for each young person charged, plus one count of disorderly residence and one count of operating without a proper liquor license. (The last charge stems from allegations that teens paid to attend the party.)

A Class 1 misdemeanor carries a maximum $1,000 fine and up to one year in jail.

The day after the party, police drained the home's pool because officers who broke up the party heard items being thrown into it. Nuñez said bags of marijuana and a 9 mm gun clip were found at the bottom of the pool.

Marni's Choices [4]

"I think from the time I started school, probably all the way back to kindergarten, I had this need to please. I had to have the best drawings, I had to read the fastest, I had to be one of the best students. The turning point didn't really happen until high school. Then I met Will. He was just plain bad, but since I'd been so 'good' all my life, Will intrigued me. He asked me out. He made me feel like I was off on some kind of adventure.

"Because I wanted Will to like me, I started acting differently. I began to dress downright sleazy. I would go out with him and his friends. They drank, so I drank. I started smoking, convincing myself it made me look cool. I caked on the makeup, thinking I looked more sophisticated. I partied more, I stayed out later. I'd ditch school.

"Pretty soon my parents and I got into these brutal arguments. I'd sneak over to Will's in the middle of the night just to get away from them. Of course, that made them angrier. Will would give me a drink, saying it would make me feel better. I also let him talk me into having sex, even though I wasn't ready. I felt guilty and drank more to cover up how trampy I felt.

"My grades started getting really bad. That caused a total mess with my parents. They knew I'd started drinking, but I don't think they knew how bad it was.

"This will give you an idea: I'd gone to a party one night, after a serious fight with my parents. I got so smashed I couldn't even walk. Will and some other friends dropped me off at home after the party. My parents were out, fortunately. But when they came home, they found me in a pool of my own vomit, passed out.

LET'S TALK

1. In the movie *Clueless*, Cher looks down on drinking and taking drugs at school or on an everyday basis, but she thinks it's OK to drink and take drugs at a party. What do you think? Why?

2. How would you describe in general terms teens who attend keg parties as described in the story. How about the adults who "supervise" such parties?

---

4 Shortened from Elizabeth Karlsberg, *Teen* (March, 1993), p. 30.

"Later in the week, my mom made me go to an **AA** (**Alcoholics Anonymous**) meeting. I started crying when I realized what this meant. I guess deep down I knew I had a problem with alcohol.

"It's been almost a year since I've had a drink. I've started to see where my need to please made me not have a mind of my own. I am starting to feel better about me again—and that's the best feeling in the world."

LET'S TALK

1. Why do you think Marni started drinking? Why do you think many teens start drinking?
2. Tell about a dangerous or illegal incident you know of that was caused by teenage drinking.

DO THIS!

Find out more about Alcoholics Anonymous and Alateen in your area. How do these organizations help people stop drinking?

Decisions Regarding Driving

Accidents are the leading cause of death for 15–24-year-olds in the United States. Such accidents include motor vehicle accidents, water-transport accidents, air and space accidents, railway accidents, falls, drownings, and accidents caused by fire, firearms, electrical current, accidental poisoning, and the inhalation or ingestion of objects.

Some teen accidents are the result of driving under the influence of alcohol (**DUI**). Other accidents are the result of reckless driving and irresponsible choices. Teens who drive drunk or recklessly usually do so because they are inexperienced and/or because they don't think about the possible consequences. Just like the boy described in the following letter (which was written anonymously), they figure a fatal accident will never happen to them.

"Please God, I'm Only 17." [5]

The day I died was an ordinary school day. How I wish I had taken the bus. But I was too cool for the bus. I remember how I wheedled the car out of Mom. "Special favor," I pleaded. "All the kids drive."

When the 2:50 school bell rang, I threw all my books in the locker. I was free until 8:40 tomorrow morning! I ran to the parking lot, excited at the thought of driving a car and being my own boss. Free!

5 As seen in a *Dear Abby* column by Abigail Van Buren. Distributed by *Universal Press Syndicate.*

It doesn't matter how the accident happened. I was goofing off—going too fast. Taking crazy chances. But I was enjoying my freedom and having fun. The last thing I remember was passing an old lady who seemed to be going awfully slow. I heard the deafening crash and felt a terrible jolt. Glass and steel flew everywhere. My whole body seemed to be turning inside out. I heard myself scream.

Suddenly I awakened; it was very quiet. A police officer was standing over me. Then I saw a doctor. My body was mangled. I was saturated with blood. Pieces of jagged glass were sticking out all over. Strange that I couldn't feel anything.

Hey, don't pull that sheet over my head! I can't be dead. I'm only 17. I've got a date tonight. I'm supposed to grow up and have a wonderful life. I haven't lived yet. I can't be dead.

Later I was placed in a drawer. My folks had to identify me. Why did they have to see me like this? Why did I have to look at Mom's eyes when she faced the most terrible ordeal of her life? Dad suddenly looked like an old man. He told the man in charge, "Yes, he is my son."

The funeral was a weird experience. I saw all my relatives and friends walk toward the casket. They passed by, one by one, and looked at me with the saddest eyes I've ever seen. Some of my buddies were crying. A few of the girls touched my hand and sobbed as they walked away.

Please—somebody—wake me up! Get me out of here! I can't bear to see my mom and dad so broken up. My grandparents are so racked with grief they can hardly walk. My brothers and sisters are like zombies. They move like robots. In a daze, everybody. No one can believe this. And I can't believe it, either.

Please don't bury me! I'm not dead! I have a lot of living to do! I want to laugh and run again. I want to sing and dance. Please don't put me in the ground. I promise if you give me one more chance, God, I'll be the most careful driver in the whole world. All I want is one more chance!

Please, God, I'm only 17!

DO THIS!

Find out how many teen accidents occurred in your community during the past 12 months. (Police reports and newspaper files can aid your research.) How many of these accidents were caused by alcohol? by reckless driving? by speeding? How many of these accidents were fatal? Report your findings to the class.

F.Y.I.

In 1995, 38 people died in Florida in late-night accidents involving teenagers. Out of concern for the safety of inexperienced drivers, the state legislature passed the "Cinderella Law." The law, which took effect July 1, 1996, prohibits 16-year-olds from driving between 11 p.m. and 6 a.m. unless they're headed to or from work or are accompanied by someone 21 years old.

Decisions Regarding Drugs

A 1993 survey reported that 4.9 percent of all 12–17–year–olds had taken marijuana; 0.4 percent had taken cocaine; 0.5 percent had used hallucinogens; 0.2 percent had tried heroin; 0.5 percent had taken stimulants; 0.2 percent had taken sedatives (sleeping pills); 0.2 percent had taken tranquilizers, and 0.7 percent had taken analgesics (pain killers). Since that survey, numerous studies have confirmed that drug use among pre-teens and teens is on the rise. In 1994, a survey by the University of Michigan revealed these facts:

◆ More teen athletes are taking anabolic steroids and growth hormone to improve their performance.

◆ Marijuana use among eighth graders has doubled since 1991.

◆ More 13- and 14-year-olds than in the recent past are experimenting with cocaine, LSD, stimulants, and inhalants.

◆ Nearly 50 percent of American twelfth graders admit to using drugs.

To make wise decisions regarding drugs, it is important to know the facts. The following table provides some basic information.

Types of Drugs and Their Effects

Type of Drug	Effects
LSD (lysergic acid diethylamide)	Scrambles the brain so that the user becomes disoriented, violent, or suicidal. After the drug "trip," people sometimes have recurring hallucinogenic flashbacks. LSD may also alter the genetic code the user passes on to his or her children.
Marijuana (pot, MaryJane, grass)	Can cause long-term mood disorders, loss of ambition, lack of concentration and focus. Can also cause high blood pressure. Blunts (marijuana cigars) multiply by 10 the harmful effects of a marijuana cigarette.
Crank (Methamphetamine, speed), Ice (a rock crystal form of speed), and Ecstasy (a "designer" form of speed).	Are highly addictive; can cause heart, liver, and lung damage.
Heroin (opium)	Is one of the most addictive drugs. Taken over time, it destroys the body and the brain if the user doesn't first die from an overdose.
Cocaine (crack)	Very addictive. Causes permanent damage to liver, lungs, brain, and nasal septum. Also causes paranoia, depression, coma, and death.
PCP (angel dust)	Leads to bizarre and violent behavior. Can destroy thinking ability, memory, and fine-motor function.

LET'S TALK

1. Why is taking drugs a violation of the fifth commandment, "You shall not kill"?
2. Rate the drug problem at your school in comparison with what you understand to be the drug problem at other high schools in your area.

All drugs, legal and illegal, present some degree of danger. Some drugs are **addictive**, which means the user needs to take more and more of the drug to get the same high. Making the decision to try one type of drug often leads to trying other, more dangerous drugs. A 1995 report of the *Congressional Quarterly Researcher* points out that teens who use pot are 85 times more likely to try cocaine than those who do not use pot. Even more frightening is the increased possibility of getting **AIDS**. *Anyone*—even a first-time drug user—who shares a needle for intravenous drug injections is at high risk for contracting the AIDS virus.

Decisions Regarding Tobacco

Many teens smoke or chew tobacco because they think it's the "in" thing to do. Here is the situation one high school freshman recently faced:

Ask Jack [6]

Dear Jack:

I overheard some guys talking about what they like in girls, and I got really upset. Most of them mentioned smoking, drinking, and partying. Are guys only interested in girls who drink and party? Because if that's the case, I think I'll go through high school dateless! I'm a freshman. Will I have to wait until college to have a date?

Clean Cut, N.J.

Dear Clean Cut:

There's absolutely nothing wrong with not drinking and smoking. It shows that you care about yourself and your body. When a bunch of guys get together, there is always some room for tall tales and male bravado. Don't worry too much about what you overheard. Any guy worth your time isn't going to be concerned with whether, or how much, you smoke and party! It's important that you stick to your own principles, rather than letting others influence you. That way, you'll present yourself as someone who is confident and enjoys life—just the kind of person most guys love to hang out with!

6 "Ask Jack" *Teen* (April, 1995), p. 18.

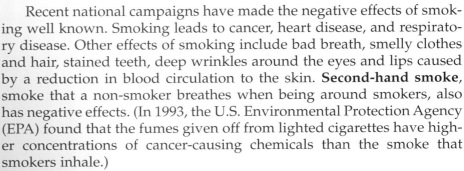

For Your Eyes Only

1. If you have ever taken drugs, why did you? What might tempt you to take drugs in the future?

2. Do you think it is "cool" to smoke or chew tobacco? Why?

Recent national campaigns have made the negative effects of smoking well known. Smoking leads to cancer, heart disease, and respiratory disease. Other effects of smoking include bad breath, smelly clothes and hair, stained teeth, deep wrinkles around the eyes and lips caused by a reduction in blood circulation to the skin. **Second-hand smoke**, smoke that a non-smoker breathes when being around smokers, also has negative effects. (In 1993, the U.S. Environmental Protection Agency (EPA) found that the fumes given off from lighted cigarettes have higher concentrations of cancer-causing chemicals than the smoke that smokers inhale.)

Despite these anti-smoking campaigns, tobacco use among teenagers is on the rise. A 1993 survey reported that 9.6 percent of all 12- to 17-year-olds had smoked cigarettes and 2 percent had used smokeless tobacco. According to the Centers for Disease Control and Prevention (CDC), more than eighteen percent of female high school seniors smoked in 1993.

Why are so many teens choosing to use tobacco, despite the facts? Some people believe it is the influence of slick cigarette ads. A 1996 study by Richard Pollay, a marketing professor at the University of British Columbia, discovered that teenagers are three times more receptive than adults to cigarette ads. Furthermore, teens tend to smoke the most heavily advertised brands—Camel, Marlboro, and Newport.

DO THIS!

In a group, analyze the ads for tobacco in one of the following media:

◆ TV sporting events,

◆ Magazines,

◆ Radio,

◆ Billboards and posters,

◆ Buses.

What messages do the ads give about tobacco? In what ways are the ads directed to teens?

Decisions Regarding Inhalants

After alcohol and tobacco, inhaling certain drugs is third in popularity for teens who use drugs. **Huffing** is a term that refers to breathing in fumes of household products, such as hair spray or lighter fluid, through the mouth. **Sniffing** is a term that refers to breathing in fumes straight from the bottle, from a coated cloth, or by heating them. **Bagging** refers to breathing household products through a paper bag.

Products most frequently inhaled by teens include aerosol sprays, air freshener, ammonia, asthma inhalers, bleach, car wax, cooking spray, drain cleaner, furniture polish and wax, gasoline, glue, hair spray, insecticides, lighter fluid, moth balls, oven cleaner, paint, spray paint, and turpentine.

Inhaling such products is very dangerous. Negative effects of inhaling include brain damage, bone marrow damage, liver and kidney damage, short-term memory loss, hearing loss, limb spasms, and damage to the reproductive organs. In addition, inhalants can bring on sudden death due to a heart attack or to oxygen deprivation. The facts, according to a recent British study, are scary: Three out of every 10 teens die the first time they try inhaling.

Why do teens start inhaling? Some do it because of peer pressure. Their friends are doing it, and they want to fit in. Other teens inhale because they like the high it produces. They don't realize the dangers or how their behavior is affecting them. Consider the following real-life story:

Lori's Story [7]

"I just turned 15 when I first started huffing. It was summer, and I was out one night with a friend who worked at a theater. They used gum remover to clean chewing gum from the floors and seats. He grabbed a few cans of the stuff and a bunch of friends decided to inhale it. I just couldn't get enough of it. The high only lasts about 20 seconds, but it was so good, I just wanted more. That night, we finished off four cans between all of us.

"I really loved the high I got from huffing, so I started getting cans every day. My friends started to notice that I had really bad mood swings. My grades dropped. I fought everyday with my dad. I got more cocky and angry when I was huffing, so our fights were pretty bad.

"One night, I finished a whole can of gum remover in about 15 minutes, which is way too fast. I was worried and crying, because it felt like the high was never going to go away. It felt way too intense for too long. But even after that nightmare, I still kept huffing. I was hooked.

"Things hit bottom when I arrived at a meeting of a teen group I belong to and they did an **intervention** on me (that's when friends and family all get together and confront a user by telling her exactly how they feel about her using). Just to see all these people around me that really cared about me, telling me I was changing, really scared me out of doing it.

"Since I quit huffing, my grades have definitely gotten better. I have my best friend back and even my relationship with my dad is better now."

LET'S TALK

1. Why do you think Lori first agreed to huffing?

2. In your experience, how prevalent is inhaling among teenagers in your school or neighborhood?

A 1993 survey reported that 1.4% of all 12 to 17 year olds had used inhalants.

—1995 *Statistical Abstract of the United States.*

F.Y.I.

---

7 Shortened from Sandy Fertman, "The truth about huffing," *Teen* (September, 1995), pp. 74ff.

F.Y.I.

For more information and advice about inhalants, call one of the following organizations:

◆ National Inhalant Prevention Coalition—800-289-4237.

◆ National Clearinghouse for Alcohol and Drug Information—800-SAY-NOTO.

◆ Exodus Recovery Center Hotline—800-829-3923 or 800-488-6939.

Becoming a Wise Person

Just saying "no" to alcohol, reckless driving, drugs, tobacco, and inhalants isn't enough to make you wise. Wise people also know *why* it is a good idea to say "no." As you have been learning in this chapter, the first step in becoming a wise person involves getting all the facts and considering all the consequences. Getting the facts helps you know the right thing to do. You can get such knowledge from published sources and in drug education programs.

Prayer is the second thing you can do to help you make right decisions. As the Venerable José Escriva once said, "Never make a decision without stopping to consider the matter in the presence of God." The Venerable Charles de Foucauld agrees: "In everything, ask yourself only what the Master would have done, and do that."

Another important way you can know the right thing to do is by listening to your **conscience**. Your conscience is the ability within you that helps you discern right from wrong. Listening to your conscience is an absolutely necessary part of making a good decision. According to the *Catechism of the Catholic Church*: "Moral conscience, present at the heart of the person, enjoins him . . . to do good and to avoid evil. It also judges particular choices, approving those that are good and denouncing those that are evil" (1777).

Fourth, becoming wise involves the actual choice: choosing to do the right thing, choosing to follow your conscience. This part of wisdom requires more than knowledge; it also requires **courage**.

The fifth part of becoming wise is your willingness to be accountable for any decisions you make and for their consequences. **Accountability** means taking responsibility for your actions and not blaming others for your problems. Although blaming others, in some cases is justified, it usually is not productive. In the end, it's your life. Through God's gift of free will, your decisions and actions shape your future.

A sixth step in becoming wise means having the courage to admit when you've made a mistake. It means learning from the mistake and applying what you have learned to future situations. Wise people know that even bad choices do not mean "the end of the world." Thus, they continue to persevere, despite these setbacks.

One more important part of becoming wise involves having a willingness to share what you have learned with others. As psychologist Dr. Hap LeCrone explains, "Wisdom becomes practical when it is useful and is used to help others." Wise people know when it is "right" to give advice and when it is more appropriate to remain silent. Whenever they give advice, it is always sound because it is based on real-life experience.

> **NOTABLE QUOTABLE**
>
> "The mere inclination to do the right thing is not in itself enough. We have to know what the right thing to do is. We need wisdom."
>
> —William Bennett,
> *The Book of Virtues*

For Your Eyes Only

Think back on a wise decision you made. How were the seven parts of becoming wise (getting all the facts, praying, listening to your conscience, making a choice, being accountable for the choice, having courage to admit mistakes, sharing what you learned with others) present in that decision?

The Courage to Choose Well

Remember, making wise decisions not only requires accurate knowledge; it also requires courage. Courage is a virtue that enables you to stand bravely by your conscience and convictions, even when others are pressuring you to do something else. Furthermore, courage is a virtue that allows you to admit your mistakes and not be crushed by them.

People who sin, who "fall off the bandwagon," are not losers. They are God's own people, capable of great heroism. That is why organizations based in the twelve steps of Alcoholics Anonymous encourage their members to say daily the following Serenity Prayer: "O God, grant me the serenity to accept the things I cannot change, the courage to change the things I can, and the wisdom to know the difference." With God's help, you can be courageous in the decisions you make. You can grow in divine wisdom.

LET'S TALK

Share an example of someone you know personally or from the news who showed courage in making a wise decision.

Prayer 🐾

For Your Eyes Only

One way I will try to grow in wisdom this week is . . .

LEADER: Lord, knowledge, responsibility, and courage are three aspects of making wise decisions. As we now come together to reflect, let us pray that your Holy Spirit will fill us even more with the gift of wisdom.

READER 1: Romans 11:33–36

READER 2: Proverbs 3:13–24

ALL: Grant me, O Lord, to know what I ought to know, to love what I ought to love, to praise what delights you most, to value what is precious in your sight, and to hate what is offensive to you. Let me not judge according to the sight of my eyes or pass sentence according to the hearing of the ears of ignorant people. Instead, help me discern wisely between things visible and spiritual. Above all, make me courageous in always following what is the good pleasure of your will. Amen. ("Prayer for True Knowledge," Thomas à Kempis)

Further Activities 🐾

1. Become active in SADD, Students Against Drunk Driving. Work with others to educate students in your school about the dangers of drinking and driving.

2. Research the latest national and local statistics for alcohol and drug use. How prevalent is teen drinking in your community? at your school? What have been the effects of the drinking? Report your findings to the class.

3. Conduct an anonymous survey of students at your school. Find out what percent have tried drugs, have smoked or chewed tobacco, or have inhaled household products. Report your findings to the class. If you think a problem exists at your school, discuss how your class can go about addressing it.

4. Invite a representative from Alcoholics Anonymous or Students Against Drunk Driving to speak to students in your class about the dangers of drinking.

At Home

Some elderly people are noted for their wisdom. Have a conversation with one of your grandparents or an elderly neighbor whom you consider wise about how he or she knows right from wrong and makes good decisions.

8. Work

CHAPTER GOALS

In this chapter, you will:

◆ Explore the Christian work ethic and how its wisdom can contribute to the development of good character;

◆ See how the virtues of diligence, cooperation with others, fortitude, and perseverance relate to self-discipline;

◆ Discover ways you can grow in self-discipline and reach your own goals.

Wisdom is not only a virtue that applies to making decisions. It also has to do with our attitudes. In this chapter, we will focus specifically on a person's attitude toward work.

When you think about it, most people spend their entire lives working. For students, work includes household chores, homework, extracurricular activities, after-school jobs, and volunteer work. For adults, work includes running a household, raising children, full-time or part-time jobs, and volunteer work. Although most people work, not everyone is happy with the type or amount of work he or she is expected to do. Finding happiness through work is indeed a challenge. Only the truly wise can do it.

LET'S TALK

What are your attitudes toward time and work? Check or note any statements that apply to you.

1. When I have an hour of free time, I usually

_____ waste it and don't really do anything.

_____ use it to learn a new skill or to gain new information.

_____ exercise.

_____ pray or write in my journal.

_____ talk on the phone with friends.

2. I think the school work I have to do is

_____ worthwhile.

_____ a waste of time.

_____ too much and too hard.

_____ not relevant to real life.

3. My attitude toward helping with household chores is:

_____ mostly cheerful and willing.

_____ sometimes cheerful and willing.

_____ unwilling compliance.

_____ rebellious protest.

_____ absolute refusal.

LET'S TALK

4. Most of the time, when I am given work to do,

_____ I apply myself and try to do the best job possible.

_____ I do the minimum and just try to get by.

_____ I do more than is required because I want to make a good impression.

_____ I don't finish it.

5. When I think of the future, my goal is to:

_____ drop out of school and make money as soon as possible.

_____ graduate from high school and then work full time.

_____ go to college.

_____ go to graduate school.

F.Y.I.

In 1993, 4.8% of the total 14–17-year-old population in the United States dropped out of school. This statistic was the equivalent of one teenager dropping out of school every 9 seconds.

The Christian Work Ethic

When Christians first came to the New World in 1620, they brought with them their values and attitudes regarding work. Today we call these values and attitudes the **Christian work ethic.** Included in this work ethic are values such as self-discipline, cooperation with others, perseverance, industriousness, creativity, open-mindedness, single-mindedness, service to others, good sportsmanship, honesty, and the appreciation of education and lifelong learning.

As Christians, we believe in the dignity of work and the importance of having a positive attitude toward it. This belief is rooted in the scriptures, which tell us that creation itself is the work of God. (See Genesis 1.) Jesus and the Father perform their work in unison. (See John 14:10–11.) Jesus calls us to do the same works he does. (See John 14:12.) To do these works, we need faith. (See John 6:29.)

LET'S TALK

1. St. Thomas Aquinas once said, "Without work it is impossible to have fun." What do you think he meant by this? Do you agree or disagree with this statement?

2. Tell about a time you felt personal satisfaction after doing work.

DO THIS!

Read and discuss *The Farmer and His Sons.* Then write a moral for the story. Be prepared to discuss your moral with the class.

Scripture

Read the following passages. Discuss what you think each passage says about the Christian concept of work.

- Psalm 127:1
- Matthew 4:18–22
- Matthew 4:23–24
- John 13:1–17
- John 21: 1–14
- Acts 18:1–11

The Farmer and His Sons [1]

A farmer, being at death's door, and desiring to impart to his sons a secret of much moment, called them round him and said, "My

---

1 Quoted in William Bennett, *The Book of Virtues* (New York: Simon & Shuster, 1993), p. 370.

sons, I am shortly about to die. I would have you know, therefore, that in my vineyard there lies a hidden treasure. Dig, and you will find it." As soon as their father was dead, the sons took spade and fork and turned up the soil of the vineyard over and over again, in their search for the treasure which they supposed to be buried there. They found none. However, the vines, after so thorough a digging, produced a crop such as had never before been seen.

Self-Discipline

Two old sayings, "Hard work never hurt anyone" and "Idle hands are the devil's workshop," reveal an important aspect of the Christian attitude toward work: Good Christians have **self-discipline**, or self-control. They train themselves in work habits that, in turn, help them form good character.

According to Catholic teaching, one of the seven capital sins is **sloth**, or **laziness**. This sin is the tendency within every person to be a full-time "couch potato," someone who just wastes time. Opposing this sin is the virtue of **diligence**—the ability to tackle a task with energy and effort, with the attitude of doing one's best.

One of the responsibilities of parents is to discipline their children—to teach them moral values and attitudes, to train them in right conduct and socially acceptable behavior. School is another training ground of discipline; students learn the value of studying and hard work in order to get good grades and to advance to another level. Adults, however, are expected to discipline themselves.

Unfortunately, not all adults in our society have a true understanding of self-discipline and diligence. For example, some adults who are in positions of authority believe it is "beneath" them to do certain forms of work. As the following true story shows, what such people are really doing is using their "superior position" as an excuse for being lazy.

Man Enough for the Job [2]

An incident is told of the first American war, about an officer who sent his men to fell some trees which were needed to make a bridge. There were not nearly enough men, and work was getting on very slowly. Up rode a commanding-looking man and spoke to the officer in charge, who was urging on his men but doing nothing himself. "You haven't enough men for the job, have you?"

"No sir, we need some help."

"Why don't you lend a hand yourself?" asked the man on horse-back.

"Me, sir? Why, I am a corporal," replied the officer, looking rather affronted at the suggestion.

"Ah, true," quietly replied the other, and getting off his horse he labored with the men until the job was done. Then he mounted

---

2 Retold by Ella Lyman Cabot. Quoted in William Bennett, *The Moral Compass* (Simon & Shuster, 1995), p. 657.

NOTABLE QUOTABLES

"Nothing is small in the eyes of God. Do all that you do with love."
—St. Thérèse of Lisieux

"Genius is one percent inspiration and ninety-nine percent perspiration."
—Thomas Edison (1847–1931)

again, and as he rode off he said to the officer, "Corporal, the next time you have a job to put through and too few men to do it you had better send for the Commander-in-Chief, and I will come again."

It was General Washington.

DO THIS!

Share examples from the news of political, religious, or business leaders who exhibit self-discipline and the value of diligence. Be prepared to share three examples with the class.

Faith vs. Work

Some people wrongly use their religious faith as an excuse to be lazy. It is true that God loves us and provides us with everything we need. It is also true that heaven is not something we can earn; union with God is a gift bestowed upon us through Jesus and the Holy Spirit. On the other hand, Jesus warns that not everyone who calls God "Father" will inherit eternal life. Faith alone is not enough; we also need to put our faith into action through good works. To understand this truth more fully, consider the following folk tale from Mexico:

God Will Provide [3]

One sunrise two neighboring farmers set out for market in town. Their wagons were piled high with tomatoes that would ripen quickly in the hot noonday sun, so they pushed their horses steadily all morning, not wanting their precious cargoes to spoil on the way.

But the poor beasts were tired by the time they reached the steepest hill outside town, and strain as they might, they could not get up the slope. The wagons sat at the bottom of the hill, with the climbing sun beating down mercilessly.

"There's nothing to do but let them rest," said the first farmer, shrugging. "And come to think of it, I could use a little *siesta* myself. We've been on the road since sunup. I think I'll lie under this tree for a while."

"But you can't!" his companion exclaimed. "By the time you wake up, your load will be ruined."

"Don't worry, my friend, God will provide. He always does. I'll just say a few prayers before I doze off." He rolled over on his side with a yawn.

The second farmer, meanwhile, strode to the back of his wagon and, putting his shoulder to the rear, began to shove as hard as he

3 William Bennett, *The Moral Compass* (New York: Simon & Shuster, 1995), p. 266.

could. He yelled at his horse to pull forward, but to no avail. The farmer pushed till the veins stood out on his neck, and he cursed at the top of his lungs, but his cart ascended the hill not one inch.

Just then the Lord and St. Peter passed along the road as they sometimes did, for often they walked abroad in order to look into people's hearts. The Lord saw the frantic, swearing farmer struggling with his load. He smiled and laid a kind hand on the wheel, and at once the cart rose to the top of the hill.

The Lord passed on with St. Peter at his side. The Gatekeeper's gaze bent downward, as if he were pondering their every step.

"I don't understand," he said at last. "Why did you help that man? Even as we came upon him, we heard him cursing most irreverently. And yet you did not help his friend, who offered his prayers for your help."

The Lord smiled.

"The man I helped cursed, it's true, but not with his heart. That is just the way he talks to his horse. In his heart, he was thinking fondly of his wife and children and aged parents, who depend on his labor and need him to return with some profit for his toil. He would have stayed there pushing all day. His friend, on the other hand, calls on me only when he believes he needs me. What he thinks of is sleep. So let him have his nap."

Scripture

Read and discuss the following passages. What do they tell you about the "proper" relationship between faith and work?

◆ Matthew 20: 1–16   ◆ James 2:14–26
◆ 1 Corinthians 3:6–11   ◆ Matthew 7:21-22

Cooperation With Others

A second aspect of the Christian work ethic is the value of **cooperation**, working with others to meet a goal. While the spirit of competition can be a good motivator to get people to work hard, too much competition can be a real problem. It's a problem, for example, when people believe it is important to win at all costs, even if that means hurting others, lying, cheating, or leaving others behind.

The **synoptic gospels** tell us that, as a young adult, Jesus was tempted by the devil in the desert. One of the temptations was to be a "one-man show," to be a loner that people both feared and worshiped. Jesus, however, said "no" to this temptation. He gathered around him a group of twelve **disciples** (a word that is very close in meaning to *discipline*). Jesus made it very clear that he wanted his disciples to work together as a church to spread the good news of salvation throughout the world. Even today, cooperation is vital among church members.

LET'S TALK

1. What are the advantages of being a "team player" rather than being a "loner"? What are the disadvantages?

2. In what ways have you witnessed cooperation among church members at your parish?

Scripture

Read and discuss the following passages. What do they say about cooperation and the Christian work ethic?

- 1 Corinthians 12:14–26
- Luke 9:46–48
- Luke 22:24–27
- Romans 12:3–12
- Colossians 3:12–17

Self-Discipline and Balance

Just as too little work (laziness) is bad, so too much work (**workaholism**) is bad. Workaholics are people who are addicted to work. They can't stop; they feel guilty about resting or taking a vacation. They measure their self-worth in terms of how busy they are or how much work they accomplish.

On the other hand, people who are truly self-disciplined have the wisdom to know that they need a balance between work and play. Just as God, in the Genesis creation story, worked for six days and then rested on the seventh, wise people take time to rest and recreate.

For Your Eyes Only

Make a copy of the following line graph in your journal. Mark the spot on the line that describes your responses to the questions (1, 2, and 3).

Too Little	Just Right	Too Much

1. How much of your time each week is spent working?
2. How much of your time each week is spent resting, praying, playing, or recreating (working on a hobby, seeing a movie, etc.)?
3. How would you rank your present level of stress?

LET'S TALK

1. What are healthy ways that teens can lower the amount of stress in their lives?

2. Describe the right balance in your life between work and play.

Self-Discipline vs. Procrastination

Have you ever stayed up all night (or most of the night) cramming for a test? If so, then you know that the stress in some people's lives is not due to having too much work to do. Instead, it is due to **procrastination**. People who procrastinate keep putting off work until the very last possible moment. Then they have to do several things at once, rushing around the clock to try to make their deadline.

Pacing Oneself

Developing good work practices, such as working steadily or pacing oneself, is an important part of self-discipline. Wise students know that true knowledge is gained by studying some every day. Wise people know that accomplishing anything of value takes steady effort, one step at a time. In essence, they put into practice the wisdom found in the following fable by Aesop:

The Tortoise and the Hare [4]

A hare once made fun of a tortoise. "What a slow way you have!" he said. "How you creep along!"

"Do I?" said the tortoise. "Try a race with me and I'll beat you."

"What a boaster you are," said the hare. "But come! I will race with you. Whom shall we ask to mark off the finish line and see that the race is fair?"

"Let us ask the fox," said the tortoise.

The fox was very wise and fair. He showed them where they were to start and how far they were to run.

The tortoise lost no time. He started out at once and jogged straight on.

The hare leaped along swiftly for a few minutes till he had left the tortoise far behind. He knew he could reach the mark very quickly, so he lay down by the road under a shady tree and took a nap.

By and by he awoke and remembered the race. He sprang up and ran as fast as he could. But when he reached the mark the tortoise was already there!

LET'S TALK

1. When it comes to work, are you a tortoise or a hare? What is one practical thing you do or can do to "win the race" or meet your deadlines?

2. Share an example from your own life that shows each of the following morals:

◆ Slow and steady wins the race.

◆ Haste makes waste.

For Your Eyes Only

How much of your stress is due to procrastination?

DO THIS!

Discuss an upcoming goal or deadline you have (a research paper, an important test, etc.). Brainstorm ways you can pace yourself and finish on time, without unnecessary stress.

---

4 Quoted in William Bennett, *The Book of Virtues* (New York: Simon & Shuster, 1993), pp. 529–530.

Self-Discipline and Fortitude

LET'S TALK

Name someone you know who has exhibited fortitude along the same lines as Keri Strug.

Another characteristic of people who have self-discipline is **fortitude.** According to the dictionary, *fortitude* is "strength of mind that enables a person to encounter danger or bear pain or adversity with courage." One of the greatest recent examples of fortitude occurred in the 1996 Olympics in Atlanta.

There, 18-year-old Keri Strug and six other teenagers represented the United States in the women's team gymnastics competition. They were doing quite well, but the Russian team was very close in its scores—close enough to capture the gold medal. With only two gymnasts left to perform on the vault, the U.S. needed a score of 9.6 or higher to be sure of winning the gold.

The second-to-last U.S. gymnast, 14-year-old Dominique Moceanu, fell on both her vault landings. Now all the pressure was on 4-foot-7-inches, 88-pound Keri Strug. Keri attacked the vault with determination, but fell on the landing and injured her ankle in the process. Her score was 9.162. Though it later was determined that the U.S. had clinched the gold medal with this score, Keri didn't know this.

Rather, Keri only knew she was the U.S. team's last chance at a gold medal (which would be the first ever in Olympic history). Should she try to vault again with the hopes of winning a team gold medal, or should she nurse her ankle so she could compete later in the week in the individual all-around competition? Although Keri suspected that she had seriously hurt her ankle, she decided to overlook the pain and try one more time.

Later she told the press, "After my first vault, I heard a snap in my foot and I was scared. I couldn't walk normal. But the other girls on the team were saying, 'Come on, you can do it. Shake it off.' I couldn't tell them, 'No, you're wrong, you don't understand. Something's wrong.' It was for the gold." When my coach asked me if I could do one more vault, there was only one answer I could give. 'I will, I will, I will' I told him."

Before the next vault, Keri said a silent prayer. "Please God, help me out. I've just got to do this one more time." With even more determination than before, she ran down the ramp and completed a near-perfect vault before falling down in wrenching pain. She had suffered a third-degree lateral sprain and had torn several ligaments in her ankle, but her final vault (a 9.712) was the defining moment of the 1996 Olympics.

Self-Discipline and Perseverance

DO THIS!

1. Research and share at least three examples from the news of people who have shown fortitude. Be prepared to tell the class about these people.

2. Research and share at least three examples of Christian saints who have shown fortitude. Be prepared to tell the class about these saints.

People with self-discipline are people who place a high premium on **perseverance.** Perseverance is a virtue that enables us to keep working toward a goal despite setbacks, mistakes, failures, or discouragement. To persevere means to be persistent and not give up.

All athletes who compete in the Olympics know firsthand what perseverance means. They have devoted years of long hours to practice, trying to perfect their skills and win a medal. But what about ordinary people—people who never win a competition or achieve national fame? Here, too, even in the ordinary events of life, perseverance is a mark of good character.

It takes perseverance, for example, to continue going to church and practicing one's faith when no other friends or even family members are doing it. It takes perseverance to study throughout the semester and get good grades. It takes perseverance to stick with a friend during a crisis or difficult time. It takes perseverance to save money for college or for a car. It takes perseverance to undergo rehabilitation for a drug problem. It also takes perseverance to recover from a serious injury.

A real-life example of perseverance was the focus of *Rudy*, a recent movie. The movie shows how persistent effort can bring about the realization of even the most impossible dream. Here is the story:

Even as a kid, Rudy Ruettiger has only one dream—to play football for Notre Dame. His older brother, parents, and teachers, however, try to bring him back to the real world. After all, Rudy is not the smartest of students. As a senior, he fails civics; his other grades are not so great, either. Furthermore, Rudy is short and doesn't weigh a lot. He just doesn't have what it takes to get into college and play football.

Four years after high school, Rudy is working at a steel mill. He has only saved up $1,000 toward Notre Dame, and now his girlfriend wants to get married. After his best friend is killed in a factory explosion at work, Rudy decides it's time to go after his dream. At the bus station, his dad tries to talk him out of it. Rudy listens respectfully, but gets on the bus.

At Notre Dame, Rudy is befriended by Father Cavanaugh who helps him get into Holy Cross Junior College. Only if his grades there are good enough, will he be able to enroll in Notre Dame. Rudy studies hard with the help of a tutor. After the first semester, Rudy gets three Bs and one A. He applies for admission to Notre Dame and is turned down.

Despite his discouragement, he keeps trying. After the second semester at Holy Cross, Rudy again applies to Notre Dame. Again he is turned down. The same thing happens the third time he applies. Rudy is about to give up, when Father Cavanaugh encourages him to keep trying. Rudy agrees to make one more effort. This time he is accepted at Notre Dame.

Through similar persistence, Rudy makes the football team. Although Rudy is never chosen to play in a game, he puts more effort than anyone else into the practices. Even though the first string players use him as a punching bag, Rudy's "can do" attitude puts to shame even the most talented team members.

Coach Ara Parseghian agrees to let Rudy dress for one game during his senior year. But then there is a change in coaches. The new coach, Dan Devine, knows nothing of Parseghian's promise to Rudy. Throughout the year, Rudy's name never appears on the dress list.

In protest, many of the players resign before the last game of the season. The coach relents, and lets Rudy dress. In the last 37 seconds of the game, with the score 24 to 3 in favor of the Irish, Rudy is put into the game. His brief appearance will make no difference in the game's outcome, but still he gives it his best. Surprisingly, he makes a tackle, and when the game ends he is victoriously carried off the field by his teammates. Despite all obstacles, Rudy has achieved his dream: He has played Notre Dame football.

Examples of Perseverance

History is filled with examples of men and women who persevered against all odds and finally achieved their goals. Often, the accomplishments of these inventors, scientists, explorers, soldiers, and pioneers were more than personal moments of triumph. The accomplishments also benefited others and changed the world for the better.

One example of perseverance may be found in the life of Louis Braille (1809–1852). Louis became blind from an accident when he was three. At age 15, after being frustrated that he could not read and write like other people, Louis started working on a system of raised dots that would allow blind people to read and write. Despite opposition from many prejudiced people who thought blind people should accept their lot and not try to read or write, Louis devoted his life to pursuing his goal.

For over 25 years, Louis' work went unpraised and unrecognized. Still, he did not give up trying to make books accessible to the blind. It was not until after he died that his method of raised dots won acceptance and was taught to blind people throughout the world. To this day, because one 15-year-old would not give up his dream, the Braille system continues to enrich the lives of many visually impaired people

Another example of perseverance may be found in the life of the Scottish essayist and historian, Thomas Carlyle (1795–1881). Here is his story:

LET'S TALK

1. If Rudy had let his parents, brother, and teachers talk him out of trying to reach his goal, dream what effect would giving up have had on the rest of his life?

2. Share an example from your own life of a time you followed the old saying, "If at first you don't succeed, try, try again." What happened? Did you finally achieve your goal? How did you feel?

Writing The *French Revolution* [5]

In the early part of 1835, Thomas Carlyle finally finished work on the first volume of his *French Revolution*. Writing it had been a terrific struggle. For almost two years he had read histories and made notes in preparation for the task; then he had spent months painstakingly writing and revising his manuscript. By the time the first volume was complete, his nerves were strained and his bank account almost empty. Yet he had confidence in his work.

He was delighted when his good friend, the philosopher John Stuart Mill, offered to read the manuscript. Carlyle tied the pages up in a neat bundle and handed it to him, hoping Mill could make some helpful suggestions.

One night, when Carlyle and his wife were sitting before the fireplace, Mill staggered in and collapsed in a chair. His hands trembled. His face was ashen.

"Your manuscript," Mill stuttered. "It was wrapped in newspaper. The housekeeper thought it was trash and put it into the fire. It's burned. All of it."

It was the only copy.

A deathly silence filled the room. Then Carlyle quietly put his hand on his friend's shoulder.

"Don't feel so bad, Mill," he said gently. "I'm sure it wasn't very good. Regardless, good or bad, it's gone now, and feeling guilty will not do a thing to bring it back. Accidents like this happen. Let's think no more about it."

After Mill left, Carlyle pondered the seriousness of the matter. Not only was the manuscript gone, so were the notes he had used to write it. He had thrown them away as he wrote. The book existed only in his memory. And he was down to the last penny of his savings. He did not know whether or not he should simply abandon the project. He went to bed that night full of utmost despair. Yet the next morning he decided he would start over.

"I will not quit the game while the faculty is given me to try playing," he wrote in his journal. "Oh, that I had faith! Oh, that I had! Then there would be nothing too hard or heavy for me. Cry silently to thy inmost heart to God for faith. Surely he will give it thee. At all events, it is as if my invisible schoolmaster had torn my copybook when I showed it, and said, 'No, boy! Thou must write it better.' What can I, sorrowing, do but obey—obey and think it the best?"

And so he went back to his desk and began the daunting journey again. He wrote through the spring of that year and into the hot

For Your Eyes Only

Many great accomplishments are the result of dreams people had as teenagers. What is one dream, or goal, you would like to accomplish in your life? How do you think you will be able to accomplish this goal?

---

5 Shortened from "Thomas Carlyle and *The French Revolution*," William Bennett, *The Moral Compass* (New York: Simon & Shuster, 1995), pp. 339–340.

LET'S TALK

1. How did Carlyle show wisdom and good character in the way he responded to his friend's "accident"? Have you ever been forced to redo a job or task? How did you respond?

2. What do you think would have happened if Carlyle had not persisted in writing his book?

NOTABLE QUOTABLE

"Happiness resides in work, both physical and mental. It resides in doing things that one can take pride in doing well, and hence that one can enjoy doing."

—Aristotle

summer. By autumn he had succeeded in rewriting what was lost and turned again to the work's second volume. He wrote on and on, feverishly, stubbornly. When volume two was complete, he plunged into volume three.

Almost two years after he had given his original manuscript to Mills, Thomas Carlyle finished his great *French Revolution*. The work endures to this day as a classic of literature and a testament to one man's spirit of endurance.

Ways to Develop Self-Discipline

Self-discipline is a learned skill—not something we are born with. Here are four ways you can teach yourself the habit of self-discipline, as well as diligence, fortitude, perseverance, and cooperation—virtues associated with the Christian work ethic.

1. If you have several things to do, first tackle the one you *least* want to do. Only after you have finished that task, let yourself work on the task you *like* to do. Then the second task will be a reward, and you will have finished both!

2. Make goals—for the year, then for each month, then for each week. For example, if your year-end goal is to save enough money to buy a second-hand car, figure out how much money you will need. Divide this amount by 12 to find out how much you need to save each month. Divide this amount by 4 to find out how much you need to save each week. Write down this amount and tape it to your mirror. Every time you make a bank deposit, cross off the week you have met your goal. (This practice will help you pace yourself, give you a sense of accomplishment, and help keep you on track.)

3. Focus on whatever you're doing at the moment. If you're doing your homework, concentrate on that rather than daydreaming or wondering about an upcoming game or dance. Likewise, if you're playing or resting, concentrate on that instead of worrying about work.

4. Don't let excuses keep you from accomplishing your goals. Say "no" to excuses. Force yourself to stick to your planned schedule, even if you don't feel like it.

Following these practices will help you see that "life's greatest joys are not what one does *apart from* the work of one's life, but *with* the work of one's life."[6]

Prayer

LEADER: Work, instead of being drudgery, can be an important way we become more like God. Let us spend these few moments in prayer, asking God for the wisdom we need to grow in self-discipline.

READER 1: Sirach 6:18–31

READER 2: Sirach 6:32–37

---

6 William Bennett, *The Book of Virtues* (New York: Simon & Shuster, 1993), p. 347.

ALL: Loving Creator, help us continue steadfastly on our course throughout life, as we work, learn, and grow. Give us the fortitude and wisdom we need to keep trying to be good disciples. Help us focus our entire attention "on the finish line" as we run "toward the prize" to which you call us—"life on high in Christ Jesus." Amen. (Philippians 3:14)

Further Activities

1. Form or join a support group to encourage students to stay in school.

2. Do volunteer work at Habitat for Humanity, helping to build homes for the poor.

3. Do volunteer work in a convalescent home. Offer encouragement to people who are facing a long period of rehabilitation and recovery.

4. Write a prayer service dedicated to St. Joseph, the patron of all workers.

5. Research the life of a scientist, explorer, inventor, soldier, or pioneer who exemplifies the Christian work ethic.

6. Explore the library and other public buildings in your town or city. How and where is Braille used to help the blind? If you do not find it used somewhere you think it should be, circulate a petition among your classmates and present it at the next city council meeting.

At Home

Ask your parents to share with you one of the dreams or goals they had as teenagers. Did they accomplish this goal? Why or why not?

Part 4 Review

1. What is wisdom? What are the seven steps to becoming wise?

2. How does God's wisdom differ from human wisdom?

3. What is the difference between an amoral decision and a moral decision?

4. How does responsibility relate to wisdom? Give an example.

5. What are three reasons pre-teens and teens start drinking?

6. What is the leading cause of death for 15–24-year-olds in the United States? Explain.

7. Name three types of drugs and their effects.

8. What are the effects of smoking and/or chewing tobacco?

9. Name three types of inhalants used by some teens. Why is inhaling household products so dangerous?

10. How does courage relate to wisdom? Give an example.

For Your Eyes Only

One way I will practice self-discipline when it comes to household chores, school work, or a part-time job this week is . . .

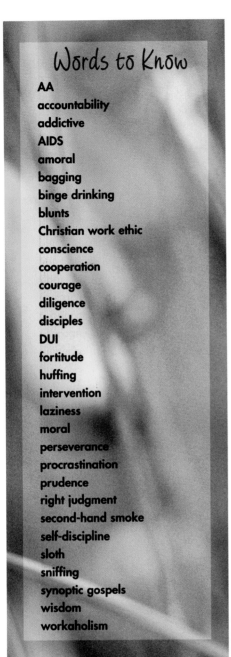

Words to Know

AA
accountability
addictive
AIDS
amoral
bagging
binge drinking
blunts
Christian work ethic
conscience
cooperation
courage
diligence
disciples
DUI
fortitude
huffing
intervention
laziness
moral
perseverance
procrastination
prudence
right judgment
second-hand smoke
self-discipline
sloth
sniffing
synoptic gospels
wisdom
workaholism

11. In your own words, explain what is meant by the Christian work ethic. What values are associated with this ethic?

12. Explain, in your own words, what is the wise and Christian attitude to have toward work, even if you are in a position of authority.

13. If salvation is a gift from God, something we can't earn, why can't we just have faith and be lazy?

14. What does Jesus' life teach us about cooperation?

15. If hard work is good, why is workaholism bad?

16. How is the fable, "The Tortoise and the Hare," an example of procrastination? an example of pacing oneself? What does the fable have to say to teenagers today?

17. How does self-discipline relate to fortitude? Give an example of fortitude.

18. How did each of the following people demonstrate perseverance?
   ◆ Rudy Ruettiger
   ◆ Louis Braille
   ◆ Thomas Carlyle

19. What are two practical ways you can develop self-discipline?

PART 5

LOVE

From the perspective of Christian character, what is love?

What does true friendship mean?

Why is generosity a sign of Christian love?

What Is Love?

There are many ways to define love. Think of a word or phrase you have heard to describe love from one of the following sources:

◆ a movie or video
◆ a popular song
◆ a friend
◆ a poem
◆ a scripture quotation
◆ a novel or short story

Share your examples and then write your own definition for love. Be prepared to share your definition with others.

Types of Love

During the first centuries of the church, Greek language and culture influenced the way Christians expressed their beliefs. For example, they used three Greek words to define three types of love. The first type of love, *phile*, refers to the warm, voluntary feeling of attachment, devotion, and tenderness that one person feels toward another. Examples of *phile* include the love between parents and children, the love between brothers and sisters, and the love between friends. The second type of love, *eros*, refers to ardent passion and sexual attraction between two people. The third type of love, *agape*, refers to an unselfish, loyal, and benevolent concern for the good of another person. This last type of love extends beyond family and friendship (relationships that are mutually beneficial) to love for strangers and enemies. Those who love this way extend their concern and help to others without ever expecting to receive any love in return.

How God Is Love

When we say that love is an attribute of God, we mean all three types of love. God loves us with parental concern, *phile*. (See Hosea 11:1–4.) God loves us as spouses love one another, with *eros*. (See Hosea 2:16–25.) God also loves us unselfishly, with *agape*, regardless of whether we respond in love or not. (See Isaiah 44:21–23; 54:8–10.)

Indeed, God is the very essence of love. (See 1 John 4:8, 16.) When it comes to the love between God and humans, God always takes the first step. God chooses us, as he chose to lead the Israelites out of Egypt and make them his people. (See Deuteronomy 7:6–8.) God's love for us lasts forever. (See Jeremiah 31:3.)

How God Loves Us

Christians believe that God shares his love by filling us with the Holy Spirit of love. (See Romans 5:5.) God's love is poured into our hearts at baptism, strengthened in the eucharist, and confirmed in confirmation. Indeed, God loves us so much that he chooses to adopt us as his own children. (See 1 John 3:1.)

God revealed his love for us by sending his only Son, Jesus, into the world to give us life. (See 1 John 4:9.) God proved his love for us by allowing Jesus to die on the cross to save us from sin. (See Romans 5:8 and 1 John 3:16.) Because of Jesus' sacrifice of himself on Calvary, nothing can ever separate us from the love of God. (See Romans 8:35–39.)

For Your Eyes Only

1. What "signs" in your life have revealed to you the love God has for you?

2. If you had to describe God's love for you with only one word—*phile*, *eros*, or *agape*—which word would you choose? Why?

129

Christians Are Called to Love

Repeatedly, Jesus called his followers to love God and one another. As Christians, we are to love God with all our hearts, souls, and strength. (See Deuteronomy 6:4). We are to love our neighbors as ourselves. (See Leviticus 19:18). We are to love one another as Jesus loved his disciples. (See John 15:9–17.)

Just as God's love for us is eternal, so we must never give up trying to reach out in love to others. Love, more than knowledge, is what builds good character and makes us more like God. (See 1 Corinthians 8:1.) Indeed, true Christians are rooted and grounded in love. (See Ephesians 3:16–17.) True love never fails; it is a virtue even greater than the virtues of faith and hope. (See 1 Corinthians 13:1–13.)

The next two chapters of this course will deal more specifically with how love shapes your character as a Christian. Chapter 9 focuses on the first two types of love—*phile* and *eros*—as they relate to friendship and sexuality. Chapter 10 looks at *agape* and its relationship with generosity.

9. Sexuality and Friendship

O ften, children take their friends for granted. A friend is simply there, someone to play with, talk with, and sometimes fight with. During adolescence, your relationship with peers takes on new significance. Not only is it important that you have a circle of same-sex friends. It is also important that you grow in your ability to develop and sustain friendships with members of the opposite sex. Such "tasks" of adolescence lay the foundation for your ability to love others as an adult. The decisions we make as teens regarding **sexuality** and **friendship** tend to have a lasting impact on the rest of our lives.

Unfortunately, many teens (and adults, as well) mistake friendship with the opposite sex to mean one thing—sex. Consider the following statistics:

◆ In 1992, 12.7% of all babies born in the U.S. were born to teenage mothers (one baby every 60 seconds). Over 30% of all babies born that year were born to unmarried women.

◆ Each year, 1 million girls under the age of 20 (1 in 10) become pregnant.

◆ Experts estimate that 40% of today's 14-year-old girls will become pregnant by the time they are 19. Forty-three percent will get pregnant at least once by the time they turn 20.

◆ The largest jump in sexual activity is among teens under 16.

◆ Pregnant girls 16 and under are the most likely to drop out of school and then to deliver the sickest and smallest babies.

◆ Nearly one in three young teenage mothers gives birth to a second child within two years.

The Church and Premarital Sex

The Catholic Church believes that **premarital sex** is wrong for a number of reasons:

◆ Sex is a wonderful gift of love that encompasses one's whole self. Sex needs a "safe" place (both geographical and emotional) in which to take place, not a cheap motel room or the back seat of a

CHAPTER GOALS

In this chapter, you will:

◆ Learn how chastity is a virtue that helps us express our sexuality in appropriate ways;

◆ Explore the characteristics of true friendship;

◆ Discover practical ways you can make new friends and become a better friend to the ones you already have.

LET'S TALK

A 1995 *Teen* magazine reader survey found that 50% of teenagers approve of premarital sex and 50% say they do not approve. About 29% of those responding say they are involved or have been involved in a sexual relationship. Approximately 48% say that they have friends who are now involved or have been involved in a sexual relationship.

1. From your experience, do you think these statistics reflect the beliefs of your peer group?

2. Besides pregnancy, what are the risks of having premarital sex?

car. Sex needs to be the expression of real, committed love—an expression that takes place over and over throughout the years. Such love is only possible within marriage.

◆ Having sex presupposes being able to handle the emotional responsibilities that go along with having sex. This responsibility is really impossible in a relationship that does not publicly include the commitment of marriage. The likelihood that the relationship of unmarried people having sex will end is strong. Then, one or both persons may end up emotionally hurt for a long time.

◆ Sexual intercourse with casual acquaintances is physically dangerous. In fact, it can be deadly. AIDS, syphilis, gonorrhea, and genital herpes are all transmitted through sexual intercourse.

◆ One of the purposes of sexual intercourse is to conceive a new life. Unmarried teens do not have the emotional maturity or financial security to begin raising children. Many teenage girls who get pregnant have **abortions,** a grave offense against the fifth commandment, "Thou shall not kill."

◆ Getting pregnant as a teenager can lead to real tragedy, as the following true story of a Catholic ninth-grader shows:

The Baby [1]

A fifteen-year-old girl tried to flush her newborn child down the toilet before tying a plastic bag around his neck and dumping him in the trash, Tucson Police Detective Karen Ives testified yesterday in Juvenile Court. The girl gave birth in the toilet at a friend's home on June 8. She left the 7-pound infant in the toilet bowl for about five minutes. Then she cut the umbilical cord with a pair of scissors and flushed, Ives said.

The girl is charged with first-degree murder and two counts of child abuse in the strangulation of her baby. The baby boy—who had a full head of black hair and weighed more than 7 pounds—was found dead Saturday morning in a large, green garbage bin near the friend's home. A man rummaging through the trash stumbled across the infant, who was wrapped in plastic and placed in a plastic bag. The boy had bruises on his neck, and an autopsy revealed he was strangled.

Sexuality—Its Virtues and Vices

Relationships change when sexual attraction is added to the mix. In adolescence, it is common for teens who despised each other as children, to suddenly be sexually attracted to each other. Remember, having sex with someone when you are not married is not a sign that you care about him or her. In fact, given the many dangers present with unmarried sex, it is really a sign that you don't care. Consider this real-life situation:

---

1 Shortened from "Girl, 15, tried to flush infant, detective says," by Kristen Cook, *The Arizona Daily Star* (June 10, 1996).

For Your Eyes Only

What emotional and physical risks of premarital sex concern you the most?

NOTABLE QUOTABLE

"Children who are born to teenage mothers are immediately at a greater risk to be involved in delinquent behavior, substance abuse, and truancy than children who have the benefit of both parents to support and raise them."

—Prosecutor Douglas Varie, Gem County, Idaho

Ask Jack [2]

Dear Jack:

For the past year, I've been dating a guy who really loves me. But a couple of weeks ago, I found out that he's been having sex with another girl. He said he has no idea why he did it. Do you think he still loves me, or should I dump him? He says that what led him to sleeping with her is the fact that I won't have sex with him. I've started to feel like I caused this whole situation. Please help.

Crushed, Ohio

Dear Crushed:

If this guy had sex with another girl, he doesn't care about you very much. No matter what he says about how much he loves you, he cheated on you. Don't make excuses for his behavior, and definitely don't take responsibility for it. Dump this guy and show him that you respect yourself too much to let anybody lie to you. Sometimes guys use sex as an excuse for their own behavior, which is totally out of line. Don't let yourself be victimized by this guy. He was wrong and he doesn't deserve you.

Healthy sexuality is not just about sex. Instead, it includes all the ways a person relates, as a male or as a female, to someone else. **Chastity** is the virtue that helps us express our sexuality in appropriate ways. For unmarried people, chastity means **abstinence** from sexual intercourse and from any act that might imply willingness to engage in sexual intercourse. For married people, chastity means sexual intercourse only with one another, and only as an honest expression of their mutual love.

Chastity is closely linked with the virtue of love. It enables us to care about and respect the other person, rather than use him or her for our own sexual pleasure (the vice of **lust**). Chastity gives us the strength to resist the vice of **fornication** (sexual intercourse between unmarried persons) and the vice of **adultery** (sexual intercourse between a married person and someone other than his or her spouse). The sixth commandment, "Do not commit adultery," is not just a commandment for married people. It is really about the call everyone has to practice chastity in their relationships.

The Virtue of Friendship

Closely related to the virtue of chastity is the virtue of friendship— the ability to form warm, loving, mutual attachments with others. Understanding the nature of true friendship is often a long, trial-and-error process. It is quite easy to choose the wrong friends or to think someone is a friend when, in fact, he or she is not.

---

2 "Ask Jack," *Teen* (April, 1995), p. 18.

The Bear and the Travelers [3]

Two travelers were on the road together, when a bear suddenly appeared on the scene. Before he observed them, one traveler made for a tree at the side of the road and climbed up into the branches and hid there. The other was not so nimble as his companion, and, as he could not escape, he threw himself on the ground and pretended to be dead. The bear came up and sniffed all round him, but he kept perfectly still and held his breath; for they say that a bear will not touch a dead body. The bear took him for a corpse, and went away. When the coast was clear, the traveler in the tree came down and asked the other what it was the bear had whispered to him when he put his mouth to his ear. The other replied, "He told me never again to travel with a friend who deserts me at the first sign of danger."

NOTABLE QUOTABLE

"Genuine friendships take time. They take effort to make and work to keep. Friendship is a deep thing. It is, indeed, a form of love."

—William Bennett, *The Book of Virtues*

True Friends

Learning how to distinguish between false friends and true friends is one of the themes of the movie, *Circle of Friends*. Another theme in the movie is chastity—learning to express one's sexuality appropriately. Here is the story line:

Bernadette (Benny, for short) is a Catholic teen who has been friends with Eve and Nan since childhood. When she attends college with them in Dublin, she learns some of the most important lessons of her life about true friendship and the importance of appropriate sexuality.

Benny meets Jack Foley, a pre-med student to whom she is sexually attracted. They tentatively strike up a friendship and learn a great deal about each other simply by talking and spending time together. They like each other a lot but do not have sex because they respect each other and want to wait until after marriage.

Eve, meanwhile, begins to date and occasionally has parties at the cottage her dead parents have left her. Nan secretly starts dating the wealthy Simon Westwood, with whom she has sex a number of times (without Eve's knowledge) in Eve's cottage.

Meanwhile, Benny's father dies and she must return home to help run the family business. There, she must fend off the unwanted advances of Sean Walsh, the sleazy assistant who wants to marry her and take over the business. When Benny discovers that Sean has been stealing money from the business, she promptly fires him.

Nan discovers she is pregnant. She expects Simon to marry her, but he's not interested. Instead, he wants her to have an abortion. Panicked,

---

3 Quoted in William Bennett, *The Book of Virtues* (New York: Simon & Schuster, 1993), pp. 271–272.

Nan thinks of a plan to get herself out of this mess. She knows that Jack is lonely without Benny, so she decides to take advantage of the situation. She finds him and seduces him. Later, she tells him she is pregnant and that he is the father. Jack agrees to marry her.

Benny is both angry and extremely hurt when she finds out that Nan and Jack have betrayed her. Then Eve discovers an old newspaper in the fireplace at her cottage. She realizes Nan must have been using the cottage to have sex with Simon. Simon is the real father of Nan's baby, not Jack. Angrily, Eve confronts Nan, and everyone finds out the truth.

After Nan leaves for England to have her baby, Jack sincerely apologizes to Benny. They agree to restart seeing each other *just as friends*, to see if Jack can prove his love for her and she can grow to trust him again.

Characteristics of True Friendship:

In *Circle of Friends*, Nan and Simon broke up when she became pregnant because the relationship was based on inappropriate sexuality, not a committed married relationship. Benny and Jack, on the other hand, were able to resume their relationship because they were truly friends.

In learning how to choose people who will be lasting friends, it is important to know some of the characteristics of true friendship. Here are four of them:

1. *True friendship changes us forever.* When we are truly friends with someone else, we honestly share who we are with that person. The relationship becomes a part of us, something that contributes to our character and identity. The following excerpt from a fictional story has toy animals as it characters, but its lessons tell about human friendship.

The Velveteen Rabbit [4]

"What is REAL?" asked the Rabbit one day, when they were lying side by side near the nursery fender, before Nana came to tidy the room. "Does it mean having things that buzz inside you and a stick-out handle?"

"Real isn't how you are made," said the Skin Horse. "It's a thing that happens to you. When a child loves you for a long, long time, not just to play with, but REALLY loves you, then you become Real."

"Does it hurt?" asked the Rabbit.

"Sometimes," said the Skin Horse, for he was always truthful. "When you are Real, you don't mind being hurt."

"Does it happen all at once, like being wound up," he asked, "or bit by bit?"

4 Margery Williams, *The Velveteen Rabbit* (New York: Platt & Munk, Publishers, a division of Grosset & Dunlap, 1987).

"It doesn't happen all at once," said the Skin Horse. "You become. It takes a long time. That's why it doesn't often happen to people who break easily, or have sharp edges, or who have to be carefully kept. Generally, by the time you are Real, most of your hair has been loved off, and your eyes drop out and you get loose in the joints and very shabby. But these things don't matter at all, because once you are Real you can't be ugly, except to people who don't understand."

"I suppose *you* are Real?" said the Rabbit. And then he wished he had not said it, for he thought the Skin Horse might be sensitive. But the Skin Horse only smiled.

"The Boy's uncle made me Real," he said. "That was a great many years ago; but once you are Real you can't become unreal again. It lasts for always."

2. *True friends know us inside out and still love us.* Real friends don't just see our exteriors; they know about and accept our interior character as well. Real friends know the real us, and they encourage our character to grow and blossom. This aspect of true friendship may be seen in the following tale from China:

The Blue Rose [5]

Once upon a time an emperor in China had one daughter. She was not only beautiful, but also wise. The emperor decided that only the man who brought her a blue rose could marry his daughter.

Many men who wanted to win the princess's hand began to try to find the blue rose. A rich merchant purchased a large sapphire that was carved to imitate a rose with petals. Although it was very expensive and beautiful, the princess rejected it.

Another suitor bought a white rose and had it dyed blue. When she saw it, the princess said, "This is a white rose. Its stem has been dipped into a poisonous dye that turned it blue. If a butterfly settled on it, it would die from the smell of the dye." And she rejected the rose.

Another artist brought the princess a china cup on which he had painted a blue rose. The princess agreed that it was the most beautiful piece of china she had ever seen. But this, too, was rejected.

One day a traveling musician visited the country. One summer evening, he sang about his joy in the beauty of the sunset. As he looked up, he saw the princess. She beckoned him to enter her garden. For hours they whispered together in the light of the stars. When the east began to grow light, she said it was time to go.

"Tomorrow, I shall come to the palace to ask for your hand," said the musician.

"I wish that was possible," said the princess, "but my father has said the man I marry must find the blue rose."

"I will find it," the musician promised. And they said good night to each other.

The next morning the musician picked a white rose on his way to the palace. He was brought to the emperor, who called his daughter. "This poor musician says that he has brought you the blue rose," the emperor told his daughter. "Has he found the rose you are searching for?"

The princess took the rose in her hands and said, "Yes, he has found the blue rose."

When everyone pointed out that this was an ordinary white rose and not a blue one, the princess answered, "I think the rose is blue. Perhaps all of you are color-blind."

The emperor decided that if the princess thought the rose was blue, it was blue. Everyone knew that she could see beauty better than anyone else in the land.

So the musician married the princess, and they lived happily ever after in a little house on the sea coast with a garden full of white roses.

3. *True friends are loyal to one another.* They can always count on one another, as the lyrics from a Whitney Houston song, "Count on Me," shows: "Count on me through thick and thin, a friendship will never end. When you are weak, I will be strong, helping you to carry on. Call on me, I will be there. Don't be afraid. Please believe me when I say, count on me."[6]

Damon and Pythias [7]

Damon and Pythias had been the best of friends since childhood. Eventually the time came for them to prove the depth of their devotion. It happened this way:

Dionysius, the ruler of Syracuse, grew annoyed when he heard about the kind of speeches Pythias was giving. The young scholar was telling the public that no man should have unlimited power over another, and that absolute tyrants were unjust kings. In a fit of rage, Dionysius summoned Pythias and his friend.

"This kind of talk is treason," Dionysius shouted. "You are conspiring to overthrow me. Retract what you've said, or face the consequences."

> **NOTABLE QUOTABLE**
>
> "It is only with the heart that one can see rightly; what is essential is invisible to the eye."
>
> —Antoine de Saint-Exupéry

> **LET'S TALK**
>
> Why do you think the princess in the Chinese folk tale chose the musician, rather than one of the other suitors?

---

6 By Babyface, Whitney Houston, and Michael Houston. Recorded by Whitney Houston and Ce Ce Winans. Copyright © 1995 ECAF Music/Sony Songs, Inc./Nippy Music Inc./Aurianna Publishing, Inc. (ASCAP) and Fox Film Music Corp. (BMI). All rights on behalf of ECEF Music and Sony Songs, Inc. administered by Sony Music Publishing. All rights reserved.

7 Shortened from William Bennett, *The Book of Virtues* (New York: Simon & Shuster, 1993), pp. 306–308.

DO THIS!

Find the lyrics to one of the following popular songs, or to another one with lyrics that speak of friendship. What do the lyrics tell you about the characteristics of true friendship?

◆ "You've Got a Friend" by Carole King

◆ "That's What Friends Are For" by Burt Bacharach and Carole Bayer

◆ "The Wind Beneath My Wings" by Larry Henley and Jeff Silbar; sung by Bette Midler.

◆ "Stand by Me" by Jerry Leiber, Mike Stoller, and Ben E. King

"I will retract nothing," Pythias answered.

"Then you will die. Do you have any last requests?"

"Yes. Let me go home just long enough to say good-bye to my wife and children and to put my household in order."

"I see you not only think I'm unjust, you think I'm stupid as well," Dionysius laughed scornfully. "If I let you leave Syracuse, I have no doubt I will never see you again."

"I will give you a pledge," Pythias said.

"What kind of pledge could you possibly give to make me think you will ever return?" Dionysius demanded.

At that instant Damon, who had stood quietly beside his friend, stepped forward.

"I will be his pledge," he said. "Keep me here in Syracuse, as your prisoner, until Pythias returns. Our friendship is well known to you. You can be sure Pythias will return so long as you hold me."

Dionysius studied the two friends silently. "Very well," he said at last. "But if you are willing to take the place of your friend, you must be willing to accept his sentence if he breaks his promise. If Pythias does not return to Syracuse, you will die in his place."

"He will keep his word," Damon replied. "I have no doubt of that."

Pythias was allowed to go free for a time, and Damon was thrown into prison. After several days, when Pythias failed to reappear, Dionysius's curiosity got the better of him, and he went to the prison to see if Damon was yet sorry he had made such a bargain.

"Your time is almost up," the ruler of Syracuse sneered. "It will be useless to beg for mercy. You were a fool to rely on your friend's promise. Did you really think he would sacrifice his life for you or anyone else?"

"He has merely been delayed," Damon answered steadily. "The winds have kept him from sailing, or perhaps he has met with some accident on the road. But if it is humanly possible, he will be here on time. I am as confident of his virtue as I am of my own existence."

Dionysius was startled at the prisoner's confidence. "We shall soon see," he said, and left Damon in his cell.

The fatal day arrived. Damon was brought from prison and led before the executioner. Dionysius greeted him with a smug smile.

"It seems your friend has not turned up," he laughed. "What do you think of him now?"

138

"He is my friend." Damon answered. "I trust him."

Even as he spoke, the doors flew open, and Pythias staggered into the room. He was pale and bruised and half speechless from exhaustion. He rushed to the arms of his friend.

"You are safe," he gasped. "It seemed as though the Fates were conspiring against us. My ship was wrecked in a storm, and then bandits attacked me on the road. But I refused to give up hope, and at last I've made it back in time. I am ready to receive my sentence of death."

Dionysius heard his words with astonishment. His eyes and his heart were opened. It was impossible for him to resist the power of such constancy.

"The sentence is revoked," he declared. "I never believed that such faith and loyalty could exist in friendship. You have shown me how wrong I was, and it is only right that you be rewarded with your freedom. But I ask that in return you do me one great service."

"What service do you mean?" the friends asked.

"Teach me how to be part of so worthy a friendship."

4. *True friends are unselfish.* Friends are willing to make great sacrifices for the welfare of each other, even to the point of risking or giving up their lives. As Jesus himself explained on the night before he died, "No one has greater love than this, to lay down one's life for one's friends" (John 15:13). This characteristic of true friendship may be seen in the following real-life stories. The first story, recorded by Cicero, took place in the fourth century B.C.E. The second story took place during the Vietnam War.

No Greater Love [8]

Whatever their planned target, the mortar rounds landed in an orphanage run by a missionary group in the small Vietnamese village. The missionaries and one or two children were killed outright, and several more children were wounded, including one young girl, about eight years old.

People from the village requested medical help from a neighboring town that had radio contact with the American forces. Finally, an American Navy doctor and nurse arrived in a jeep with only their medical kits. They established that the girl was the most critically injured. Without quick action, she would die of shock and loss of blood.

A transfusion was imperative, and a donor with a matching blood type was required. A quick test showed that neither American had the correct type, but several of the uninjured orphans did.

8 John W. Mansur, *Reader's Digest* (August, 1987).

The doctor spoke some pidgin Vietnamese, and the nurse a smattering of high school French. Using that combination, together with much impromptu sign language, they tried to explain to their young, frightened audience that unless they could replace some of the girl's lost blood, she would certainly die. Then they asked if anyone would be willing to give blood to help.

Their request was met with wide-eyed silence. After several long moments, a small hand slowly and waveringly went up, dropped back down, and then went up again.

"Oh, thank you," the nurse said in French. "What is your name?"

"Heng," came the reply.

Heng was quickly laid on a pallet, his arm swabbed with alcohol, and a needle inserted in his vein. Through this ordeal Heng lay stiff and silent. After a moment, he let out a shuddering sob, quickly covering his face with his free hand.

"Is it hurting, Heng?" the doctor asked. Heng shook his head, but after a few moments another sob escaped, and once more he tried to cover up his crying. Again the doctor asked him if the needle hurt, and again Heng shook his head. But now his occasional sobs gave way to a steady, silent crying, his eyes screwed tightly shut, his fist in his mouth to stifle his sobs.

The medical team was concerned. Something was obviously very wrong. At this point, a Vietnamese nurse arrived to help. Seeing the little one's distress, she spoke to him rapidly in Vietnamese, listened to his reply, and answered him in a soothing voice.

After a moment, the patient stopped crying and looked questioningly at the Vietnamese nurse. When she nodded, a look of great relief spread over his face.

Glancing up, the nurse said quietly to the Americans, "He thought he was dying. He misunderstood you. He thought you had asked him to give all his blood so the little girl could live."

"But why would he be willing to do that?" asked the Navy nurse.

The Vietnamese nurse repeated the question to the little boy, who answered simply, "She's my friend."

NOTABLE QUOTABLE

"Fate chooses our relatives; we choose our friends."

—Jacques Delille
(1739–1813)

DO THIS!

Read John 21:15–19 accompanied by a Bible commentary. Which form of love (*phile*, *eros*, or *agape*) did Peter use? Which form did Jesus use? What does the use of different forms of love tell you about the meaning of this passage?

Scripture

Read and discuss the following passages. What characteristics of true friendship may be found in them?

◆ The Book of Ruth   ◆ 1 Samuel 18, 19, 20   ◆ John 11:1–36

LET'S TALK

1. When was a time a friend went out of his or her way to help you? What did this gesture tell you about the friendship? about the friend?

2. What is more important to you: to have many friends or to have a few good friends? Explain.

Becoming a Better Friend

Like all skills, making friends and becoming a better friend to others takes practice. When it comes to choosing the right friends and behaving in a Christlike manner towards one's friends, it is important to do certain things well. Here are some suggestions for becoming a better friend:

For Your Eyes Only

1. Think of one friend. How are you two alike? How are you different? What makes your friendship work?

2. Who do you consider to be your best friend? Do you think this person would be willing to make a sacrifice for you? Would you be willing to make a sacrifice for this friend?

1. Concentrate on what you and the other person like in common and can do together. If you're good at tennis and your friend isn't, choose to do something else that you both feel comfortable with. (Or, you can take the time to teach your friend how to play tennis. In return, however, be prepared to let your friend teach you something new.)

2. Take turns being the leader and the follower, the talker and the listener. (True friendships are mutual. Both people have a responsibility to keep the relationship going.)

3. Do things alone as friends, but also do things as friends with others. Expand your circle of friendship. Be inclusive, rather than exclusive. Spend time in wholesome activities, in good environments. (For example, you and your friend might join a parish youth group or teen choir.)

4. Don't talk for your friend or think you have to agree on everything. Encourage your friend to be self-sufficient and independent—to be his or her own person.

5. Always treat your friend with respect, encouraging him or her to grow and to become the best person possible.

Following these practices will give you a good start at making

NOTABLE QUOTABLE

"We cannot tell the precise moment when friendship is formed. As in filling a vessel drop by drop, there is at last a drop which makes it run over, so in a series of kindnesses there is at last one which makes the heart run over."

—James Boswell
(1740–1795)

For Your Eyes Only

1. What is another thing you can do to become a better friend? Why?

2. What are some practical things you can do to meet new people?

For Your Eyes Only

One way I will either try to make new friends or to be a better friend this week is . . .

friends and becoming a better friend. However, they are no guarantee that things will be perfect. If something goes wrong—if the friendship goes sour or ends—the virtue of true friendship can still offer you hope. As Jesus advised his disciples when they experienced rejection, "Shake off the dust from your feet" and move on. (See Matthew 10:11–14.) Learn from the mistake you have made and reach out in friendship to someone else. If you are truly a person of good character, there are plenty of other people in today's world who will value you as a friend.

Prayer

LEADER: God loves each one of us as a parent loves a child, as a brother and sister love one another, and as friends love each other. Let us pray today that the virtue of love may characterize all our relationships, especially those involving friendship.

READER 1: Sirach 6:5–17

READER 2: 1 Corinthians 13:1–13

ALL: Most Holy Trinity, as God the Father, you love us as a parent. As God the Son, you love us as a brother. As God the Holy Spirit, you love us as a friend. Help us respond to your love in the way we show love toward others, especially our families, our classmates, and our friends. Help us appreciate the special gift of sexuality you have given us, and help us always to express that sexuality in appropriate ways. Amen.

Further Activities

1. Help with the Challenger Division of Little League. (Push a child in a wheelchair around the bases; help field ground balls, etc.)

2. Join Big Brothers or Big Sisters to become a friend to a child who has only one parent.

3. Donate blood at the American Red Cross or a local blood bank.

4. Sponsor a school-wide program that promotes the values of chastity, abstinence, and appropriate sexuality.

5. Work with friends on a bake sale, car wash, or other fund-raiser to donate money, diapers, or food to a local home for unwed mothers.

6. Write a letter to one of your friends, thanking him or her for the gift of friendship.

At Home

Try to take a renewed look at a sibling as a friend. Go out of your way to do something nice this week for your brother or sister.

142

10. Generosity

CHAPTER GOALS

In this chapter, you will:

◆ See how generosity is a form of Christian *agape*, a type of love Jesus practiced in his own life;

◆ Study examples of generosity in literature to see how this virtue is part of good character;

◆ Learn about some real-life examples of generous people.

Healthy people love themselves. They are concerned about their own welfare, and they try to solve their own problems. Self-interest and self-concern are necessary for survival. However, too much of a "good" thing can become bad. Too much self-concern can prevent us from caring about other people. Without even realizing it, we can become overly self-indulgent and selfish; we can become blind to the needs of others and downright stingy in the ways we respond to those needs.

A song by Phil Collins, "Another Day in Paradise," expresses these sentiments: "She calls out to the man on the street, 'Sir, can you help me? It's cold and I've nowhere to sleep. Is there somewhere you can tell me?' He walks on, doesn't look back. He pretends he can't hear her. Starts to whistle as he crosses the street; seems embarrassed to be here."[1]

LET'S TALK

1. How do you respond to someone begging on the street?
2. What is your overall attitude toward the poor?

NOTABLE QUOTABLE

"Be diligent in serving the poor. Love the poor. Honor them as you would Christ himself."

—St. Louise de Marillac

The Toughest Kind of Love

It's relatively easy to love people who love you. While *phile*—the love between parents and children, brothers and sisters, and friends—can be difficult at times, such love is much easier than loving someone you consider to be an enemy. Likewise, *eros*—the sexual relationships between two people—may have moments of conflict; but it, too, is much easier that loving someone you don't even know or like.

Indeed, the toughest kind of love is *agape*—love for others that involves sacrifice on our part and no hope of getting anything in return. In this type of love, we simply give away our time, talents, or money and expect nothing back.

Agape is the mark of a true Christian, of someone with good character. Jesus taught us the meaning of *agape* by offering himself up on the cross as a sacrifice for our sins. He also calls us to have the same type of

---

1 Phil Collins, "Another Day in Paradise." Copyright © 1989 Philip Collins Ltd (PRS)/Hit and Run Music (Pub) Ltd. Administered by Hit and Run Music (Pub) Ltd (PRS). All rights reserved.

love for others. Mother Teresa of Calcutta explained Christian *agape* in this way:

"It is very important for us to realize that love, to be true, has to hurt. I must be willing to give whatever it takes not to harm other people and, in fact, to do good to them. This requires that I be willing to give until it hurts. Otherwise, there is no true love in me and I bring injustice, not peace, to those around me.

"It hurt Jesus to love us. We have been created in his image for greater things, to love and to be loved. We must 'put on Christ,' as scripture tells us. And so, we have been created to love as He loves us."[2]

Another word for Christian *agape* is **charity**. Charity is a virtue that enables us to love others as Jesus himself loved the poor, the lepers, the lame, the blind, the grieving, the strangers, and the outcasts. Charity is the virtue that enables us to imitate the actions of Jesus who fed the hungry multitudes with a few loaves and fishes and who gave water to a thirsty Samaritan woman. (See Matthew 14:14–21, 15:32–38; Mark 6:32–44; Luke 9:10–17; John 6:1–13, 4:4–42.)

Indeed, Christians are to love others as Jesus loved. If someone wants our shirt, we are to give away our coat as well. If someone needs our help for a mile, we are to go an extra mile. Jesus especially urges us to give to those who beg and to be kind to those who cannot repay us. (See Matthew 5:40–42.)

F.Y.I.

The United States raises three to eight times more children in poverty than other western nations and has the largest and fastest growing income gap between the richest 5% and the poorest 5%.

—1995 Luxembourg Income Study

Scripture

Read and discuss each of the following passages. How does the passage exemplify *agape*, or charity?

◆ 1 Kings 17:9–24   ◆ Luke 10:25–37   ◆ Matthew 25: 31–46

---

2 Mother Teresa of Calcutta, "Give Until It Hurts." Permission to reprint may be obtained from the Missionaries of Charity, Inc.

More About Charity

Christian charity is characterized by the related virtues of **generosity, kindness**, and **compassion**. According to the dictionary, *generosity* is the unselfish (liberal or magnanimous) giving of one's time, money, and help without expectation of anything in return. *Kindness* is the gentle, sympathetic, and helpful offering of relief. *Compassion* is sympathetic awareness of others' distress, together with a desire to alleviate their suffering.

In his book, *The Moral Compass*, former U.S. Secretary of Education William Bennett explains the meaning of compassion in this way:

> Trying to put yourself into another's place, to share for a moment his or her feelings, is often the starting point of compassion. But there's more to true compassion than just emotion. To help someone, you usually have to *do* something, not just *feel* something. Compassion takes the name of action. It means exerting yourself and bestowing some effort for someone else's sake.[3]

The first Christians took seriously Jesus' words, "Be compassionate as your Father is compassionate" (Luke 6:36). They formed a real **community** with one another, sharing all things in common. They sold their property and goods, dividing everything on the basis of people's needs. (See Acts 2:44–46, 4:32–35.) They worked both as individuals and as a group to feed the hungry, give drink to the thirsty, clothe the naked, give shelter to the homeless, take care of the sick, visit those in prison, and bury the dead. Today, the church describes these last seven actions as the **corporal works of mercy**. Like the early Christians, we are called to perform these works of mercy in our own day—with generosity and love.

DO THIS!

1. With others, reenact one of the scripture passages above. Or, write and perform a short skit of a modern-day situation that is based on the passage.

2. In a small group, interview a staff member of a parish. Find out how the corporal works of mercy are presently being officially sponsored and performed in the parish. Report your findings to the class.

Generosity vs. Covetousness

Within each of us is the tendency to be selfish instead of generous. The Catholic church describes this tendency as the capital sin of **covetousness**. Covetousness is similar to greed. It is selfishness "to the max," the self-centered grasping of material possessions. It is concern only about one's own welfare.

The movie *It Could Happen to You* portrays the struggle between covetousness and generosity that resides in all of us. In the movie, Charlie Lang is a New York cop, who doesn't have change to leave a tip to Yvonne, a waitress who serves him coffee. So Charlie shows Yvonne his lottery ticket and tells her that if it wins, he'll split it with her.

As luck would have it, Charlie's ticket wins $4 million. Charlie's wife, Muriel, is furious about his promise to the waitress and doesn't want to share the money with her. Charlie decides to do the right thing: He tells Yvonne about the money and honors his promise.

Once the three people have the money, their different characters become apparent. Muriel can't spend enough money fast enough on herself—furs, jewelry, clothes, plastic surgery, a nicer home. Charlie, however, donates $10,000 to the policemen's widows fund, treats everyone to a free subway ride home, and takes the neighborhood kids to the

For Your Eyes Only

1. How have you recently shown generosity?

2. How have you recently shown kindness?

3. How have you recently shown compassion?

---

3 William Bennett, *The Moral Compass* (New York: Simon & Shuster), p. 363.

stadium to play ball. Yvonne buys the restaurant where she works. She establishes a table there for people who can't afford to pay.

Muriel, who can't understand Charlie's generosity, divorces him and marries Jack Gross, a successful businessman. She then takes Yvonne to court to get back the other half of the lottery winnings.

Yvonne and Charlie end up with no money at all, but they realize they have something more important—each other. When the people they have helped find out they are in trouble, they donate money to help them. Yvonne and Charlie are given enough money to get back on their feet and to continue being generous to others.

For Your Eyes Only

1. What would you do if you won millions of dollars?

2. What do your decisions about spending money say about your character?

F.Y.I.

In 1995, 40 million Americans lived below the federal poverty line. Over 100,000 American children were homeless. One in five children lived below the poverty line.

LET'S TALK

1. What is the difference between generous and selfish behavior? Give some practical examples.

2. St. Basil once said, "If all people would take only according to their needs and would leave the surplus to the needy, no one would be rich, no one would be poor, and no one would be in misery." Do you agree or disagree? Why?

Stories of Generosity

World literature contains many stories about *agape*, or generosity. Here are two of them:

The Gift of the Magi [4]

One dollar and eighty-seven cents. Three times Della counted it. Tomorrow would be Christmas Day and she had only $1.87 with which to buy Jim a present. She had been saving every penny she could for months, with this result.

Now, there were two possessions of the James Dillingham Youngs in which they both took a mighty pride. One was Jim's gold watch that had been his father's and his grandfather's. The other was Della's beautiful hair, which fell about her rippling and shining like a cascade of brown waters. It reached below her knees and made itself almost a garment for her.

She did it up nervously and quickly. Once she faltered for a minute and stood still while a tear or two splashed on the worn red carpet. On went her old brown jacket; on went her old brown hat. With a whirl of skirts and with the brilliant sparkle still in her eyes, she fluttered out the door and down the stairs to the street.

Where she stopped the sign read: "Madame Sofronie. Hair Goods of All Kinds." One flight up Della ran, and collected herself, panting.

"Will you buy my hair?" asked Della.

"I buy hair," said Madame. "Take yer hat off and let's have a sight at the looks of it."

---

4 Adapted and shortened from O. Henry (1862–1910), "The Gift of the Magi" Quoted in William Bennett, *The Book of Virtues* (New York: Simon & Shuster, 1993), pp. 166–170.

Down rippled the brown cascade.

"Twenty dollars," said Madam, lifting the mass with a practiced hand.

"Give it to me quick," said Della.

Oh, and the next two hours tripped by. Della was ransacking the stores for Jim's present. She found it at last. It surely had been made for Jim and no one else. It was a platinum fob chain, simple and chaste in design, properly proclaiming its value by substance alone. It was even worthy of The Watch. As soon as she saw it she knew that it must be Jim's.

When Della reached home her intoxication gave way a little to prudence and reason. She got out her curling irons and went to work repairing the ravages made by generosity added to love. Within forty minutes her head was covered with tiny, close-lying curls.

At 7 o'clock the coffee was made and the frying pan was on the back of the stove hot and ready to cook the chops.

The door opened and Jim stepped in and closed it. His eyes fixed on Della, and there was an expression in them that she could not read. Della wriggled off the table and went for him.

"Jim, darling," she cried, "don't look at me that way. I had my hair cut off and sold it because I couldn't have lived through Christmas without giving you a present."

Jim drew a package from his overcoat pocket. "Don't make any mistake, Dell," he said, "about me. I don't think there's anything in the way of a haircut that could make me like my girl any less. But if you'll unwrap that package you may see why you had me going a while at first."

White fingers and nimble tore at the string and paper. And then an ecstatic scream of joy; and then, alas! a quick change to hysterical tears and wails. For there lay The Combs—the set of combs, side and back, that Della had worshipped for long in a Broadway window. Beautiful combs, pure tortoiseshell, with jeweled rims—just the shade to wear in the beautiful, vanished hair. They were expensive combs, she knew, and her heart had simply craved and yearned over them without the least hope of possession. And now, they were hers, but the tresses that should have adorned the coveted adornments were gone.

"My hair grows so fast, Jim!"

Then Della leaped up like a little singed cat. Jim had not seen his beautiful present. She held it out to him eagerly upon her open palm. The dull precious metal seemed to flash with a reflection of her bright and ardent spirit.

"Isn't it a dandy, Jim? I hunted all over town to find it. You'll have

NOTABLE QUOTABLE

"Love is patient; love is kind."

—1 Corinthians 13:4

to look at the time a hundred times a day now. Give me your watch. I want to see how it looks on it."

Instead of obeying, Jim tumbled down on the couch and put his hands under the back of his head and smiled.

"Dell," said he, "let's put our Christmas presents away and keep 'em a while. They're too nice to use just at present. I sold the watch to get the money to buy your combs. And now suppose you put the chops on."

The magi, as you know, were wise men—wonderfully wise men—who brought gifts to the Babe in the manger. Being wise, their gifts were no doubt wise ones. And here I have lamely related to you the uneventful chronicle of two foolish children in a flat who most unwisely sacrificed for each other the greatest treasures in their house. But in a last word to the wise of these days, let it be said that of all who give gifts these two were the wisest. Of all who receive gifts, such as they are wisest. Everywhere they are wisest. They are the magi.

Grandmother's Table [5]

Once there was a feeble old woman whose husband died and left her all alone, so she went to live with her son and his wife and their own little daughter. Every day the old woman's sight dimmed and her hearing grew worse, and sometimes at dinner her hands trembled so badly the peas rolled off her spoon or the soup ran from her cup. The son and his wife could not help but be annoyed at the way she spilled her meal all over the table, and one day, after she knocked over a glass of milk, they told each other enough was enough.

They set up a small table for her in the corner next to the broom closet and made the old woman eat her meals there. She sat all alone, looking with tear-filled eyes across the room at the others. Sometimes they spoke to her while they ate, but usually it was to scold her for dropping a bowl or a fork.

One evening just before dinner, the little girl was busy playing on the floor with her building blocks, and her father asked her what she was making. "I'm building a little table for you and mother," she smiled, "so you can eat by yourselves in the corner someday when I get big."

Her parents sat staring at her for some time and then suddenly both began to cry. That night they led the old woman back to her place at the big table. From then on she ate with the rest of the family, and her son and his wife never seemed to mind a bit when she spilled something every now and then.

---

5 Adapted from the Brothers Grimm. Quoted in William Bennett, *The Book of Virtues* (New York: Simon & Shuster, 1993), pp. 143–144.

Examples of Compassion

History is filled with real men and women who showed generosity and compassion in their actions. For example, Florence Nightingale was a nurse during the Crimean War (1854) between the allies (France, England, and Turkey) and Russia. She exhibited great courage, compassion, and generosity to save the sick and wounded. Another example, Clara Barton (1821–1912) was a Civil War nurse who founded the American Red Cross. Because of her selfless service of the wounded, she was known as the "Angel of the Battlefield."

There are many other real-life examples of generosity as well. Consider the following people:

Margaret Haughery (1813–1882)

Margaret Haughery was an Irish immigrant and Catholic laywoman who moved to New Orleans from Baltimore in search of health for her husband. When both her husband and child died, Margaret ironed clothes for a living. She began helping the children of the Pydras Orphan Asylum. Eventually, Margaret became a wealthy businesswoman, but she never stopped helping the orphans. When she died, she gave her life savings of $30,000 to orphans throughout the city. Today, in the old business part of New Orleans, there is a statue of a woman sitting in a low chair, with her arms around a child who leans against her. The statue, which was dedicated in 1884, is called the Margaret Statue. It was one of the first memorials erected to a woman in the United States.

Joseph Damien de Veuster (1840–1889)

Belgium-born Joseph Damien de Veuster spent most of his life as a priest living with and helping the lepers in Molokai, one of the Hawaiian islands. The lepers were outcasts and were greatly feared by most people because of their terrible disease. Father Damien was neither afraid nor stingy in his kindness toward the lepers. He gave everything to help them, even his own health. He also died of leprosy.

St. Martin of Tours (316–397)

While serving in the military, Martin of Tours helped a poor, shivering beggar by cutting his own cloak in half and giving it to the man. Today Martin is a patron saint of France.

St. Nicholas (d. c. 350)

Nicholas—the bishop of Myra, a poor diocese in Asia Minor—inherited a fortune from his parents. One day, as he passed by the house of a poor family, he heard the father lamenting the fact that his three daughters would never be able to marry because he had no dowry to give them. That night, Bishop Nicholas secretly went back to the man's house and left three golden bars, one for each girl. Because of his anonymous generosity, the three girls were able to get married. (The bishop eventually became known as St. Nicholas, the forerunner of today's Santa Claus.)

NOTABLE QUOTABLE

"Wherever there is a human being, there is an opportunity for kindness."

—Seneca

St. Maximillian Kolbe (1894–1941)

Maximillian Kolbe was a Polish priest who was imprisoned at the concentration camp Auschwitz because of his outspoken views against the Nazis. One day, a prisoner escaped from the camp. In retaliation, the Nazis lined up the prisoners and told them they were going to select one to die in place of the escapee. They chose a man, who begged for his life because he had a wife and small children. Father Kolbe did not know the man, but he felt sorry for him. He volunteered to die in his place. The Nazis accepted his offer, and slowly starved him to death.

Generosity Is a Habit

Generosity, like all virtues, is a habit. We don't reach adulthood and suddenly start to be generous. Instead, our ability to be generous starts in childhood and is improved on during adolescence. Here are the stories of two real-life teens who are already showing generosity in their actions:

A Tucson Teen [6]

Johnny Serrano, 14, has a simple answer for why he became a teenage volunteer.

"I was bored at home." Rather than waste hour upon hour at home each day, Johnny volunteers to work with intermediate students at Kern Elementary School.

Johnny Serrano said he may apply for a job with the city someday, but he's usually too busy playing with the kids at the midtown school to think about too much else. Despite a cast protecting a broken knuckle, Serrano was a willing "pitcher" in an afternoon game of kickball earlier this week at the school.

"It's fun being with the kids," he said.

A Massachusetts Teen [7]

In 1993, thirteen-year-old Amy Kumpel decided to do something to help homeless children in her community—Stoneham, Massachusetts. With some of her friends, she started Kids Helping Kids, a group that aimed to raise funds for homeless children by auctioning celebrity-autographed patchwork pillows.

After obtaining autographs from a number of celebrities (David Letterman, Jay Leno, Oprah Winfrey, Brian Austin Green, Candice Bergen, Bill Cosby, Hillary and Bill Clinton, Tipper and Al Gore, the cast of "Cheers," and the cast of "Home Improvement," to name a few), the girls met every Monday to iron, cut, stitch, sew, and stuff pillows.

Once the patchwork pillows were assembled, the girls needed to find a location for their auction. After the profile about Kids

F.Y.I.

During 1995 and 1996 in Tucson, AZ, some 320 volunteers, ages 11 to 18, participated in Youth Volunteer Corps projects ranging from school clean-ups and graffiti removal to creating arts and crafts with cancer-stricken children.

---

6 Adapted from Raina Wagner, "Volunteer programs seek teens," *The Arizona Daily Star* (May 19, 1996), C1.

7 Adapted from *Teen* (November, 1993), p. 36.

Helping Kids appeared in the Boston Globe, a number of prestigious hotels in the Boston area offered to host the event. The auction took place at the Betet Ballroom in Boston's Ritz-Carlton Hotel.

The results? The auction raised several thousand dollars for the Inn at Spot Pond, a family homeless shelter in Stoneham. Amy and her friends at Kids Helping Kids were also nominated as a group candidate for the 1994 Noxzema Extraordinary Teen Awards program.

Generosity to a Fault

Do you remember the tightrope analogy used earlier in this course? Well, having the right balance also applies to generosity (as well as to all the other virtues we've been talking about). Although it doesn't happen often, it *is* possible to be "generous to a fault," or too generous. Some people are so busy "saving the world" and volunteering for projects to help others that they neglect their own responsibilities to themselves and their families. As William Bennett so wisely observes, "like all virtues, compassion must be tempered, and it must be informed by a good measure of reason."[8] While genuine Christian charity—sacrificial generosity, kindness, and compassion—should be extended beyond our families, friends, town, and nation, another aspect of charity is equally important. As an old saying appropriately notes, "True charity begins at home."

Prayer 🌿

LEADER: Let us spend these few moments in prayer, reflecting on the many different examples of generosity we have learned about. Let us ask God to help us be more generous and loving and to follow the example of Jesus.

READER 1: John 15:12–17

READER 2: Ephesians 4:31–5:2

READER 3: 1 Peter 4:8–10

ALL: Jesus, you gave up everything for us, including your life. Help us grow more selfless and more spontaneous in the way we give our time, talent, resources, and money to help others. Help us keep on giving, even when it hurts. We ask this in union with your Holy Spirit of love. Amen.

Further Activities 🌿

1. Develop a plan whereby you and your friends can help the homeless and/or poverty stricken children in your area.

2. As a class, sponsor a school-wide fundraiser for the Muscular Dystrophy Association, the March of Dimes, Easter Seals, the American Cancer Society, or the American Heart Society.

For Your Eyes Only

One way I will practice Christian generosity this week is . . .

---

8 William Bennett, *The Moral Compass* (New York: Simon & Shuster, 1995), p. 364.

Words to Know

abstinence
adultery
agape
charity
chastity
community
compassion
corporal works of mercy
covetousness
eros
federal poverty line
fornication
friendship
generosity
kindness
lust
phile
premarital sex
sexuality

3. Volunteer at a community food bank, clothing bank, soup kitchen, or homeless shelter.

4. Sponsor canned food drives or clothing drives to help victims of a recent disaster.

5. Help at the St. Vincent de Paul Society, the Goodwill, or the Salvation Army.

6. Research the following places to find volunteer programs for teens: your city or county parks and recreation department, the library, hospital, museum, nursing home, school, and parish. Report your findings to the class.

At Home

Go out of your way to be generous to a family member.

Perform an act of kindness or helpfulness and do not ask for anything in return.

Part 5 Review

1. What are the three different types of love? Give an example of each.

2. How does God love us in each of the three ways?

3. What is chastity?

4. What does chastity mean for unmarried people? for married people?

5. In your own words, explain how sexual relationships and friendships are connected?

6. What are four characteristics of true friendship?

7. What are two ways you can make new friends and/or become a better friend?

8. What advice would Jesus give if a friendship sours or a relationship ends? Why?

9. What is the difference between healthy self-love and unhealthy self-love?

10. Which of the three types of love is the hardest to practice? Why?

11. What is one way Jesus showed *agape* to others?

12. What do you think the parable of the Good Samaritan means for Christians today?

13. What are the seven corporal works of mercy?

14. What does the movie *It Could Happen to You* say about the relationship between generosity and good character?

15. Select two individuals from chapter five who are examples of generosity. What did they do? What have you learned from them?

16. Is it possible to be too generous? Explain.

PART 6

M ERCY

What is mercy?

How are peace, patience, and nonviolence related to mercy?

Why do people of good character forgive rather than hold a grudge or retaliate?

153

What is Mercy?

The dictionary defines *mercy* as "lenient compassion or **forbearance** toward an offender." Merciful people are patient with the imperfections and mistakes of others. They forgive and show leniency toward those who hurt them, even though they are not obliged by justice to do so.

God's Mercy

According to Christian teaching, mercy is an essential attribute of God's character. This belief, which occurred rather late in the development of the **Hebrew scriptures**, was adopted and enlarged upon by Jesus. Whereas parts of the Hebrew scriptures depict God as an exacting judge who is quick to punish evildoers and to reward the virtuous, Jesus presents the gentle and compassionate side of Abba in his teaching. The Father of Jesus is merciful and gracious, "slow to anger and abounding in kindness" (Psalm 103:8). God's mercy is constant and enduring. (See Psalm 136.)

For Your Eyes Only

How do you imagine God? Use the following scale. Zero represents a God who is quick to punish. Ten represents a merciful, gracious God. Mark and explain the spot that most closely describes your perception of God.

0	5	10
_____	\\ _____\\

LET'S TALK

1. Share an example from a novel, short story, or movie in which one person showed mercy toward another or toward an animal. What happened? What did you think of the person's character?

2. Share an example of someone you know who showed mercy, either toward you or toward another person.

Jesus Shows God's Mercy

Although the God the Father is just, God's mercy is *larger* than justice. This attribute of the Father may be seen in the way Jesus treats the adulterous woman. **Scrupulous** people are about to stone the woman to death for her sin—a punishment seen as just under Jewish law. Jesus, however, saves the woman from death and refuses to punish her. Instead, he gives her a "second chance" and urges her not to sin again. (See John 8:1–11.)

God's mercy is closely related to pity and compassion. Jesus shows us this type of mercy when he violates Jewish law to feed his hungry disciples and to cure people on the **Sabbath**. He shows mercy to them and says that meeting the needs of people is more important than keeping this particular law. (See Matthew 12:1–8; 12:9–15.)

God's mercy is peaceful and nonviolent. Jesus shows us this aspect of mercy on the night before his death. After Judas has betrayed him and the soldiers are carrying him away, Jesus tells Peter to put away his sword and not to react with violence. Jesus mercifully reattaches the soldier's severed ear. (See Matthew 26:50–54 and Luke 22:47–53.)

Divine mercy is further shown in the way God continually forgives sinners. Instead of living in constant fear of a God who will condemn

For Your Eyes Only

Describe a time in your life when someone gave you "a second chance." How did that gesture of mercy affect your self-concept? How did it affect your behavior?

us if we do wrong, Jesus says we can approach God and ask for **forgiveness**. With the psalmist, we can say, "Have mercy on me, O God, in your goodness; in the greatness of your compassion, wipe out my offense" (Psalm 51:1-2).

Jesus demonstrates this aspect of God's mercy when he forgives sins, overlooks the betrayal of Peter, forgives those who crucify him, and, with his dying breath, forgives a thief who is crucified with him. (See Matthew 9:1–8, John 21:15–19, and Luke 23:32–43.)

Our Call To Have Mercy

Jesus is very clear about the response we are to have to God's mercy. Because God has mercy on us, we are to be merciful toward others. As Jesus explains in the Sermon on the Mount, "Blessed are the merciful, for they will receive mercy" (Matthew 5:7). He further elaborates on this message in his parable of the unmerciful servant. (See Matthew 18:21–35.) God will forgive us and be merciful toward us in the same measure that we forgive others and show mercy to them. (See Matthew 6:12, 14.)

In the next two chapters of this course, you will be exploring further the virtue of mercy and its relationship to good character. Chapter 11 deals with the aspect of mercy relating to peace, patience, and nonviolence. Chapter 12 deals with the aspect of mercy relating to forgiveness.

Scripture

Discuss what each of the following passages says about the mercy we are to have toward others.

◆ Matthew 7:1–5   ◆ Matthew 5:38–39   ◆ Matthew 12:15–21

For Your Eyes Only

In what ways have you felt God's mercy in your own life or in the life of your family?

11. Peace and Patience

CHAPTER GOALS

In this chapter, you will:

◆ See how weapons, violence, and retaliation are a way of life for many people in today's world;

◆ Discover examples of people who have shown peace and patience;

◆ Learn ways you can deal with anger, deal with conflict, and avoid situations of violence.

The dictionary defines **peace** as "tranquillity; quiet; calm; freedom from disturbance; and harmony with others." **Patience**, a related virtue, is "long-suffering, forbearance, or steadfast calmness in the midst of stress, trials, or provocations." Both peace and patient endurance are related to the virtue of mercy. Christians believe that they are two fruits of the Holy Spirit. Whenever these two virtues are present in a person, God is also present. (See Galatians 5:22.)

A good starting point to understanding peace and patience is to look at what these virtues are *not* and why they are so often absent in our present-day society.

Survival of the Fittest

The three R's used to refer to academics—reading, writing and 'rithmatic. Today, many people think the three R's in life mean retribution, revenge, and retaliation—survival of the fittest. This mindset is shown powerfully in the movie *Boyz n the Hood*. Tre Styles, a young African-American in the film, is suspended from school for three days for fighting. He doesn't see that he's done anything wrong. Whenever there's a problem, fight about it—that's what everyone else does. As part of Tre's punishment, his mother makes him go live with his dad.

When his father shoots an intruder, Tre thinks he is "cool" for owning and using a gun. Mr. Styles, however, tries to get Tre to see that violence is not "cool" or "macho." Real men treat others with respect, not violence.

In the neighborhood, Tre makes friends with Ricky, Doughboy, and Chris—three boys who value guns, violence, and breaking the law. They are intent on living life "to the max" now, partly because they have no sense of a future. The results are predictable—Doughboy goes to prison for stealing; Chris ends up in a wheelchair when he is shot by a rival gang; Ricky becomes an unwed father before he is out of high school.

By the time Doughboy gets out of prison, the neighborhood situation has gotten even worse. Gangs regularly cruise Crenshaw Blvd., looking for trouble. When Ricky is killed by a rival gang, Tre is faced with the decision of his life—to seek revenge or to choose peace and **nonviolence**. Despite his father's pleas for the latter, Tre must make up his own mind. He knows that what he decides will determine not only his present character, but also his entire future.

LET'S TALK

1. Why do you think some people think violence is "cool" and being a peacemaker is "weak"?

2. Do you agree or disagree with the "law of the jungle," that only the fittest survive? Explain.

3. What do you think would happen if Tre joined Doughboy and Chris in retaliating for Ricky's death? What are some of the possible consequences?

Violence—A Way of Life

"Violence as a way of life" is represented in the lyrics of "Gangsta's Paradise," a 1996 Grammy award-winning song that speaks of being careful of how you "talk" and "walk" so as not to wind up circled by police chalk, a way to describe being murdered.[1]

Hard Cold Facts

The hard cold facts of today's society portray a grim picture, much in contrast to the gospel message of peace and patience.

Weapons

In 1993, almost 24% of all those arrested in the U.S. for carrying weapons were teenagers.[2] During the same year, about 135,000 students carried guns to school daily. One-fifth of all students reported carrying a weapon.[3] In 1995, a gun took the life of at least one young person every two hours—the equivalent of a classroom full every two days.[4]

In a 1995 poll conducted by *Teen* magazine, half of all high-school and junior-high students said weapons could be found on students at their campus. Fifty-nine percent of those polled said they could get a gun if they wanted one.

While some people think that violence is characteristic of ethnic neighborhoods, the statistics do not confirm this stereotype. The fact is: white families are twice as likely to have guns in the house and one-third more likely to subscribe to the gorier cable TV channels with a proliferation of violence than non-white households.[5]

Violent Crimes

In 1993, over 350,000 juveniles (ages 10–17) were arrested for violent crimes. About 3,500 of the arrests were for murder, over 44,000 for robbery, over 54,000 for weapon violations, and almost 69,000 for **aggravated assault**.[6]

In 1994, young people committed 13% of all the violent crimes in the United States. Young males between the ages of 15 and 24 committed 6,800 murders and were 16 times more likely than young males living in other industrialized nations to be murdered themselves. According to the U.S. Dept. of Justice, the number of teenage murderers tripled between 1984 and 1994 even though the teenage population remained stable. The number of girls under 18 arrested and charged with violent crimes went up 103% between 1984 and 1994. Juvenile murderers used guns in eight out of ten cases.

The reasons for murder and violent crimes have become increasingly trivial. Consider, for example, what happened in Chicago during

---

1 By Artis Ivey, Jr., Larry Sanders, and Doug Rasheed. Performed by Coolio featuring L.V. Copyright © 1995 Jobete Music Co., Inc./Black Bull Music, Inc. (ASCAP). All rights reserved.
2 From 1995 *Statistical Abstract of the United States.*
3 From *Creative Classroom* (October, 1993).
4 From *Teen* (August, 1995).
5 From 1995 *Statistical Abstract of the United States.*
6 From 1995 *Statistical Abstract of the United States.*

the winter of 1995–96. Two boys—one 12 and one 13—dropped a five-year-old out of a fourteenth-story window because he wouldn't steal candy for them.

Gang Warfare

Joining neighborhood and ethnic gangs is the way of life for many pre-teens and teenagers today. Boys and a rapidly increasing number of girls join gangs primarily for social reasons—friendship, a sense of belonging and identity, and security. What happens instead is that these boys and girls become involved in a life of constant warfare—turf battles, drug dealing, drive-by shootings, and grand theft auto. Consider the real-life story of one girl caught up in a gang:

Regina [7]

In Los Angeles, Regina has been in the Playgirl Gangsters for several years. To join the gang, Regina had to fight two gang members at once for a count of 60, ending up bloodied and bruised. In return, she got a new gang name, a tattoo, and a group of 20 or 30 girls willing, in theory at least, to kill and die for her. At her peak, Regina estimates she stole some four cars a day to steal the parts for cash or merely to take joyrides. Although she's been caught six times, she's never been convicted.

Three years ago, she painted on a mustache, darkened her face with makeup, and hid her hair under a baseball cap to set out on her first "mission." A rival male gang member had fired a sawed-off shotgun through the passenger window of a car driven by one of Regina's "homegirls," killing her friend's 12-year-old brother. "He was after my girlfriend," Regina says of the gang rival, "but figured she'd suffer more if he blasted her little brother's brains." The muscles in Regina's throat tighten. "I found the guy at a back-yard beer party, bragging about the killing. I went up to him and said, 'This is the big payback from the 'hood.' Bam, Bam! Shot him twice with a nine millimeter. Should have seen the look on his face—he couldn't believe this was happening! I ran to my car, rubbed off my mustache with baby oil, tore off the guy clothes—underneath I had my girl clothes—then burned outta there."

Regina's tale is a typical one. Like many female gang members, she comes from a poverty-stricken neighborhood where fathers are

---

7 Shortened and adapted from Gini Sikes, "Girls in the 'hood." *Scholastic Update* (February 11, 1994), p. 20ff.

LET'S TALK

What would you have done if you were Dumar Stokes? Was going to get his gun the right thing to do?

For Your Eyes Only

Have you ever been attracted to or belonged to a gang? Why?

absent and mothers struggle to make a living, leaving children to fend for themselves. To Regina, gangs (also called posses or crews) offer a kind of alternate family structure. "In my neighborhood, we're having our own personal Vietnam War." she says. "Only it doesn't end."

Forcible Rape

In 1993, close to 5,500 juveniles (ages 10–17) were arrested for forcible **rape**.[8] According to the Worldwide Web, the statistics in 1996 were worse: In the U.S., a woman was raped every 1.3 minutes. Ninety-two percent of the rape victims were acquainted with their attackers.

The horrible nature of these violent crimes becomes even more evident when you look at specific crimes. For example, consider what happened during the winter of 1995–96 in New York. Two teenage boys and a young woman locked up a 13-year-old girl, repeatedly raped and tortured her, then hung her up in a closet by her heels before she managed to escape. Also consider the following news story:[9]

LOS ANGELES—The crimes are awful: the gang rape of a 13-year-old girl and the slaying of a beloved 82-year-old neighborhood woman. The prime suspect is even more shocking: a boy just past his 12th birthday, whose alleged acts are so violent that his own mother turned him in after police identified him by name on live television.

"She did the right thing. It was not easy for her. She had the character and the courage to turn him in," police Capt. Tom Lorenzen said Friday.

The boy, is a shade under 5 feet tall, less than 100 pounds, slight of build, very young-looking. He was identified on live television after police obtained a court order granting permission to name the minor. He is the main suspect in the gang rape of a 13-year-old girl and the shooting death of Viola McClain, who was known as "everybody's mama."

Monday, police said, the boy and several other boys and men abducted the 13-year-old girl and forced her into an abandoned house. Behind the boarded-up windows, the girl was raped and tortured for up to two hours, police said. In an apparent attempt to kill her, some of the gang attempted to set fire to the house. They dragged a mattress used in the attack outside and set fire to it.

That's when McClain's grandson Dumar Stokes, 33, smelled smoke. He saw two boys running from the fire and confronted them. The boy told Stokes: "If you don't get out of the way, we'll smoke you." Stokes went inside his grandmother's house to get his own gun, but before he got outside, his grandmother walked onto the porch. She was hit in the neck by a bullet and died in the emergency room.

---

8 From 1995 *Statistical Abstract of the United States.*
9 Shortened from "Boy, 12, accused in rape, killing," *Associated Press* (August 4, 1996).

Turn the Other Cheek

The message of Jesus—to turn the other cheek when someone hurts us—is hard to swallow when we are grieving and angry. And yet, that is when we most need to heed the gospel and turn to the virtues of peace and patience, for they are the only hope we have of ending violence.

Consider the following real-life story in American history:

Jackie Robinson [10]

On October 23, 1945, Branch Rickey, general manager of the Brooklyn Dodgers, signed a contract with Jackie Robinson, a black player, to play with the Montreal Royals in the International League. Until then, no black had played major-league baseball in the twentieth century.

It didn't take long for the **bigots** to react to the appearance of Robinson on a baseball field occupied by white players. During spring training in Sanford, Florida, civic leaders demanded that Jackie get out of town. The insolent demand infuriated Robinson, but he remembered his promise with Branch Rickey. For three years, no matter what happened, he would not retaliate or fight back. Without a word, Robinson left town.

During a spring training game at De Land, Florida, Jackie tried to score from second base on a hit. He had to slide home to make it. As the umpire called him safe, a policeman ran up and ordered Jackie off the field. "We ain't havin' Nigras mix with white boys in this town," the policeman said. "I said to git!" Without a word, Jackie left.

During the regular season, Jackie's first hit for Montreal was a home run. But acceptance did not come easily. The rival players were violently hostile. Opposing pitchers threw at him continually. Time after time, Jackie hit the dirt, got up, brushed himself off, and said nothing. He was constantly insulted by opposing players who called him vile names that were unprintable—but he said nothing.

"As long as you are in baseball," Branch Rickey told Robinson, "you will have to conduct yourself as you are doing now. That is the cross you must bear."

Robinson agreed. He was determined to take it all and fight back only on the diamond with base hits, stolen bases, and great fielding plays.

He did this so well that he helped the Montreal Royals win the International League pennant and the Little World Series in 1946.

[10] Adapted from Hal Butler, "The Man Who Broke the Color Barrier," *Sports Heroes Who Wouldn't Quit* (New York: Julian Messner, a division of Simon & Schuster, Inc., 1973).

Jackie, the batting champion with a .349 average, was named Rookie of the Year.

The next year, Jackie was assigned to play first base for the Brooklyn Dodgers. Some of the team members protested. During the season, National League pitchers threw at him. Efforts were made to spike him on the bases. Vicious insults flowed from the dugouts of opposing teams. Even off the field, Robinson experienced troubles. In some cities where the Dodgers played, Robinson was not allowed to stay in the same hotel with the other players; there were restaurants he was forbidden to enter. But Robinson exhibited a courage few men have been called on to show. He took it all, never losing his temper, never striking back, even though many times he was tempted to hit back with his fists.

The hostility toward Jackie Robinson reached a high point on May 6, when the St. Louis Cardinals were scheduled to play the Brooklyn Dodgers. A group of Cardinal players decided they would go on strike and refuse to play the game because of Robinson's presence. If that succeeded, they intended to mobilize players on other teams and call a general National League strike.

Fortunately, a sports writer on the *New York Herald Tribune* exposed the plot against Robinson before it happened, and Ford Frick, then president of the National League, took immediate and bold action. He sent a stinging ultimatum to the players planning to strike. As a result, the strike was canceled.

One day during a game, Pee Wee Reese, the Dodger shortstop from Kentucky, jogged over from his position to talk to Robinson. He placed his hand gently on Jackie's shoulder as he talked, and a newspaper photographer shot the picture. The photo appeared in newspapers across the country, and the fact became known that Reese, among all the Dodger players, was the most sympathetic toward Robinson's difficult problem. He saw in Robinson a superb ballplayer, and the color of his face mattered not.

By mid-season there were signs that most of the Dodgers were beginning to accept Robinson on an equal footing. The reason was obvious. Robinson, despite his troubles, was playing spectacular ball, and his play won him the respect that was due him. It required a superman to play good baseball under the tensions that gripped Robinson throughout the critical year, and Jackie proved himself to be a superman. In his first major-league season, he hit .297, collected 12 home runs, and stole 29 bases. In the World Series that followed against the New York Yankees, he contributed seven hits in 27 times up for a .259 batting average. When the season ended, Jackie Robinson was named the National League Rookie of the Year.

In 1997, to mark the fiftieth anniversary of Jackie Robinson's debut with the Dodgers, major league baseball retired his number 42 on every team, an honor that is unprecedented in any sport.

LET'S TALK

1. When did you have to "turn the other cheek"? What happened? Why did you choose to respond the way you did?

2. Have you ever been in a situation where you should have turned the other cheek and did not? Explain what happened.

NOTABLE QUOTABLE

"Nonviolence is the answer to the crucial political and moral questions of our time; the need for us to overcome oppression and violence without resorting to oppression and violence."

—Martin Luther King, Jr. (1929–1968)

Other Real-Life Examples

Fortunately, there are heroic examples of young people in this world who are choosing peace and patience rather than violence. Such young people are not "sissies," "wimps," or "chickens." Instead, they are exhibiting great self-control and courage. They are showing great strength of character.

Here are three examples:

Alejandro Fernandez [11]

He was tired of the funerals. He was tired of the eulogies—for fellow gang members, for neighbors, for a brother. "They always said the same thing: 'What a pity, but it was just a matter of time,'" Alejandro Fernandez, 24, recalled. "I knew I had to change my life, or someday the priest would be talking about me."

Fernandez left his "banda" in a shanty-town on the edge of Mexico City four years ago and took up with a new group, where members looked to the future rather than over their shoulder for the next bullet.

At Urban Courage, an international coalition of former gang members seeking to reroute their lives, Fernandez said he made a discovery. "Life doesn't have to be violence, only violence," he said. "I think I always knew it but didn't really believe it."

Urban Courage, based in Mexico City, brought the former gang members to Istanbul as part of a program to acknowledge groups that are making a difference in cities around the world.

"These kids have all the pathologies of kids from the war zone, because in fact that is what it often is like," said Helen Samuels, the group's international director.

Her interest in trying to defuse gang violence began when her daughter's friend was killed by a gang in Los Angeles because she leaned on their car by mistake.

El Rio Teens [12]

For nine months, feelings of anger, frustration, and sorrow were released as young artists painted bright blues, reds, and yellows on the wall at El Rio Health Center. With paint brushes in hand,

---

11 "Gang kids' stories open eyes at UN urban summit," *Associated Press* (June 7, 1996).
12 Melissa Prentice, "Mural honoring grief, peace dedicated to teens," *The Arizona Daily Star* (May 19, 1996), p. B3.

young people from Barrio Anita and Barrio Sovaco met there each Saturday to grieve for two young neighborhood boys shot to death last year.

More than thirty young painters added a part of themselves—a brightly colored Aztec dancer, the Virgin Mary, a young Chicano family, red roses and clouds—to the mural. The mural was dedicated yesterday in memory of Peter Valenzuela Jr., 15, and Joseph Campos, 12. Joseph was accidentally shot in the head June 19 by his 14-year-old brother. Less than a month later, Peter was walking with a group of friends when he was killed in a drive-by shooting.

"The friends of both kids were overwhelmed by grief," said Judy Bernal, whose son Joaquin, 15, was Peter's friend. "We knew if the kids didn't channel their grief into something positive, it would likely become self-destructive."

So she and her husband, Julio Bernal, an artist, started handing out paint brushes. And the close-knit group of children and teens got to work.

"This got them together, and it gave them a common purpose," she said. "These kids are often misidentified as gang members. But this gave them the opportunity to say, 'That is how you see us, but this is how we really are. Look what we can accomplish.'"

Yesterday more than 100 community members gathered near the completed mural to pray, sing, and dance with traditional Aztec dancers, to honor the young artists for not reacting to the tragedies with violence.

"Everyone is dying," said Yndia Campos, Joseph's sister and one of the teens who dedicated many weekend hours to the project. "We wanted to prove to everyone that we want to stop the violence."

"We wanted to take the anger out this way instead of retaliation," Mateo Otero, 16, said.

"Instead of taking away from the community, we wanted to try to give something back," agreed Jesse Cruz, who never missed a Saturday painting session.

Alvindee Bell [13]

Nineteen-year-old Alvindee Bell was a student in Los Angeles, when the following incident happened. Leaving work one day in March, Bell heard screams. The strapping young man rescued a teenage girl from an attacker who was later charged with sexual **battery**. Bell, a developmentally disabled youth who participates in the Special Olympics, received a city council commendation for his bravery. Says city attorney Lynn Magnan-Donovan: "This has reaffirmed my faith in human beings. He responded to a situation where others wouldn't."

---

13 "Local Heroes," *Time* (June 17, 1996), p. 26.

Christian Strategies of Peace

People of good character try to live by the beatitude, "Blessed are the peacemakers, for they will be called children of God" (Matthew 5:8). Such people do not run away from conflicts. They handle the normal feeling of anger in a positive way. They confront these challenges head on. They face them with courage and perseverance.

Being a peacemaker in today's world involves three commonsense strategies. These strategies include dealing with anger, dealing with conflict, and avoiding situations that might lead to violence or rape.

Dealing With Anger

Anger itself is neither good nor bad. It is simply a feeling, an emotion. However, anger does become sinful when it controls us—when we become enraged to the point that all we want is revenge, retaliation, and violence. Anger also becomes sinful when we take out our anger on an

innocent person (for example, a businesswoman is angry at her boss, but doesn't dare let him know it; instead, she comes home and takes out her anger on her children).

Thomas Jefferson once offered this advice regarding anger: "If you are angry, count to ten before you do anything, and if you are very angry, count to a hundred." It is good advice to follow. Only when we are calm and in control of our emotions (rather than vice versa) can we have the presence of mind to figure out the best solution to our problems. That is why the Roman statesman, Titus Maccium Pautus, once wrote, "Patience is the best remedy for every trouble."

A second strategy for dealing with anger is to attend to it immediately, rather than letting it fester. Usually what happens to unattended anger is that it escalates until we "blow up" like a volcano. That is why the old sayings "never let the sun set on your anger" and "never go to bed angry" are also good to follow.

A third strategy for dealing with anger is trying to put yourself in the other person's shoes. As an old Indian saying goes, "Don't judge someone else until you've walked a whole day in his or her moccasins." Trying to see another person's point of view is a good way to dissipate your own anger. It shows that you respect the other person and are willing to dialogue together toward a peaceful solution. Once you know *why* a person said or did something that angered you, you may tend to have more compassion or mercy toward him or her.

A fourth strategy for dealing with anger is to get out your frustrations in healthy ways. Hit a punching bag or pillow instead of a person. Spend your excess energy by jogging instead of making life miserable for those around you.

A fifth strategy for dealing with anger is to postpone a confrontation with the person you are angry at until you have had a chance to calm down. Once your feelings of rage subside, you can be more rational and calm in the way you approach the situation and, chances are likely, you'll get better results.

Dealing With Conflict

Someone once said, "Life is full of conflict. The only time we won't experience conflict is when we are dead." People of good character learn to deal with conflict by solving problems. The five steps of problem solving are as follows:

1. *Determine if the situation is a mere misunderstanding or a true conflict.* Sometimes we get angry because we "think" a person intentionally hurt us. That person may not even be aware of what he or she said or did. People of good character ask questions to determine the whole story before they react. They try to clarify points of misunderstanding.

2. *If there is true conflict, focus on the point of disagreement.* Focus on the present point of disagreement, not on all the things the person has done in the past that have irritated you. People of good character stay focused. They listen to the other's point of view, while also clarifying their own interest and needs. Finding out *why* another person has done something may help you see a solution.

3. *Work together to look for possible solutions.* Dialogue, don't demand or dictate. People of good character try to maintain an atmosphere of partnership with the other person in a conflict. Both sides must agree to a solution that is mutually beneficial. If one side "wins" and the other "loses," there will still be conflict and anger.

4. *Be flexible.* If Plan A doesn't work, then look for a Plan B—a solution that both people can agree to.

5. *Be patient and persevere until an acceptable solution is reached.* People of good character don't quit or give up when their first efforts to

solve a problem fail. They keep trying. If they reach a point where they realize they can't resolve the conflict on their own, they agree to have a neutral third party intervene.

Above all, people of good character are patient with themselves. They realize that they won't always be perfect, that sometimes they'll make mistakes. They also realize that they can learn from their mistakes and move on. In short, they are not only merciful toward others. They are also merciful with themselves.

Avoiding Violence and Rape

People of good character try to avoid situations that might lead to violence or rape by taking the following actions:[14]

1. *Examine your feelings about and values regarding violence or sex ahead of time.* Don't be swept away by the emotions of the moment. For example, don't threaten violence and then at the last minute try to back out. Likewise, don't "make out" heavily on a date and then at the last moment say "no."

2. *Set limits to what you will and will not tolerate.* For example, it's OK to let your friends know that you don't want to be with them when they are carrying a weapon. Likewise, it's OK to walk away if things get out of hand on a date.

3. *Don't give mixed messages.* For example, don't give the impression that sometimes it's OK to get revenge and other times it's not. Likewise, don't let a date think that "no" really means "yes." Always be clear. Mean what you say. Be consistent.

4. *Be alert to nonverbal messages you may be giving.* You may be sending nonverbal messages with your posture, clothing, tone of voice, gestures, and eye contact. For example, the wearing of gang colors in a rival gang's neighborhood is asking for trouble. Likewise, dressing immodestly can give the impression that you are sexually promiscuous.

5. *Actively participate in deciding where to go and what to do.* This rule especially holds true when you are with your group of friends or on a date. Cruising a street known for fighting is not a good idea if you don't want to fight. Likewise, spending time alone together in a bedroom or hotel room on a date is not a good idea if you don't want sex.

6. *Don't do anything you don't want to do.* Don't go along with the crowd because you are too afraid to protest. Don't face the possibility of rape because you are too "polite" to get out of a dangerous situation.

7. *Avoid situations where alcohol, drugs, and weapons are present.* Alcohol and drugs impair people's ability to reason and make calm judgments. Their use can lead to unwanted violence and sex.

LET'S TALK

Discuss a typical conflict teens have with parents, such as wanting to stay out later than parents want. Role-play the teen/parent conflict. Go through the five steps of problem solving to show an appropriate way to deal with conflict.

NOTABLE QUOTABLES

"Let your understanding strengthen your patience."
—St. Peter Damian

"Why lose your temper if by doing so you offend God, annoy other people, give yourself a bad time, and have to find it again in the end?"
—Venerable José Escriva

---

14 Adapted from Jean O'Gorman Hughes and Bernice Sandler, *Project on the Status and Education of Women, Association of American Colleges* (April, 1987).

For Your Eyes Only

One way I will try to be a peacemaker this week is . .

8. *Get to know other people's values before you go out with them.* This holds true for both a group's values and an individual's values. For example, get to know the other person's values before you go out on a date with him or her. And be up front about your own values. If things get out of hand while you are with the group or on the date, don't be afraid to seek out a safe ride home with someone you can trust.

Following these suggestions for dealing with anger, dealing with conflict, and avoiding situations of violence and rape may not solve all the world's problems. But they will be a good way for you to grow in good Christian character and enhance your ability to be merciful. They will help you learn to be a peacemaker in all your relationships, a true child of God.

Prayer

LEADER: As we come together today in prayer, let us praise God for showing us mercy and patience. Let us pray that we may imitate the actions of Jesus as we say, "Peace be with you."

ALL: And also with you.

READER 1: Matthew 26:47–56

READER 2: Colossians 3:12–15

ALL: Lord, make me an instrument of your peace. (*Prayer of St. Francis*)

Further Activities

1. Find out who was awarded the Nobel Peace Prize for the past five years and why. Report your findings to the class.

2. Donate blood in a Red Cross blood drive to help the victims of violence.

3. Research one of the areas of unrest and violence in the world today. Then draw up a proposal for peace. Discuss the situation and your plan with the class.

4. Watch a TV show you enjoy. Record the number of times guns or other weapons are used to threaten or inflict violence. Share your findings with the class.

5. Find out which movies were the "top box office hits" last week. How many of these movies contained violence? Share your findings with the class.

At Home

Try to be a peacemaker when there is an argument or fight between two family members. If you have hurt someone in the family or done something wrong, be the first to apologize.

12. Forgiveness

CHAPTER GOALS

In this chapter, you will:

◆ Learn about four types of forgiveness—the forgiveness of God, forgiving oneself, forgiveness in personal relationships, and societal forgiveness;

◆ See heroic examples of people who forgave others;

◆ Understand how the sacrament of reconciliation is an opportunity for forgiveness and grace.

Forgiveness is another gift related to the virtue of mercy. Jesus practiced and taught the gift of forgiveness in his ministry.

For example, Jesus forgives the sins of a paralyzed man because of the man's faith. (See Matthew 9:2; Mark 2:5; Luke 5:20.) Jesus forgives a sinful woman who washes his feet with her tears. (See Luke 7:36–50.) Jesus forgives his executioners, as well as one of the thieves who is crucified with him. (See Luke 23:32–43.) After his resurrection, Jesus forgives Peter for denying him three times. (See John 21:15–19.)

In his teaching, Jesus places great importance on forgiveness. He tells his followers to forgive one another. (See Matthew 6:14; Mark 11:25; and Luke 17:3.) They are to do this not just once or twice, but "seventy-seven times." (See Matthew 18:21–22.) Furthermore, Jesus confers upon the twelve apostles the power to forgive sins. (See John 20:21–23.)

Scripture

Read and discuss one of the following parables of Jesus that deal with forgiveness. What does the parable mean? How does the parable apply to your life?

◆ The Unforgiving Servant (Matthew 18:23–35)

◆ The Merciful Father/Prodigal Son (Luke 15:11–32)

◆ The Pharisee and the Publican (Luke 18:9–14)

Types of Forgiveness

In this chapter, we will be talking about four types of forgiveness: God's forgiveness of us, our forgiveness of ourselves, the forgiveness needed in personal relationships, and societal, or social, forgiveness.

God's Forgiveness

Basic to Christianity is the belief that God forgives us, even when we don't deserve it. God loves us and values us so highly that God sent Jesus to die for our sins and to win for us eternal redemption.

Forgiving Oneself

You know that Jesus stressed the importance of *loving* our neighbor as ourselves. For Jesus, such love includes *forgiving* our neighbor as we forgive ourselves. Some people find it much easier to forgive other people than to forgive themselves. If they make a mistake or do something wrong, they hate themselves and continually put themselves down. They don't let themselves ever forget the time they "messed up."

DO THIS!

Plan a skit based on the parable you discussed in the previous activity. The skit should involve contemporary teenagers involved in a "real-life" situation related to the teaching of the parable.

169

Being sorry for our sins is indeed a necessary ingredient of Jesus' call to "repent, and believe in the good news" (Mark 1:15). But Jesus did not intend that we hate ourselves or continually "beat ourselves up" for our vices, mistakes, and omissions. Instead, Jesus calls us to be gentle with ourselves, just as God is a gentle, loving shepherd with us. (See Matthew 18:12–14 and Luke 15:3–7.) We are to forgive ourselves and move on because God has already forgiven us.

One saint who understood this type of forgiveness was St. John Vianney. Here is his story:

St. John Vianney (1786–1859)

John was a very poor student, but he desperately wanted to be a priest. He tried to study and to get decent grades, but it was impossible. He just wasn't as bright as everyone else in the seminary. Throughout school, John suffered the ridicule of others and the humiliation of continually failing. Finally, the seminary ordained him in an exasperated effort to get rid of him.

John was sent to the poorest parish in all of France, the rural community of Vianney. Parishioners there laughed at John's simple-mindedness and were quick to criticize him. John, however, did not respond to them with hatred. Instead, he started to spend time with them in the confessional. At first, people came to Father John because they thought he was too "dumb" to exact much from them in the way of penance. But slowly, they began to realize that John was a man of great wisdom and insight. He had the uncanny gift of reading their hearts and getting right to the problem.

John's confessional came to be known, not as a place for a meaningless ritual, but as a place of true conversion and forgiveness. People began to flock to John's church from all of France, seeking to talk with him. They came to respect and to admire him greatly, for he helped them truly accept God's forgiveness by forgiving themselves.

F.Y.I.

Today, John Vianney is the patron saint of parish priests and confessors. His feast day is August 4.

LET'S TALK

1. Which do you think is harder to do—to forgive yourself or to forgive someone else? Why?

2. Tell about someone you know who is able to get right to the heart of the problem and offer helpful advice.

3. What could you say to help convince skeptical teens of the meaning and purpose of the sacrament of reconciliation?

Forgiveness in Personal Relationships

Someone once remarked, "*Falling* in love is easy. What's really hard is *staying* in love." Usually when people fall in love, they only see the other person's good points. The person seems "perfect." When time goes on, however, it becomes apparent that neither person in the relationship is perfect. Each one has faults. Inevitably, each ends up hurting the other in some way—either big or small. That is why staying in love requires much more than the emotion of love; it also requires the hard work of forgiveness.

Consider the following lyrics of an Amy Grant song, "That's What Love Is For." How do they point to the importance of forgiveness in personal relationships? "Believing in the one thing that has gotten us this far. That's what love is for. To help us through it, that's what love is for. Nothing else can do it. Round off the edges, talk us down from the ledges, give us strength to try once more. That's what love is for." [1]

Societal Forgiveness

The virtue of mercy is often at odds with the virtue of justice when it comes to society's ability to forgive a person of a crime. Originally, serving time in prison was seen as both a punishment and as an opportunity to reform, or rehabilitate, oneself for the better. The ultimate goal was the criminal's reunion with society—living as a productive citizen.

Unfortunately, societies are not always willing to "forgive and forget," even after the criminal has served his or her time and has been paroled. "Once a criminal, always a criminal," is the type of thinking that leads to discrimination against many ex-convicts.

The following story, which deals with the subject of societal forgiveness, was written in the nineteenth century. Its message about the need for societal forgiveness is as relevant now as it was then, as attested by the story's recent success as an award-winning Broadway musical.

Les Misérables [2]

Jean Valjean was a wood-chopper's son, who, while very young, was left an orphan. His older sister brought him up, but when he was 17 years of age, his sister's husband died, and upon Jean came the labor of supporting her seven little children. Although a man of great strength, he found it very difficult to provide food for them as a wood-chopper.

One winter day he was without work, and the children were crying for bread. Jean went out in the night, and, breaking a baker's window with his fist, carried home a loaf of bread for the famished children. The next morning he was arrested for stealing, his bleeding hand convicting him.

For this crime he was sent to the galleys with an iron collar riveted around his neck, with a chain attached, which bound him to his galley seat. Here he remained four years; then he tried to escape, but was caught, and three years were added to his sentence. Then he made a second attempt, and also failed, the result of which was that he remained 19 years as a galley slave for stealing a single loaf of bread.

LET'S TALK

How do the song's words, "Round off the edges, talk us down from the ledges" relate to the words of Jesus in Matthew 7:1–5? How do both quotations relate to the virtue of forgiveness?

---

1 By Mark Mueller, Michael Omartian, and Amy Grant. Recorded by Amy Grant, *"That's What Love Is For."* Copyright © 1991 by MCA Music Publishing, a division of MCA, Inc., Moo Maison, All Nations Music, and Age to Age Music, Inc. All rights for Moo Maison controlled and administered by MCA Music Publishing, a division of MCA, Inc. All rights reserved.

2 From Victor Hugo, *Les Misérables.* Shortened from the excerpt, "The Good Bishop," found in William Bennett, *The Book of Virtues* (New York: Simon & Shuster, 1993), pp. 644–46.

When Jean left the prison, no one would receive him. Everyone knew him to be an ex-convict and a dangerous man. Finally, he wandered to the house of the good bishop. The bishop was a simple, loving man, with a great heart, who thought nothing of himself, but loved everybody.

When he entered the bishop's house, Jean identified himself as an ex-convict and asked: "Will you give me a little food and let me sleep in the stable?"

The good bishop said: "Sit down and warm yourself. You will take supper with me, and after that sleep here. You are my brother."

After supper the bishop took one of the silver candlesticks that he had received as a Christmas present and, giving Jean the other, led him to his room where a good bed was provided. In the middle of the night Jean awoke with a hardened heart. He remembered the silver knives and forks that had been used for supper and made up his mind to steal them. So he took what he could find, sprang into the garden, and disappeared.

When the bishop awoke and saw his silver gone, he said: "I have been thinking for a long time that I ought not to keep the silver. I should have given it to the poor, and certainly this man was poor."

At breakfast time, five solders brought Jean back to the bishop's house. When they entered, the bishop, looking at him, said: "I am glad to see you. I gave you the candlesticks, too. Why did you not take them?"

Jean was stunned by these words. So were the soldiers. "We thought he had stolen the silver and was running away."

But the good bishop only said, "Let him go. The silver is his. I gave it to him."

So the officers went away.

"Is it true," Jean whispered to the bishop, "that I am free? I may go?"

"Yes," he replied, "but before you go, take your candlesticks."

Jean trembled in every limb and took the candlesticks like one in a dream.

"Now," said the bishop, "depart in peace, but do not go through the garden, for the front door is always open to you day and night."

Jean looked as though he would faint.

Then the bishop took his hand, and said: "Never forget you have promised me you would use the money to become an honest man."

He did not remember having promised anything, but stood silent while the bishop continued solemnly:

"Jean Valjean, my brother, you no longer belong to evil, but to good. I have bought your soul for you. I withdrew it from black thoughts and the spirit of hate and gave it to God."

The bishop's action of forgiveness had a profound effect on the rest of Jean's life. He *did* change his life around. He became an honest citizen who was compassionate and forgiving toward others.

Despite Jean's rehabilitation, however, the inspector hunting him could never forgive him. The words **clemency** (acting mercifully with regard to lessening the severity of a punishment) and **pardon** (excusing an offense without exacting a penalty) were not in this man's vocabulary. He saw Valjean only as a criminal, and he became obsessed with finding Jean and taking him back to prison. The inspector's inability to forgive Jean eventually affected his ability to forgive himself. In utter frustration, he committed suicide one night.

DO THIS!

1. One of the corporal works of mercy is to visit the imprisoned. Learn how the Catholic church is involved in prison ministry (either adults or juveniles) in your local area. Also find out if there are any ways teens can become involved in this ministry.

2. Research information about the juvenile justice system and how juvenile offenders are "rehabilitated." Share your findings with the class.

Capital Punishment

Capital punishment is the state-approved killing of a convicted criminal for serious crimes he or she has committed. The death penalty has been a state-sanctioned and, in some cases, church-sanctioned punishment for centuries. During the time of Jesus, Jewish law allowed a woman caught in adultery to be stoned to death (although Roman law did not permit such a sentence to be carried out). According to Roman law, non-Romans and slaves could be crucified as punishment for crimes such as murder, robbery, piracy, treason, and rebellion. Jesus was crucified for the religious crime of **blasphemy**, ultimately translated as treason and rebellion against the Roman government. With him were crucified two men convicted of robbery.

In the Middle Ages, many people (mostly women) were burned at the stake for being convicted of witchcraft. During the Inquisition, some Catholics were burned at the stake for committing the sin of **heresy**. St. Joan of Arc was burned to death for this supposed "crime."

Today, capital punishment is a hotly debated topic. **Abolitionists,** people who argue against capital punishment, often stage peaceful protests on the night of state executions. They are opposed by **retributionists,** people who uphold capital punishment.

The debate over capital punishment involves a number of important values:

For Your Eyes Only

Has anyone mercifully forgiven you, even though you didn't deserve it?

LET'S TALK

1. What is your opinion on the likelihood that a criminal can be rehabilitated?

2. How comfortable would you feel working at a job where a known ex-convict was also working? How comfortable would you feel living next door to an ex-con?

◆ the sanctity of all human life,

◆ the protection of society—the lives of innocent people,

◆ the preservation of law and order in society, and

◆ the achievement of justice (a fitting punishment for a crime committed).

The U.S. bishops have taken a strong stand against capital punishment. They argue that it is not right to treat violence with further violence. Human life—from conception to natural death—should be respected, regardless of what a person does.

A recent movie focused on the subject of capital punishment and its relationship to Christian forgiveness. The movie is about a real-life religious woman working in Louisiana. Here is the movie's story line:

Dead Man Walking

Sister Helen Prejean has never been inside a prison, but when death-row inmate, Matthew Poncelet, writes to her, she writes back, offering comfort. In return, Poncelet asks her to visit him.

Somewhat warily, Sr. Helen goes to the prison to visit Poncelet. What she finds is not likable: Poncelet shot two teenagers who were parked at a lover's lane, after stabbing and raping the girl. Furthermore, Poncelet is prejudiced against African-Americans, the very people Sr. Helen works with in the St. Thomas projects.

Poncelet maintains his innocence—that his partner shot the teens, not him. He further cites the injustice that has been done: His partner in crime got a sentence of life in prison; he, on the other hand, got the death sentence. Poncelet pleads with Sr. Helen to file a motion he's written for mercy to the Appeals Board.

Sr. Helen gets more and more involved. She agrees to get Poncelet a lawyer and to try to talk his mother into speaking on his behalf at the pardons board hearing.

At the hearing, Mr. and Mrs. Delacroix, the parents of the slain boy, and Mr. and Mrs. Percy, the parents of the slain girl, are on hand to make sure Poncelet does not get clemency. They want him to pay for what he did to their children. In their eyes, he deserves to die.

The Pardons Board denies clemency and schedules Poncelet's execution in one week. Sr. Helen agrees to be his spiritual advisor—someone who will be with him up to and throughout the execution.

Sr. Helen, who is opposed to the death penalty, continues to push for appeals in the Federal Court. Meanwhile, she has to bear the hatred of both the Percys and the Delacroixes, who can't understand how she could support Poncelet. "I'm just trying to imitate Jesus," she tries to explain to them. "Every person is worth more than his or her worst acts." They, however, strongly disagree. "You can't befriend our enemy and be our friend, too," they tell her.

Despite Poncelet's disrespect and continued denial of guilt, Sr. Helen does not quit trying to get him to see how he has seriously hurt the lives of many people, including his own family. "Admit the truth," she pleads with Poncelet. "Go to your death as a man, not as a victim. Apologize for what you've done and receive God's forgiveness."

Not until a half hour before his execution does Poncelet take responsibility for killing the two teens. The Federal Appeals Court denies clemency, and Sr. Helen has to watch as Poncelet is taken to the death chamber and strapped to the table where the lethal injection will take place. Before his death, Poncelet asks the Percys and Delacroixes for their forgiveness.

After burying Poncelet and spending time with his grieving family, Sr. Helen continues to spend time with Mr. Delacroix. They pray together, asking for the grace to forgive Poncelet and what he did. "I don't have your faith," Mr. Delacroix tells Sr. Helen. "I still have a lot of hate. But maybe we could help each other find a way out of the hate."

Examples of Forgiveness

Although it is very hard to forgive others who have hurt us or our loved ones, such mercy is possible. Here are three people whose stories attest to this possibility. One is a saint, the other is a pope, and the third is an ordinary gas station worker.

St. Maria Goretti (1890–1902)

Maria Goretti was born into a poor farming family in Italy. The family was so poor that they had to share a small house with Mr. Goretti's business partner and the partner's son, Alessandro Serenelli. One day when Maria was 12, Alessandro tried to rape her while they were alone in the house. When Maria resisted him, he grew so angry that he stabbed her repeatedly. When Maria's parents came home, they found her covered with blood and barely alive. She told them what had happened, but she also said, "I forgive Alessandro. I forgive him with all my heart; and I want him to be with me in heaven."

Maria died several days later. Alessandro, unrepentant of his crime, was sent to prison. While there, he had a vision of Maria that changed his life. He realized the terrible wrong he had done, and he felt sincere sorrow. Many years later, when he was finally released from prison, the first thing Alessandro did was to visit Mrs. Goretti and beg her forgiveness for killing her daughter. He spent the rest of his life working for Maria's canonization, which happened in 1950.

Pope John Paul II

In 1980, Pope John Paul II wrote the **encyclical**, *Dives in Misericordia* (On the Mercy of God). The encyclical is a testament to the Christian belief that "God is rich in mercy" (Ephesians 2:4) and that "God's mercy is . . . from generation to generation (Luke 1:50). In the letter, Pope John Paul II discusses the importance of personal and societal forgiveness.

> Society can become "ever more human" only when we introduce into all the mutual relationships which form its moral aspect the moment of forgiveness, which is so much the essence of the gospel. Forgiveness demonstrates the presence in the world of the love which is more powerful than sin. Forgiveness is also the fundamental condition for reconciliation, not only in the relationship of God with humans, but also in relationships between people. . . .

> For this reason, the Church must consider it one of her principal duties . . . to proclaim and to introduce into life the mystery of

---

For Your Eyes Only

1. What is your opinion on capital punishment?

2. If someone killed one of your family members, do you think you could forgive the murderer? Explain.

DO THIS!

Find out how many prisoners are presently on "death row," either in your state or across the nation. Research how many executions have taken place in your state since the U.S. Supreme Court reinstated the legality of capital punishment in 1976.

mercy, supremely revealed in Jesus Christ.... It is precisely in the name of this mystery that Christ teaches us to forgive always. (*Rich in Mercy*, #2216, #2218–19)

Less than six months after writing this encyclical, Pope John Paul II was challenged to put his words into action. On May 13, 1981—five days before his 61st birthday—the pope was nearly killed by an assailant's bullets. Mehmet Ali Agca, a 23-year-old Turkish national who had escaped from prison in 1979, fired upon the pope at close range as he entered St. Peter's square. Pope John Paul II was seriously wounded in the abdomen, right arm, and left hand.

The pope underwent emergency surgery to remove three sections of his intestines. For three days, he ran a high fever and remained on the critical list. On day four, he got out of bed and publicly forgave Agca.

Agca, who had also wounded two tourists in the attack, expressed regret for shooting the tourists. But he said he was not sorry for shooting the pope.

Pope John Paul II remained in the hospital until June 3. The wound was more serious than first believed, however, and the pope was re-hospitalized from June 20 until August 14. During that time, he underwent further intestinal surgery.

At first, Agca insisted he acted alone. On July 19, 1981, he went on trial in an Italian court. He was convicted and sentenced to life in prison. Throughout 1982 and 1983, Agca changed his story. He began telling Italian investigators that he received instructions to kill the pope while in Bulgaria and was helped both by Bulgarian secret service agents and KGB members from the Soviet Union. He claimed to be acting as part of an assassination plot planned by three Bulgarians and three other Turks to protest the pope's outspoken support of the Solidarity Trade Union in Poland. (The six men were later acquitted for lack of proof.)

On June 22, 1983, some Turkish anti-Christians abducted Emanuela Orlandi, the 15-year-old daughter of a Vatican employee. The kidnappers called the Vatican and demanded Agca's release from prison in exchange for Emanuela's life. For two months, Vatican officials tried to negotiate with the kidnappers. The pope himself pleaded for her life. On August 29, 1983, John Paul II prayed publicly for the release of Emanuela Orlandi. At the same time, he prayed for Mehmet Ali Agca—thus fulfilling a demand posed by the kidnappers.

By September 23, the kidnappers dropped their demand for Agca's release. Tragically, Emanuela was never heard from again. Nor was her body ever discovered.

Despite all that had happened, Pope John Paul II met with Mehmet Ali Agca in his prison cell on

NOTABLE QUOTABLE

"The saints had no hatred, no bitterness. They forgave everything."

—St. John Vianney

December 27, 1983. The men talked for 20 minutes, and again the pope forgave him. Four years later, Pope John Paul II continued to extend his forgiveness to Agca by meeting with Muzeyen Agca, his mother.

Dennis Tapp [3]

OAKLAND, CA: The first time they met, David Magris pumped two bullets into Dennis Tapp, leaving him partially paralyzed for life. The second time they met, they embraced. In between those two meetings lies the story of a convict who returned from death row and a victim who overcame debilitating injuries to forgive his attacker.

"It made me feel better to be able to forgive," Tapp says. "I'd rather have that than hatred in me."

For his part, Magris still doesn't fully understand how the man he left for dead can wish him well in life. But he's grateful.

Rewind to a June night in 1969: Magris was out with three acquaintances, celebrating his twenty-first birthday with a one-night crime spree. Tapp, then 26, was working the graveyard shift at his father's gas station in Vallejo.

"Two men came up to the service station and knocked on the door," Tapp recalls. "They asked for keys to the bathroom. I said, 'Bathroom's open.'" The next thing he knew, he was looking down the barrel of a sawed-off carbine. "I opened the safe. I gave them my wallet," Tapp says. "They said 'turn around.' I turned around, and the first bullet hit me right in the middle of the back. Another bullet hit me right on my shoulder, and I was paralyzed from the waist on down."

Magris would later say, "I panicked. I just started pulling the trigger and got out of there."

Tapp was the second victim that night. Magris and his cronies had first stopped at another gas station where they ordered the attendant to fill a bag with money and then abducted him and drove to the outskirts of town. There, one of Magris' accomplices fired several shots into the attendant's back. Unlike Tapp, he did not survive.

The two trigger men were ultimately sentenced to die in San Quentin's gas chamber. But in 1972, Magris and 107 other inmates were moved off death row after the U.S. Supreme Court outlawed the death penalty. Magris decided to make good on his second chance. He got counseling and eventually earned a college degree. In 1985, he was paroled.

Meanwhile, Tapp had been fighting his own battle to stay alive. He came to after the shooting to find himself "on the floor, bent over a heater and bleeding. I called the operator, and the operator had the phone call traced. At the same time, I asked God to forgive the

3 Michelle Locke, "Forgiveness binds victim to assailant," *Associated Press* (May 20, 1996).

men who did this to me," says Tapp, a devout Catholic. He ended up partially paralyzed, minus his right kidney and in need of several liver operations. Eventually, he walked again, although he still has a limp.

Today, Tapp is married and spends much of his time volunteering at a nearby hospice. Although each step is a reminder of that night in 1969, his opposition to the death penalty has never wavered.

After he was freed from prison, Magris immediately engaged in a battle against the death penalty. Then he became a subject in an ABC-TV "20/20" report that followed the fate of those paroled from death row. Asked if he wanted to meet Tapp, Magris agreed. Forty-five minutes later he found himself knocking on a motel-room door.

"We were both afraid of each other because we were both afraid one of us might have a gun," says Tapp.

"It seemed like the light of God was on him," Magris recalls. "He asked me if there was anything I wanted to say, and I said, 'Yes, I apologize for my part in this crime. You didn't have that coming.'"

Tapp says the look in Magris' eyes convinced him the apology was for real. "I said, 'David, I forgive you.'"

"I was incredibly moved," Magris now says. "That kind of forgiveness is to be not just honored, but respected and admired and hopefully replicated."

Celebrating Forgiveness

Like all virtues, our ability to forgive grows with practice. The more times we forgive, the greater becomes our ability to forgive. The same truth applies to being forgiven. The more times we accept forgiveness from God and from others, the greater becomes our ability to become a better person and to stay in touch with God's will for us.

Accepting and celebrating God's forgiveness is paramount in the sacrament of reconciliation. The sacrament goes by many names. In fact, the official name is the sacrament of **penance**. A common name for the sacrament, **confession**, emphasizes the importance of confessing our sins and feeling sorry for them. Penance, on the other hand, emphasizes the importance of making amends for the wrong we have done.

Using the name reconciliation helps us to remember that the sacrament is a celebration of forgiveness—a tangible experience that reminds us that God loves us despite our sins and imperfections.

When approached properly, the sacrament of reconciliation can be a truly moving experience. It can be a time of learning—of seeing more of the truth about ourselves. It can be a time of healing—of letting the Good Shepherd love us and carry us back to the fold. It can be a time of joyful success—of knowing that we are "back on the right track" and making true progress.

It is wise for Catholics to celebrate forgiveness in the sacrament of reconciliation as often as possible. Not only is the sacrament necessary

LET'S TALK

1. Place yourself in the place of Maria Goretti, Pope John Paul II, or Dennis Tapp. How would you respond if similar crimes were committed against you?

2. Tell about a person you know who lives Jesus' words: "Love your enemies and pray for those who persecute you" (Matthew 5:43–44).

NOTABLE QUOTABLE

"To err is human; to forgive is divine."

—Alexander Pope (1688–1763)

for the absolution of mortal sins, it is an opportunity for character growth as well. Armed with the felt experience of God's forgiving love, we can more easily face the struggles of everyday relationships with hope and confidence. We know, in our hearts, that nothing—not even our worst actions—can ever keep us from the forgiving love of God.

Prayer

LEADER: We sometimes find it difficult to forgive. To forgive others, we must experience a conversion—from anger and hatred to sincere understanding and clemency. As we gather today in prayer let us ask Jesus for the grace to follow his example and to be merciful toward everyone, even our persecutors and enemies.

READER 1: Luke 17:3–4

READER 2: Luke 18:9–14

ALL: Have mercy on us, O God, in your goodness. In the greatness of your compassion, wipe out our offenses. At the same time, open our hearts to show mercy toward those who have sinned against us. Teach us to forgive always and never to hold a grudge. We ask this in union with your Son, Jesus, and your Holy Spirit. Amen. (based on Psalm 51)

Further Activities

1. A proposal has been made to televise the execution of criminals. Debate whether or not watching a televised execution would (1) change people's opinions about the morality or immorality of the death penalty and (2) deter violent crime.

2. In a small group, research and list all the methods that have been used to impose the death penalty in the U.S. Share your findings with the class.

3. Find out whether or not your state has the death penalty. If so, what form of capital punishment is used? When was the last execution? Stage a debate about whether or not you think your state's law should be changed.

LET'S TALK

1. When have you celebrated the sacrament of reconciliation?

2. How is the sacrament of reconciliation related to having good character? to developing good character?

4. Prepare a reconciliation service that can be celebrated by your class. Lead the class in this service. If possible, invite one or more priests to hear individual confessions.

At Home

Make a conscious effort to let someone in your family know that you have forgiven him or her for a past hurt.

For Your Eyes Only

One way I will either ask for forgiveness or try to forgive this week is . . .

Words to Know

abolitionist
aggravated assault
anger
battery
bigots
blasphemy
capital punishment
clemency
confession
encyclical
forbearance
forgiveness
Hebrew scriptures
heresy
mercy
nonviolence
pardon
patience
peace
penance
rape
retributionist
Sabbath
scrupulous

Part 6 Review

1. Define mercy.
2. In what ways is God merciful?
3. Why is peace a mark of good character?
4. Do you think violence is valued or not valued by many people in today's world? Give two examples to support your view.
5. Why do some pre-teens and teens join gangs?
6. What was Jesus' teaching regarding violence?
7. Give one example from the text of a teen who is trying to follow Jesus' teaching regarding peace.
8. What is the difference between the emotion of anger and the sin of anger?
9. What are two healthy ways to deal with anger?
10. What are the five steps in dealing with conflict?
11. What are two ways teens can help themselves avoid violence or rape?
12. When did Jesus teach the virtue of forgiveness by his actions, by forgiving someone?
13. According to Jesus, what is our duty regarding forgiveness?
14. What are four types of forgiveness?
15. Why is forgiveness needed in personal relationships?
16. What values are involved in the debate about capital punishment?
17. Tell how one of the following people exemplified forgiveness: (A) St. Maria Goretti, (B) Pope John Paul II, (C) Dennis Tapp.
18. What are two other names for the sacrament of reconciliation?

PART 7

JUSTICE

What is justice?

Why are fairness and equality important to people of good character?

What does good citizenship have to do with good character?

What Is Justice?

Another attribute of God is **justice**. According to the dictionary, *justice* is that which is "proper, fair, and correct." It is a sense of what is right, of what "should" happen. Justice meets a standard, or requirement, of decency—whatever is seen as equal and fair.

The word used in the Bible for justice is *sedakah*, which means "righteousness," innocence, or right conduct before the law. To seek righteousness or justice is to seek God, who alone is just. (See Isaiah 45:21 and 51:1.)

God's Justice

Throughout the Bible, God is portrayed as righteous and as loving justice. (See Isaiah 30:18; Jeremiah 9:23; Psalms 33:5 and 99:4.) God is a just judge, whose every judgment is fair and right. (See Psalm 7:11 and 1 Peter 2:23.) God punishes the wicked and rewards the good. (See Matthew 13:24–30, 36–43 and 25:31–46.) God blesses those who are righteous (Psalm 5:13). God hears the cry of the just. (See Psalm 34:16.) God gives justice to the needy. (See Exodus 22:21–27.)

Because God is just, God perfectly keeps the covenant established with Abraham, Jacob, Joseph, and David. God is forever faithful to the covenant, even when humans are not.

Jesus is the justice of God, both the fulfillment of the original covenant and the embodiment of the New Covenant. (See Hebrews 12:24.) Jesus' death is both righteous and saving. (See Romans 5:18.) It brings us a righteousness we could not acquire on our own through mere obedience to the law. (See Romans 3:11, 21–25.)

Because of the salvation won by Jesus, every Christian receives the gift of justice through the Holy Spirit at baptism. God's gift of justice brings us life in the spirit. (See Romans 8:10.) This life, also known as the "kingdom of God," is a reign of justice. (See Isaiah 9:1–7; 11:1–9 and Romans 14:17.) It includes all people (Matthew 22:1–14; Luke 14:16–24), especially the poor (Luke 6:20), the hungry (Matthew 14:13–21), the sick (Luke 13:10–17), the contrite (Luke 7:36–50), and the lowly (Luke 9:46–48).

NOTABLE QUOTABLE

"Just are the ways of God."

—John Milton
(1608–1674)

Scripture

In a small group, read the scripture passages found in the text above. Write a one sentence summary for each passage.

For Your Eyes Only

1. Describe an experience that you associate with the term *justice*?

2. Name one person you associate with the term *justice*?

Our Call to Justice

Because justice is an attribute of God, people in right relationship with God are also just. For this reason, the Bible describes both King David and King Solomon as "righteous" men. (See 1 Kings 3:6 and

10:9.) Joseph, the man betrothed to the virgin Mary, and Jesus are also described as "just" men. (See Matthew 1:19; Acts 3:14; 1 Peter 3:18.)

Justice, along with prudence, temperance, and fortitude, is a **cardinal virtue**; it is basic to all the other **moral virtues** that make up good character. Justice is a fundamental part of all successful relationships—with God, with other people, and with ourselves.

The justice we are to have toward God is summarized in the first three of the Ten Commandments. We are to worship God alone; we are to respect God's name; we are to keep holy the Sabbath. Accordingly, in the preface to the eucharistic prayers at Mass, we acknowledge that "it is 'right' to give God thanks and praise."

The justice we are to have toward others is summarized in the last seven of the Ten Commandments. We are to respect the rights of others—to authority, to life, to marriage, to property, and to a good reputation. Furthermore, we are to treat others as we ourselves would want to be treated, the essence of the Golden Rule described by Jesus in Matthew 7:12.

Indeed, God demands that we act justly toward others. (See Deuteronomy 16:20 and Micah 6:8.) We are to make justice our aim, just as Jesus demanded justice of Zacchaeus, who treated unfairly those from whom he collected taxes. (See Luke 19:1–10.)

In this section of the course, we will be discussing two types of justice—**commutative justice** and **contributive justice**. Commutative justice, the subject of Chapter 13, is a type of justice that calls for fairness and equality in all agreements and exchanges between individuals. Contributive justice, the subject of Chapter 14, is the type of justice that obliges us to participate in society and work for the common good of all people. In other words, this type of justice obliges us to be good citizens—both of our own nation and of the world.

NOTABLE QUOTABLE

"For the kingdom of God is not food and drink, but righteousness and joy in the Holy Spirit."

—Romans 14:17

Scripture

Discuss how each of the following passages relates to justice.

◆ Matthew 5:6   ◆ Matthew 5:10   ◆ Matthew 6:10

13. Fairness and Equality

Have you ever heard a small child say, "It isn't fair!" when he thought his sister got a bigger piece of cake? Have you yourself ever complained that life isn't fair when your parents said you couldn't do something? The concept of justice, our perceived need to get our fair share, does not lessen as we get older. Consider the following real-life story:

The Challenge of Being Fair [1]

It was the day of the Senior Class picnic, and Janet had to let her sister Diane have the car. What a come-down! She had to get a ride with someone instead of driving up in her own wheels. Why did that little snot sister have to get the car? She was only going to drive to work, where the stupid car would sit parked all day.

"It's not fair!" Janet yelled. She threw the keys on the floor and stomped out of the kitchen. Her mother let Janet cool off a little, then sat down in the living room with her. "I am sorry you are so upset, but you need to understand a few things. First, it is not your car; we bought it for both of you. Second, a lot in life isn't fair, so get used to it. Third, I am not telling you to give Diane the car; I am asking you to because your sister needs to get to work. Finally, your friends aren't going to throw you to the wolves just because you have to get a ride from someone else. If they did, what kind of friends would they be? Look, we just can't afford cars for both of you."

Janet got the point. She was disappointed that she wouldn't be able to show off the car to her friends, but they knew about the car anyway. And she was going to the picnic. "Okay," Janet said. "Diane gets the car for work. But it cuts both ways, right? Sometimes, I get the car."

"Right," her mother agreed. "That's the whole idea."

1 Elizabeth Caldwell, *Teenagers!* (San Diego, CA: Silvercat Publications, 1996), pp. 16–17.

DO THIS!

Identify at least one situation that involves justice and fairness in each of the following areas: family, school, work, city or town, nation, world. When you have finished, share your list with the class.

CHAPTER GOALS

In this chapter, you will:

◆ Learn about commutative justice—the type of justice that calls for fairness in exchanges between individuals;

◆ See how different forms of discrimination oppose the concept of fairness and equality;

◆ Learn from the example of Jesus and several Christians how to treat others with fairness and equality.

LET'S TALK

1. According to Janet's mom, "a lot in life isn't fair." Do you agree or disagree? Give examples to support your opinion.

2. Society has many different rules for adults and teenagers. For example, teens under a certain age cannot legally drive, drink alcohol, or smoke tobacco. Many communities have curfews that dictate the time teens must get off the streets. Do you think these rules are fair or unfair? Explain your reasoning.

Commutative Justice

The type of justice that calls for fairness and equality in all exchanges between individuals is called *commutative justice*. Commutative justice applies to work contracts, marriages, rental agreements, school grades, family life, payment for purchases, and just about everything else involving daily life and your relationship with other people.

Underlying the concept of commutative justice is the belief that every person—regardless of age, gender, race, sexual orientation, or religious preference—has dignity, worth, and certain rights. Thomas Jefferson eloquently expressed this belief in *The Declaration of Independence* when he wrote:

"We hold these truths to be self-evident, that all men are created equal, that they are endowed by their Creator with certain unalienable Rights, that among these are Life, Liberty, and the pursuit of Happiness."

Unfortunately, the ideals of fairness and equality are not always attained in human relationships. Too often, certain people become the targets of **discrimination**—hatred that is based on their race, ethnic background, age, gender, health status, sexual orientation, or religious beliefs. These people are not given equal opportunity when it comes to housing, jobs, and higher pay despite their individual qualifications and accomplishments.

What causes people to discriminate against people who are somehow different from them? Some people believe the source of discrimination is biological, something that everyone is born with. It is perhaps a survival mechanism that naturally causes us to distrust strangers or people unlike us. The ancient writers of the book of Genesis believed that divisions among people were caused by human pride. God created different languages so that the people, who were trying to raise the Tower of Babel to the heavens and so make themselves equal to God, would be unable to complete it. (See Genesis 11:1–9.) The following folk tale from Africa offers an insightful explanation for the continuation of the discrimination:

Frog-child and Snake-child [2]

Once upon a time, the child of the Frog was hopping along in the bush when he spied someone new lying across the path before him. This someone was long and slender, and his skin seemed to shine with all the colors of the rainbow.

"Hello there," called Frog-child. "What are you doing lying here in the path?"

"Just warming myself in the sun," answered the someone new, twisting and turning and uncoiling himself. "My name is Snake-child. What's yours?"

---

2 Shortened from "Why Frog and Snake Never Play Together," in William Bennett, *The Book of Virtues* (New York: Simon & Shuster, 1993), pp. 284–286.

"I'm Frog-child. Would you like to play with me?"

So Frog-child and Snake-child played together all morning long in the bush.... After a while they both grew hungry and decided to go home for lunch, but they promised each other to meet again the next day.... Then they each went home.

"Look what I can do, Mother!" cried Frog-child, crawling on his belly.

"Where did you learn how to do that?" his mother asked.

"Snake-child taught me," he answered. "We played together in the bush this morning. He's my new friend."

"Don't you know the Snake family is a bad family?" his mother asked. "They have poison in their teeth. Don't ever let me catch you playing with one of them again. And don't let me see you crawling on your belly, either. It isn't proper."

Meanwhile, Snake-child went home and hopped up and down for his mother to see.

"Who taught you to do that?" she asked.

"Frog-child did," he said. "He's my new friend."

"What foolishness," said his mother. "Don't you know we've been on bad terms with the Frog family for longer than anyone can remember? The next time you play with Frog-child, catch him and eat him up. And stop that hopping. It isn't our custom."

So the next morning when Frog-child met Snake-child in the bush, he kept his distance.

"I'm afraid I can't go crawling with you today," he called, hopping back a hop or two.

Snake-child eyed him quietly, remembering what his mother had told him. "If he gets too close, I'll spring on him and eat him," he thought. But then he remembered how much fun they had had together, and how nice Frog-child had been to teach him how to hop. So he sighed sadly to himself and slid away into the bush.

And from that day onward, Frog-child and Snake-child never played together again. But they often sat alone in the sun, each thinking about their one day of friendship.

For Your Eyes Only

How prejudiced are you towards people who are different from you? Where do you think your ideas and attitudes came from? Were you born with them or were they taught to you?

LET'S TALK

Prejudice and discrimination often are passed from one generation to the next. Share an example that supports this statement.

Forms of Discrimination

Some people believe that discrimination ended in the United States following the civil rights movement of the 1960s. Unfortunately, that isn't true. In today's world, there are many forms of discrimination. For example, **racism** continues. Racism is discrimination against others because of their racial identity. **Anti-Semitism** is a type of racial discrimination that targets people who are Jewish. **Xenophobia** is discrimination against others because they are newcomers or immigrants. **Sexism** is discrimination primarily against women because of their gender, although "male bashing" is a type of reverse sexism. **Homophobia** is discrimination against homosexuals because of their sexual orientation. Another type of discrimination targets people who have the AIDS virus.

A number of recent movies have a theme involving the injustice of discrimination. Among them is a movie about the **Holocaust**, Nazi Germany's attempt to kill the entire Jewish race in Europe. Here is its story line:

Schindler's List

In September, 1939, after the German army has defeated Poland, Jews there are forced to relocate. In Krakow, Oskar Schindler decides there is a fortune to be made by taking advantage of this situation. He goes to the German government with a plan to hire Jews for an enamelware factory he wants to build.

By 1941, Schindler has started up a factory with the help of a Jewish accountant named Itzhak Stern. He begins to hire a number of Jews, based on Itzhak's recommendations.

Outside the factory, conditions are worsening for the Jews. They are forced to live in ghettos and to wear the Star of David on their clothing.

These ovens were used to burn the bodies of victims of Nazi slaughter, at Oswiecim, Poland.

In 1943, the Germans "liquidate" the Polish ghetto, killing many Jews and sending the others away to a work camp. There, the SS commander kills them at will. Schindler, however, bribes the commander to get certain Jews out of the camp. He is kind toward the Jews, not because he is pro-Jewish, but because they are good for his business.

By April, 1944, the Germans have killed 10,000 Jews. They decide to close down the Krakow labor camp and send all the Jews to Auschwitz, where they will be killed.

F.Y.I.

During World War II, almost 4 million Jews were killed in concentration camps. Another 2 million Jews were killed by the Nazis in other ways. By the end of the war, about 72% of the Jewish population in Europe had been killed.

LET'S TALK

Describe a positive shift in your opinion of a person or group of people different from you. How did it occur?

Oskar Schindler doesn't have to get involved. He can simply take his profits and leave Poland, never to think about the Jews again. But he has begun to view the Jews as people. Some of them he even counts as friends. He doesn't want them to die. So he decides to take his workers to Czechoslovakia to start a munitions factory there. Using his entire profits, Schindler buys the lives of 1,100 Jews—on the pretext that he needs them to work in his new factory.

At the factory, Schindler makes sure that none of the shells his workers are producing can actually be fired. He allows the Jews to celebrate the Sabbath and their other religious rituals.

By the time the war ends, Schindler is financially broke. He must now hide from the Allies, who will accuse him of being a Nazi sympathizer and persecutor of the Jews. Before he leaves town, his Jewish workers donate the gold from their dental fillings to make a ring for him with the inscription, "Whoever saves one life saves the world in time." The workers also sign a letter explaining his generosity to them, in case he should be captured.

At the end of the movie, the camera shifts to the present-day grave of Oskar Schindler. Past it file hundreds of people—the real-life descendants of the Jews he saved—who owe their lives to this one man who refused to give in to the hatred and prejudice surrounding him.

DO THIS!

Read one of the following books to find out more about the Holocaust:

◆ *The Diary of Anne Frank* by Anne Frank;

◆ *Mila 18* or *Exodus* by Leon Uris;

◆ *Night* by Elie Wiesel; or

◆ *The Winds of War* by Herman Wouk.

Prepare a report on the Holocaust for the class.

NOTABLE QUOTABLE

"[The Holocaust] will forever remain a shame for humanity. . . . Once again I issue an appeal to all people, inviting them to overcome their prejudices and to combat every form of racism by agreeing to recognize the fundamental dignity and the goodness that dwell within every human being and to be ever more conscious that they belong to a single human family, willed and gathered together by God."

—Pope John Paul II, *Apostolic Letter on the Fiftieth Anniversary of the Outbreak of World War II*, September 14, 1989.

Racial Discrimination

According to the *1995 Statistical Abstract of the United States*, 71% of American teenagers are white Americans, 14% are African-Americans, 1% are Native Americans, 3% are Asian-Americans, and 11% are Hispanic-Americans (Mexican, Puerto Rican, Cuban, Central and South American). Prejudice among each of these groups against other races still runs strong, as evidenced by the following newspaper articles:

Incident in the Bronx [3]

In January, 1992, four white teenagers attacked two black children in the Bronx. The teenagers beat the children and stole three dollars. Then they cut the girl's hair and sprayed both children with white shoe polish. "You'll be white today!" the attackers shouted.

Symbols of Hate in Chicago [4]

Chicago—The pupils at the Keller Regional Gifted Center here were hustled into the building Friday morning as soon as they got off of their yellow school buses. Usually, they linger a few minutes before the bell rings. But the principal, Cynthia B. Dougal, did not want the children outside.

The night before, wood chips from the playground at the multiracial school had been meticulously arranged in a 50-foot-by-20-foot swastika on the blacktop a few feet from the swing set. In addition to the swastika, a large Confederate flag design, Nazi lightning bolts, and the initials K.K.K. were also built out of the wood chips.

It was at least the third time this school year that racial hatred was smeared on the grounds of the elementary school. The school, in which 60 percent of the pupils are black, is in the predominately white, working-class Mount Greenwood neighborhood on the Far South Side. Most of the pupils are bused to the school traveling up to 40 minutes each way. Many say the trip is worth it; Keller has among the highest math and reading scores in the state.

In the fall, two high school freshmen were charged with scrawling swastikas and racial slurs on the playground equipment. "The haters have gotten slicker since then," Dougal said. She guessed that by using the wood chips already on the playground, they might have been trying to avoid prosecution, since they were not damaging any property. But the police department said whoever made the swastikas could still be charged under hate-crimes statutes.

3 Shortened from *Associated Press* wire (January 8, 1992).
4 Shortened from "Chicago school besieged by symbols of hate," The *New York Times* (May 27, 1996).

LET'S TALK

What do you think is the difference between "freedom of expression," which is guaranteed by the U.S. Constitution, and a hate crime? In what ways were the two incidents on this page an example of a hate crime rather than freedom of expression?

F.Y.I.

K.K.K. are initials that stand for the Ku Klux Klan, a group founded and perpetuated in hatred of African-Americans, Jews, and Catholics.

AIDS Discrimination

Between 1982 and 1994, over 45,600 persons age 13 to 29 died of AIDS. In addition to being critically ill, some of these teenagers and young people also had to endure the injustice of discrimination. Here is one teen's story:

Ryan White (1971–1990) [5]

Ryan White was a normal kid, with just one exception: He was born with **hemophilia**. Periodically, he needed a blood transfusion. After the transfusion, life usually returned to normal again.

But this time was different. At age 13, Ryan accidentally received a transfusion of tainted blood. As a result, he was infected with the AIDS virus. When students, parents, and school officials found out about Ryan's condition, hysteria broke loose. He was banned from attending school in Russianville. And for the next two years, Ryan was shunned by neighbors, relatives, schoolmates, and teachers. All the people mistakenly believed that they or their children could get AIDS just by being around Ryan.

As time went on, things got worse. No one would sit near the family in church. Then the family received threatening phone calls. Finally, a bullet was fired through the Whites' front window.

When Ryan's story hit the news, he developed a new group of friends: including Marlo Thomas, Barbara Bush, Jesse Jackson, Elton John, Donald Trump, and Howie Long. Because of the influence of these friends, Ryan became a national spokesperson for AIDS education. Wherever he went, he told people the truth about AIDS and how it could and could not be spread.

Ryan eventually won a court battle to attend school. But when he returned to school, he found that he was the butt of "Ryan White

---

5 *San Francisco Chronicle* (May 12, 1991), p. E-4.

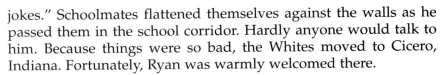

For Your Eyes Only

What do you think your attitude and actions would be if you found out that a classmate was HIV-positive or had AIDS?

jokes." Schoolmates flattened themselves against the walls as he passed them in the school corridor. Hardly anyone would talk to him. Because things were so bad, the Whites moved to Cicero, Indiana. Fortunately, Ryan was warmly welcomed there.

"I never really believed that Ryan would die of AIDS," his mother said a year after his death. "I thought that God would send us a miracle. I believe now that God did send us a miracle in Ryan. Miracles come in different forms—it's not always long life. Sometimes a miracle is what a person is able to do with life."

F.Y.I.

Discrimination against Ryan White did not end with his death. More than once, his grave and tombstone were vandalized by people filled with prejudice and hatred.

The Example of Jesus

Jesus lived in a society that was filled with prejudice and discrimination. The Jews, for example, looked down on their cousins, the Samaritans, because they had intermarried with surrounding Gentile tribes. Many Jews hated the Romans, whose government ruled their country and whose tax collectors pressed them for money. The Samaritans and Romans were equally discriminatory against Jews.

Within the Jewish community itself, prejudice and discrimination also existed. The upright Pharisees, for example, discriminated against public sinners; men discriminated against women; the rich discriminated against the poor; the healthy discriminated against the sick, and adults discriminated against children.

Jesus, however, taught his followers to have a more inclusive view of life. God, Jesus taught them, is the Father of everyone (Matthew 6:9). God's kingdom is like a banquet in which all people, including the poor and the outcasts, are welcome (Matthew 22:1–14; Luke 14:16–24).

In his actions, Jesus lived what he taught. He did this in the following ways:

◆ He chose poor fishermen and a tax collector to be among his twelve apostles (Matthew 4:18–22; 9:9–13);

◆ He cured the servant of a Roman centurion (Luke 7:1–10);

◆ He welcomed and respected small children (Mark 10:13–16);

◆ He associated with sinners (Luke 7:36–50);

◆ He mingled with lepers and people with other illnesses (Luke 5:12–16; 17:11–19);

◆ He treated Samaritans with respect (John 4:4–42);

◆ He dealt fairly with foreigners (Luke 8:26–39; Matthew 15:21–28); and

◆ He treated women both as equals (Luke 4:38–39; 8:43–48; 13:10–17; John 20:11–18) and as friends (Luke 10:38–41; John 11:1–44).

LET'S TALK

1. If Jesus were alive today, who are some outcasts you think he would reach out to and include?

2. Relate an experience of someone talking and acting as if he or she was "better than" you. How was this attitude conveyed? How did it make you feel?

Hungering for Justice

Since the very beginning of the Church, Christians have tried to follow Jesus' example and to reach out to people of all races and nations. On Pentecost, for example, the apostles preached to a crowd of people from the entire Roman empire who heard them in their native languages (Acts 2:1–12). The first Christians also sold their property and made sure the needs of the poor were taken care of (Acts 4:32–5:16). Early Church writers, such as St. Basil and St. Ambrose, wrote about the obligations of justice and the rights of the poor.

Many of the saints we honor today were involved in doing justice. St. Martin de Porres served black slaves in Peru. St. Elizabeth of Hungary gave away her riches to feed the poor. St. Vincent de Paul and St. Louise Marillac helped the poor of Paris with food, clothing, and shelter. St. Frances Cabrini and St. John Neumann both helped poor immigrants who came to America. St. Katherine Drexel worked with Native Americans and African-Americans. Blessed Junipero Serra tried to improve the lives of the indigenous peoples of California.

In 1979, the U.S. bishops wrote the first of many important **pastoral letters** on the evils of prejudice and discrimination. This letter, *Brothers and Sisters to Us*, calls all Catholics to follow the example of Jesus and the saints in reaching out with fairness and equality to people of all races. Here is some of what the bishops wrote:

> Racism is a sin: a sin that divides the human family, blots out the image of God among specific members of that family, and violates the fundamental dignity of those called to be children of the same Father (#9). Mindful of its duty to be the advocate for those who hunger and thirst for justice's sake, the Church cannot remain silent about the racial injustices in society and in its own structures (#7).

In today's world, many people continue to hunger and thirst for justice. Inspired by the beatitudes of Jesus, they strive to be fair to others and to make justice a reality for everyone. They approach the goal of justice by taking one small step at a time—knowing that all their efforts, even small ones, can help to bring about God's reign of fairness and equality.

Here are two real-life stories of young people today who truly hunger for justice and are helping to make God's reign a reality:

DO THIS!

Research the life of one of the saints mentioned on this page. Report your findings to the class.

Rebuilding in Alabama [6]

Boligee, Ala.—The two-day drive from Washington, D.C., to Greene County in the heart of Alabama's black belt felt like a journey back through time. Three decades ago, during the summers of 1964 and '65, I had driven south to work in the civil rights movement in Mississippi and Alabama. Now I was returning in early July with my 15-year-old son, Jody Avirgan, to join a Quaker-run project rebuilding three of the black churches destroyed by arsonists since December 1995.

A fourth Baptist church in the area is being rebuilt by the Mennonites.

While my son pounded nails, I talked with old-timers and activists, blacks and whites, about what has changed, what's remained, and why there is the upsurge in hate crimes.

Many are numbed by a sense of *déjà vu*. At the Civil Rights Institute in Birmingham, advisory board member Carolyn McKinstry, 47, said, "When I started hearing about these church burnings, it became very real it was happening again. You always think things won't happen again."

In 1963, McKinstry was attending Sunday school in Birmingham's 16th Street Baptist Church when a bomb exploded, killing four young girls. "I lost four friends that day, and it instilled a lot of fear in me," recalled McKinstry. "Church burnings. Church bombings. It's like the ultimate in evil."

"As happened in the '60s, thousands of people from around the world have responded," said Harold Confer, 55, a Washington builder. Confer heads Washington Quaker Work Camps, which is spearheading this reconstruction project, the first in the country. Volunteers from across the United States and as far away as Tanzania and Yugoslavia have arrived in tiny Boligee, population 300, and turned "a modest summer work camp program into a movement."

NOTABLE QUOTABLE

"Justice is truth in action."
—Benjamin Disraeli
(1804–1881)

LET'S TALK

What do you think a 15-year-old like Jody Avirgan might learn from the experience of rebuilding the church?

6 Martha Honey, "Rebuilding burned church is a first step," *The National Catholic Reporter* (August 23, 1996), pp. 6–7.

The School Mascot [7]

Three Pueblo High School seniors—Maria Francisco, Margaret Jose, and Renee Montana—have no regrets about seeking a new image for the school mascot, the "Warrior." The trio led an effort to change the school mascot because they felt the figure was stereotypical and insulting to their ethnic heritage. The Warrior had been the school's mascot since 1955.

From the controversy, Native American students on the campus came together, and the issue was resolved by talking and not violence, with input from many students talking and working together. "It was courageous," said Jose. "We had it underground for so long. This was the first year it really came out."

The school's Tribal Images organization, made up of—although not limited to—Native American students, raised the issue, saying the feather-clad mascot was an insult to Native Americans. The issue went to a student body vote, and while the outcome was not completely what Tribal Images sought, the mascot's image is more generic, although it is still a human figure.

"From this experience, we learned that there is racism out there," Jose said. Francisco, 18, Tribal Images president, said racism surfaced only after the mascot issue was raised. Montana, 19, said for the first time students from across the southside campus came up to the fellow Native American students and "asked our point of view."

Francisco and Jose, 18, are full-blooded Tohono O'odham; Montana is half Hispanic.

Francisco said instead of getting violent at the height of the controversy, "We spoke as adults rather than speaking as children. We didn't get angry or upset."

Each mourns the loss of language and tradition and hopes to set an example for children who are following them. As they leave high school and further their education, each young woman plans to learn her native language fluently.

Jose, whose first language is O'odham, studied her native tongue at Pueblo and would like to return to her home at North Komelik on the reservation to educate youngsters about their language and culture. "I want to talk to the younger kids and tell them not to be afraid to speak the language. Know who you are. Be proud of who you are," Jose said.

LET'S TALK

1. Do you think the practice of pro sports' teams keeping names and mascots like Indians, Braves, and Redskins is racist towards Native Americans? Defend your position.

2. What are situations of injustice that exist in your local community? What is already being done to correct the situation? What can you do to help?

---

7 Sara Hammond, "Trio led drive to change Pueblo's mascot," *The Arizona Daily Star* (May 19, 1996), p. 45.

Prayer 🍀

LEADER: Today as we come together in prayer, let us remember that every one of us is a precious child of God, someone with dignity and rights. Just as we want others to treat us fairly and as an equal, so too, we are called to be just and fair in all our dealings with others. Let us pray now, that God's gift of justice may take root in us and blossom.

READER 1: Psalm 111

READER 2: 1 Corinthians 12:12–27

ALL: Our Father in heaven, help us to realize that we are all your children, regardless of our different ages, genders, races, nationalities, or sexual orientations. Help us reach out in fairness and equality to everyone and express justice in our daily actions. This we ask, following the example of your son Jesus and filled with the gift of your Holy Spirit. Amen.

Further Activities 🍀

1. Sponsor a multicultural day at your school that will showcase the clothing, food, and customs of the different racial groups in your local area.

2. Volunteer at an AIDS hospice to help victims of AIDS and their families.

3. Join a parish or community program to help immigrants learn English as a second language.

4. Work with a small group to discuss practical ways you can eliminate prejudice at your school.

5. If your school or parish has a social justice committee, become active in it. Let your classmates know about upcoming events or projects and how they, too, can get involved.

6. Volunteer an hour or two each month to help at the local St. Vincent de Paul society.

7. Attend a cultural event in your local area to find out more about the traditions and customs of another race.

At Home 🍀

This week, if there is a disagreement or argument among family members, try to work out a solution that is fair to everyone.

For Your Eyes Only

One way I will try to act justly this week is . . .

14. Good Citizenship

At birth, you automatically became a citizen of your country. You also became a citizen of the world. Such **citizenship** means that you have certain rights and responsibilities as a member of society. The virtue of good citizenship is the basis of contributive justice, the type of justice that obliges all persons to be active and productive in society, to contribute to the well-being and protection of others.

Examples of good citizenship, or contributive justice, include keeping the laws of society, voting, participating in politics, running for political office, working as an individual and in groups for the betterment of others, and contributing in any way—especially through volunteer **public service**—to social betterment.

LET'S TALK

1. How is each of the following actions an example of good citizenship? How does each action contribute to the well-being or protection of others?
   ◆ Working at a voting booth.
   ◆ Picking up litter and trash along a highway or county road.
   ◆ Registering voters.
   ◆ Running for a position on the city council.
   ◆ Re-staking trees at a local park after a storm.
   ◆ Obeying traffic laws and speed limits.
   ◆ Participating in a local or national political party.
2. Brainstorm examples of good citizenship at your school. Be prepared to share your list with the class.

The Common Good

Developing your own good character is never an isolated or selfish act. Instead, it is a part of good citizenship; it is something that contributes to the well-being of others. Indeed, the virtue of good citizenship implies the belief that we are all called to build community with others. Good character built on good citizenship helps to build good community.

Furthermore, people of good character believe they have an obligation to contribute to the **common good** of all members of society. This obligation is also known as **solidarity**. Solidarity is the recognition that we are all responsible for the welfare of the human family, regardless of national, racial, or economic differences.

Individual Rights

Good citizenship begins at home—first in your local community and then across the nation. Good citizens obey civic laws and participate voluntarily in public life because they respect the rights of others and want to ensure for themselves the same rights. Some of these rights may be found in the first ten amendments of the U.S. Constitution. The amendments, called the **Bill of Rights**, guarantee all U.S. citizens the following:

◆ Freedom of religion, speech, the press, peaceful assembly, and petition to the government for a "redress of grievances."

◆ The right to keep and bear arms.

◆ The right to privacy in one's own home, without soldiers being housed there.

◆ Freedom from unreasonable searches and seizures.

◆ Freedom from being tried twice for the same crime; the right not to give testimony against oneself; the right not to have private property taken for public use without just compensation.

◆ The right to a fair and speedy trial; right to an impartial jury; the right to legal counsel.

◆ The right to a jury trial in civil cases.

◆ Freedom from excessive bail or fines; freedom from cruel or unusual punishment.

DO THIS!

1. In a small group, read and discuss the first ten amendments of the U.S. Constitution. Give practical examples of the rights found in these amendments.

2. View the video *The Client*. Afterwards, discuss in a small group which laws and constitutional rights are involved in the story. Why is it important to Mark and his lawyer that these laws and constitutional rights be upheld?

3. Make a "Bill of Rights" for students at your school. Share your list with the class.

The Common Good

Although all people have a right to life, liberty, and the pursuit of individual happiness, good citizens realize that sometimes they must sacrifice these individual rights for the common good. As William Bennett, explains:

"Good citizens are those who know and live up to their duties by exercising virtues such as responsibility, loyalty, self-discipline, work, and friendship. . . . They are willing to sacrifice their own interests, even their own lives, for the good of the rest."[1]

Good citizens realize that they—in their lifetime—may never reap the benefits of their hard work and social involvement. But they continue to work anyway, for the good of those who will follow in their footsteps. This aspect of good citizenship is illustrated well in the following poem by Will Allen Dromgoole:

---

1 William Bennett, *The Moral Compass* (Simon & Shuster, 1995), p. 593.

The Bridge Builder [2]

An old man, going a lone highway,
Came, at the evening, cold and gray,
To a chasm, vast, and deep, and wide,
Through which was flowing a sullen tide.
The old man crossed in the twilight dim;
The sullen stream had no fears for him;
But he turned, when safe on the other side,
And built a bridge to span the tide.
"Old man," said a fellow pilgrim, near,
"You are wasting strength with building here;
Your journey will end with the ending day;
You never again must pass this way;
You have crossed the chasm, deep and wide—
Why build you the bridge at the eventide?"
The builder lifted his old gray head:
"Good friend, in the path I have come," he said,
"There followeth after me today
A youth, whose feet must pass this way.
This chasm, that has been naught to me,
To that fair-haired youth may a pitfall be.
He, too, must cross in the twilight dim;
Good friend, I am building the bridge for *him*."

LET'S TALK

1. How would your world be different today if past U.S. citizens had not (A) fought to abolish slavery? (B) worked for women's right to vote? (C) defeated Nazi Germany in World War II?

2. What does the poem say to you about your own life as a citizen?

Civic Responsibility

Good citizens don't just complain about what their local, state, or federal governments are doing or are not doing. Instead, such people get involved. They try to change things they feel need to be changed. They participate and try to make things better for everyone. This sense of involvement and action is called **civic responsibility**.

In a small group, read and discuss the following newspaper article. How are the people in the article showing civic responsibility? How are they working to make things better for everyone?

Interstate Poison [3]

Five train cars laden with pesticide-contaminated dirt from the San Francisco Bay ended up on the wrong train and were detoured in Tucson for five days. The errant rail cars were intended for Waste Management Inc.'s garbage landfill in Mobile, 30 miles south of Phoenix.

A dozen demonstrators, including members of the Southwest Center for Biological Diversity and the Student Environmental Action Coalition, called for the Legislature to ban such waste from

---

2 William Bennett, *The Book of Virtues* (New York: Simon & Shuster, 1993), p. 223.
3 Shortened from Keith Bagwell, "Carloads of DDT-tainted soil park 5 days on southside," *The Arizona Daily Star* (September 10, 1996), p. 1B.

199

the state. "We need legislation that will make this stuff hazardous waste," said Al Byrd. "If the Legislature won't act, we're calling for Pima County and the city of Tucson to adopt more stringent standards."

While the DDT-contaminated dirt is classified as hazardous waste under California laws, it is permissible under Arizona's less stringent standards.

Shane Jimerfield, a Southwest Center spokesman, said the DDT-laden soil will be dumped with regular garbage and without any special precautions. "It's crazy. DDT is a major reason the bald eagle was an endangered species, and it's been banned for 23 years," he said. "This stuff has been here since Wednesday, close to a lot of neighborhoods—kids could climb up on these cars and get it all over them."

Forty-two carloads of DDT-contaminated soil arrived at the Mobile landfill and were dumped last week. They are the first of an expected 800 to 1,100 loads needed to carry 160 million pounds of DDT-tainted soil from California to Mobile.

DDT (dichlorodiphenyltrichlorethane) causes cancer, damages immune and reproductive systems and accumulates in the body. The chemical remains dangerous for 150 years or more.

Loyalty and Patriotism

Good citizens embody the virtues of **loyalty** and **patriotism**. Loyalty, according to the dictionary, is faithful allegiance to a person or government. Patriotism is love for and devotion to one's country. The opposite of such virtues is **treason**, the offense of attempting to overthrow the government or to assassinate or injure the country's leader.

The obligation to be loyal to one's city or country is age-old. In ancient Athens, for example, young Greeks were expected to take the following oath of patriotism when they reached the age of 17.

The Athenian Oath [4]

We will never bring disgrace on this our City by an act of dishonesty or cowardice.

We will fight for the ideals and Sacred Things of the City both alone and with many.

We will revere and obey the City's laws, and will do our best to incite a like reverence and respect in those above us who are prone to annul them or set them at naught.

We will strive increasingly to quicken the public's sense of civic duty.

Thus in all these ways we will transmit this City, not only not less, but greater and more beautiful than it was transmitted to us.

4 Quoted in William Bennett, *The Book of Virtues* (New York: Simon & Shuster, 1993), p. 217.

The principles found in this oath may also be found in the *Pledge of Allegiance*, written by Francis Bellamy in 1892: "I pledge allegiance to the flag of the United States of America and to the republic for which it stands, one nation, under God, indivisible, with liberty and justice for all." The principles are also found in the *American's Creed*, written by William Tyler Page in 1918: "I believe it is my duty to my country to love it; to support its Constitution; to obey its laws; to respect its flag, and to defend it against all enemies."

Jesus and Citizenship

Jesus was crucified for supposed treason against the Roman government. (See Luke 23:2–4.) Biblical testimony, however, does not support this charge against Jesus. In his dialogue with Pontius Pilate, Jesus says, "My kingdom is not from this world" (John 18:36). Earlier, Jesus taught his followers, "Give to the emperor the things that are the emperors, and to God the things that are God's" (Matthew 22:21). As far as we know, Jesus was a model citizen who expected his followers to be the same.

NOTABLE QUOTABLE

"Ask not what your country can do for you; ask what you can do for your country."

—John F. Kennedy (1960)

LET'S TALK

1. On a scale of 1 to 10 how able and willing are you to perform the following patriotic duties:

◆ recite the Pledge of Allegiance

◆ sing the National Anthem

◆ correctly hand and fold the flag?

Church and State

In the very beginning of the church, the Roman government considered Christians to be dangerous subversives—people who were not good citizens because they gave their primary allegiance to God rather than to the nation.

When the Roman Emperor Constantine converted and made Christianity the state religion in the early fourth century, the division between Christianity and politics eventually became obliterated. Many Church leaders also became civic leaders. Over the centuries, this mingling of religion and politics led to much corruption and to the mistaken notion that God's kingdom was the same as earthly power and riches.

Both the Protestant Reformation and the Catholic Reformation sought to restore the church to its original role of bringing about God's kingdom of justice and peace.

Colonists who came to America wanted to guarantee freedom of religion, but at the same time, they often discriminated against Catholics. They were afraid that the allegiance of Catholics to the pope in Rome would be greater than their allegiance to the nation. Loyal citizens did not want the United States to be under the domination of the Vatican. For this reason, Catholics were often prevented from holding high public offices. It was not until 1960 that the nation elected its first Catholic president, John F. Kennedy. The election was a big step forward to recognizing that Catholics not only could be good citizens, but, in conscience, had a duty to be good citizens.

Today, the constitutional principle of separation of church and state attempts to separate religion and politics. Public schools, for example, are not allowed to teach one specific religion or to force their students to say mandatory prayers. The church itself encourages the separation. Most bishops have urged pastors not to preach in support of particular political actions from the pulpit or to seek to influence their parishioners to vote for a certain political party. Instead, the bishops have urged pastors to encourage parishioners to register to vote, to become informed on the issues and the candidates running for office, and to vote according to Christian principles. Furthermore, Pope John Paul II has forbidden priests and religious from running for public office, in an attempt to keep the roles of civic leadership and spiritual leadership from again becoming blurred.

LET'S TALK

1. Do you think priests ought to preach a Sunday sermon on the moral implications of any of the following: legalized abortion, U.S. immigration policies, affirmative action, euthanasia or physician-assisted suicide? Have you ever heard a priest preach on any of these—or any other "political" topics?

2. Do you think a Catholic today would face discrimination in a national election for a high public office?

3. To whom do Catholics owe first allegiance—their church or country?

NOTABLE QUOTABLE

"[Doing justice] is not an optional or peripheral part of our faith. Nor is it new. It is at the heart of our faith, and it is deeply rooted in the gospel. As Christians we are, by definition, a community of people who have a mission to transform the world on behalf of justice and human dignity."

—Archbishop John Roach (1991)

World Citizenship

Good citizenship involves more than patriotism to one's country. It also involves a global mentality, a sense of world citizenship.

You don't have to make a trip to Disneyland's "It's a Small World" exhibit to realize that everyone in the world is connected to everyone else. Every day—thanks to telecommunications satellites, international businesses and financial institutions, and the worldwide web—the world is getting smaller and smaller. In order to survive in today's world, we need a sense of global solidarity—seeing everyone as our neighbor, as someone deserving of justice.

As Martin Luther King, Jr., once said, "Injustice anywhere is a threat to justice everywhere. We are caught in an inescapable network of mutuality, tied in a single garment of destiny. Whatever affects one directly, affects all indirectly." In other words, what happens to people on the other side of the world somehow also affects us.

Although world citizenship and global justice involve many topics, we will only be discussing three in the remaining pages of this chapter—global development, international human rights, and world peace.

Global Development

In addition to national boundaries, our world is divided by economic boundaries. Some countries belong to the "haves"—countries that have abundant natural resources and the technology necessary to use these resources. Other countries belong to the "have nots"—countries that have few natural resources and inadequate technology.

Sociologists further divide the world's countries into three groups—the **First World**, the **Second World**, and the **Third World**—based on their economic success. The First World, which consists of industrialized or developed countries with a market economy, includes the United States, Canada, Western Europe, Australia, Japan, South Africa, and Taiwan. The Second World, which consists of industrialized countries that are presently or were previously under communism (a command economy), includes China, the Commonwealth of Independent States, and Eastern Europe. The Third World, which consists of poor, non-industrialized countries, includes Southeast Asia, India, most of South America, and most of sub-Saharan Africa.

In the Third World, the least developed countries (LDCs) are the most poverty stricken. The average income is less than $200 per year, two-thirds of the adults are *illiterate*, and the people have the lowest life expectancies on the planet. Here are some further statistics about the Third World, based on a 1990 United Nations report:

◆ More than 1 billion people live in absolute poverty (less that $370 per year).

◆ 100 million people are homeless; many people with homes live in substandard housing with inadequate sanitation and unsafe drinking water.

◆ 800 million people go hungry every day; another 500 million people experience periods of hunger throughout the year.

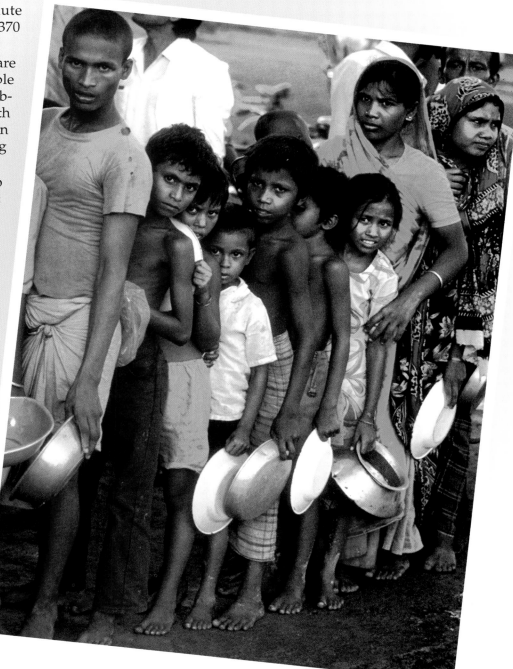

Such statistics are hard to imagine. That is why the World Development Forum developed this simpler analogy: If our world were a village of 1,000 people, 60 of those people would control half the income. Five hundred people would be hungry. Six hundred would live in shantytowns, and 700 would be illiterate.

Injustice is often the root cause for global inequality and the misery of the Third World. Many Third World countries were once colonies of developed countries that exploited them for their resources and cheap labor and unintentionally introduced diseases into the human and animal populations.

Furthermore, many Third World countries owe huge debts to developed nations. They have to spend so much of their national budgets on interest payments that they have relatively little money to spend on needed improvements at home.

The virtues of justice and global citizenship obligate richer nations to help poorer ones—through foreign aid, trade, financial help, investments, and development programs. The U.S. bishops explain this obligation in the following way:

> As followers of Christ, we are challenged to make a "fundamental option for the poor"—to speak for the voiceless, to defend the defenseless, to assess life styles, policies, and social institutions in terms of their impact on the poor. This "option for the poor" means . . . strengthening the whole community by assisting those who are most vulnerable. As Christians, we are called to respond to the needs of all our brothers and sisters, but those with the greatest needs require the greatest response. [5]

F.Y.I.

Over 18 million people died during 1990 from starvation. In the same year, 900–960 million people throughout the world could not read or write.

LET'S TALK

1. How could a teen today live out the "option for the poor" that the bishops talked about?

2. Do you agree that richer nations (and persons) are *obligated* to help poorer ones?

International Human Rights

In addition to the rights guaranteed to U.S. citizens by the Constitution, it is important to realize that *all* people have certain rights, regardless of what country they live in.

This realization of global justice was finally put into writing in 1948 by the United Nations. In its *Declaration of Human Rights*, the United Nations assembly declares that *every* citizen of *every* nation has the right to life, liberty, freedom from personal attack, freedom from slavery and arbitrary arrest, a fair trial, the assumption of innocence until proven guilty, freedom from **torture**, freedom of conscience and religion, freedom of opinion and expression, privacy, family, correspondence, freedom to participate in community life, education, a standard of living adequate for maintaining health and well-being, peaceful assembly,

---

5 National Conference of Catholic Bishops, *Economic Justice for All*, #16.

and participation in government. Every year, the U.N. Commission on Human Rights meets in Geneva to examine human rights violations—including slavery, religious intolerance, unlawful detention without a trial, and forcible confinement in mental hospitals.

In addition to its *Declaration of Human Rights*, the United Nations wrote another document, called the *Geneva Conventions*. This document outlines the right of all prisoners of war (POWs) to be treated humanely and to receive medical treatment. According to the document, no physical or mental means of coercion can be used on POWs.

Today, another item can be added to the list of international human rights—the right of all people to freedom from **terrorism**. According to the dictionary, *terrorism* is any act that intends to kill people and destroy property indiscriminately and to create a climate of fear and insecurity. Throughout the world, acts of terrorism have interfered with people's right to assemble peacefully, to travel, to safety, and to life itself. Consider these recent examples: the bombing of the World Trade Center in New York, the bombing of the Federal Building in Oklahoma, and the bombing of Centennial Park at the 1996 Summer Olympics in Atlanta. In all these cases, innocent people died unjustly.

> **DO THIS!**
>
> Report on one of the acts of terrorism listed on this page or another example approved by your teacher. What happened? What were the effects, both physical and psychological?

> **F.Y.I.**
>
> Another group that is trying to promote justice and protect human rights is Amnesty International. The group works to guarantee fair trials for all political prisoners and to abolish the use of torture. For more information about this organization, write to:
>
> Amnesty International USA
> 322 Eighth Ave.
> New York, NY 10001

> **LET'S TALK**
>
> Why is an act of terrorism—for any reason—an act of injustice?

World Peace

Although peace is a fruit of the Holy Spirit, fighting and armed combat seem to be part of the human condition. On any day throughout the year, it is highly probable that fighting and armed combat are taking place somewhere in the world. If one nation is not fighting with another nation, then different groups of people within the same nation seem to be waging civil **war** and killing one another.

Technically, *war* is an armed conflict involving one or more governments and causing the death of 1,000 or more people per year. Although Jesus called his followers to live as peacemakers, the Catholic church acknowledges that there are times when war is justified. Such justification especially occurs when the war is being waged to defend one's homeland or the human rights of people who cannot otherwise defend themselves.

The U.S. bishops, in their 1983 pastoral letter, *The Challenge of Peace*, further outline the qualifications of a "just" war. Here are some principles they uphold:

◆ Offensive war of any kind is not morally justified, but defensive wars are.

◆ Nuclear war is *never* morally justified.

◆ It is not morally justified to direct conventional weapons at whole cities or civilian areas for the purpose of mass destruction.

The bishops go on to say that "Peacemaking is not an optional commitment. It is a requirement of our faith. We are called to be peacemakers, not by some movement of the moment, but by our Lord Jesus" (#333). In other words, Christians are called to be good world citizens by working toward world peace.

The importance of global citizenship and world peace is the underlying theme of the science-fiction movie *Independence Day*. Here is the story-line:

Independence Day

On July 2, President Thomas Whitmore learns that a huge space ship is heading toward earth. Before long, 36 smaller ships, each 15 miles in width, leave the mother ship and place themselves above various locations around the world.

Simultaneously, David Levinson, a brilliant scientist who is working at a New York cable company, discovers that the alien mother ship is using the earth's communication satellites to coordinate the smaller ships and to establish a countdown to a massive world-wide attack. In just 7 hours, the attack will occur.

> ## F.Y.I.
>
> In 1991, the U.S. and the Commonwealth of Independent States possessed 40,000—50,000 nuclear weapons, including short-range missiles, intercontinental ballistic missiles (ICBMs), neutron bombs, and "smart" bombs. There were enough weapons to kill every person living on earth 12 times.

> ## NOTABLE QUOTABLE
>
> "No more war! War never again!"
>
> —Pope Paul VI, Address to the U.N., October 4, 1965

The President, not wishing to cause mass hysteria, tells the American public via the emergency broadcast system not to panic and to wait until it is known what the aliens want. Meanwhile, he evacuates the Vice President, cabinet members, and joint chiefs of staff to Norad, a high-security military base. He also calls his wife Marilyn and tries unsuccessfully to get her to leave L.A., where she is being interviewed.

David, whose ex-wife Connie is with President Whitmore in the White House, drives to Washington, D.C. to warn them of what is coming. After the "Welcome Wagon" helicopters sent to greet the aliens are annihilated, the President tells the American public to leave the targeted cities at once. He, along with Connie David, his daughter, and other trusted advisors get out just in time. When the countdown reaches zero, the space ships destroy Los Angeles, New York, Washington, D.C., and other major cities throughout the world.

While still in his plane, the President tries to launch a counterattack. Captain Steven Hiller is among the Marine pilots from El Toro who are sent to attack the space ships. Their weapons, however, prove ineffective against the ship's protective shield. Meanwhile, the President learns that Norad and El Toro have both been destroyed. Furthermore, his wife's helicopter never made it to Dallas.

At Area 51, a top-secret government facility in Nevada, President Whitmore learns more about the aliens and what he is up against. The aliens are like locusts who hop from planet to planet, using up all the natural resources. They want humans to die so they can take over the earth for themselves.

The President realizes that if the earth is to survive, all nations will have to put aside their petty differences and band together in a counter-offensive. He organizes the attack, using Morse code to get the message to Russia, Japan, Britain, and the Middle East. To realize his plan, he calls for the generous and selfless service of David Levinson, Steven Hiller, and dozens of civilian pilots, including former Vietnam veteran Russell Case.

Eventually, the strategy works. The ship over Area 51 is destroyed, as are the other ships stationed around the world. From now on July 4 will not be just an American holiday, but a world holiday celebrating our freedom from annihilation—our right to live on this planet.

Good Citizenship and You

There are many ways you can become involved in society and work for justice—both locally and on an international level.

Fortunately, you will not have to "reinvent the wheel" to get started. Many different groups that are trying to better the world and to bring about justice already exist. For example, Bread for the World strives to end world hunger. *Pax Christi* works for world peace. The Catholic Worker Movement provides social services to the poor in the United States.

Volunteering for some form of public service is an important way you can benefit society and, at the same time, grow in good character and responsible citizenship. That is why Congress initiated a national public service award specifically for teens. The Congressional Bronze Award is given to 14-to-16-year-olds who have spent 100 hours in voluntary public service and 50 hours in learning a skill, physical fitness, and going on an expedition. The Congressional Silver Award, for 16-to-18 year olds, requires twice as much work as earning the bronze. Here is what four teens did in 1996 to win the awards:

◆ David Haefner, 15, helped out at the University of Arizona Ecology and Evolution Lab, capturing and feeding wild grasshoppers and collecting data on their eggs. He was also active in the U.S. Navy Sea Cadet Corps, which he said taught him discipline and responsibility.

◆ Erin O'Meara, 16, volunteered at both the Goodwill Thrift Shop and the Tucson Arts District, where she had already helped out for about three years.

◆ Amanda Calahan, 16, camped for a week with underprivileged children and served as a counselor's assistant at the Youth Haven Camp in Picacho. She's polishing up her sign language at Pima Community College and plans to go to Mexico and build houses in poor areas as part of a mission trip through her church.

◆ Theodore Wall, 17, helped new 4-H members learn about animals. He also volunteered at the Tucson Medical Center for two summers, working in the recovery and operation areas. [6]

As you can see from these examples, there are many different ways you can help to better your community and the world. Basically when it comes to justice, two things are important: (1) becoming informed about the situation and what needs to be done, and (2) getting involved, doing what you can to make a contribution.

NOTABLE QUOTABLE

"Not only is volunteerism of benefit to society, it helps individuals become more responsible citizens."

—Regan Ruelas, Class of 1996, Amphitheater High School, Tucson, AZ

Prayer 🐾

LEADER: Today as we come together for prayer, let us remember that God is just and that we, too, are called to do justice. Let us pray for the grace to become informed and to get involved as good citizens—both of our local community and of our world community—so that the rights of all people may be protected.

READER 1: 1 Corinthians 12:4–11

READER 2: Ephesians 2:19–22

ALL: Loving and just God, help us be informed and involved citizens who work for the common good. Help us be generous and selfless in serving the needs of others and helping to build a more just and peaceful world. May we help your kingdom come and your will be done on earth as it is in heaven. Amen.

For Your Eyes Only

One way I will become more informed about justice issues and begin to get involved this week is . . .

---

6 For more information about the congressional awards or these teens, see Hanh Kim Quach, "Four teens win congressional public service awards," *The Arizona Daily Star* (September 9, 1996), pp. 1B–2B.

Further Activities 🎋

1. Prepare a report on the work of one of the following organizations: Bread for the World, Catholic Relief Services, Peace Corps, UN Development Program, UN Food and Agriculture Organization (FAO), International Money Fund (IMF). How does the group work to promote justice on an international level?

2. Write a report about the peacemaking efforts of one of the following people: Franz Jaegenstaetter, Dorothy Day, Aung San Suu Kyi.

3. Write a report about one of the following women and how she was a good citizen: (A) Queen Esther (in the Bible), (B) Judith (in the Bible), (C) St. Joan of Arc. Answer: "How can this woman be a role model of good citizenship for teens today?"

4. Research local public service projects that teens can become involved in. Inform the class of these volunteer opportunities. Encourage everyone in your class to become involved in some way.

At Home 🎋

The next time your family gathers for a meal, discuss a recent world event that involves justice.

Part 7 Review

1. What is justice? What is the difference between commutative justice and contributive justice?

2. In what ways is God just?

3. What do the Ten Commandments have to do with justice?

4. What is the belief underlying the concept of commutative justice?

5. What are three different theories regarding *why* people discriminate against those who are different?

6. What are three different forms of discrimination?

7. What was the Holocaust? Why was it unjust?

8. What is a hate crime? How does it differ from "freedom of expression"?

9. In terms of prejudice and discrimination, what was Jesus' society like?

10. Give three examples of actions of Jesus that countered prejudice and discrimination.

11. Give two examples of people in the church who have hungered for justice by trying to reach out to people suffering discrimination.

12. What do the U.S. bishops say about our call to fairness and equality in their pastoral letter, *Brothers and Sisters to Us*?

Words to Know

anti-Semitism
Bill of Rights
cardinal virtue
citizenship
civic responsibility
common good
commutative justice
contributive justice
discrimination
First World
hemophilia
Holocaust
illiteracy
justice
loyalty
moral virtue
pastoral letter
patriotism
public service
racism
Second World
sexism
solidarity
terrorism
Third World
torture
treason
war
xenophobia

13. What are three examples of an action that shows good citizenship, or contributive justice?

14. What is solidarity? Why is solidarity an important component of contributive justice?

15. What are four rights guaranteed to U.S. citizens in the Bill of Rights?

16. What was the position of Jesus regarding citizenship?

17. How does the phrase, "It's a small world," relate to good citizenship and contributive justice?

18. According to church teaching, what should the relationship between rich nations and poor nations be?

19. According to church teaching, when is war justified? When is it not justified?

PUTTING IT ALL TOGETHER

What does it mean to be a "whole" person?

What does it mean to be holy?

How do you rate your own Christian character?

Becoming Whole

If you have ever put together a puzzle of 1,000 or more pieces, you know it is something that takes a great deal of time, trial-and-error, patience, and perseverance. Each small piece contains a truth, reality, or meaning all its own. And yet each piece seems like nonsense until it is put together with other pieces to make one large, cohesive whole.

In a way, this course has been like the pieces of a giant puzzle. You have been given information about goodness, power, wisdom, love, mercy, and justice—attributes of God and attributes that make up good character. To understand the truth or reality of each attribute, it has been necessary to study each one separately. Each attribute, however, is only part of the whole picture. Just as God is not any one of these or any other attributes, neither is good character composed of only one attribute. Good character involves putting together all the pieces; it means becoming **whole**.

Knowing about all the pieces that compose good character is not enough. We still need to assemble the puzzle. We need to practice all the virtues, to integrate them into our every thought and action. Without this **integration** of all the virtues, good character is incomplete, as the following story shows:

The Heedless Man [1]

There was once a man who, like most of us, knew in his heart and mind the way to Heaven. He knew he should love his neighbor as himself, honor his parents, and deal with all people honestly. He knew to help the needy and defend the innocent. He knew humility and patience and self-restraint were the way of the wise.

And this man surely tried to do all these things—but only once in a while. He would help a friend if he happened to remember the friend was in need, or say a prayer of thanksgiving if convenient, or give money to the poor if stricken with a guilty conscience. But most of the time he was too busy with his own affairs.

The habits he practiced impressed themselves upon his soul. He developed the shortcoming of heedlessness. Opportunities for exemplary behavior came and went; occasionally he seized them, but usually he did not even notice the chance to do good.

Then one day he died. As he climbed the path toward **Paradise**, he looked back at his life. He recalled the times he had loved and aided his fellow creatures and judged them sufficient.

When he reached the towering gates of Heaven, though, he discovered they were locked. A voice sounded from the air.

"Watch carefully," it warned. "The gates open only once every ten thousand years."

The man stood wide-eyed and trembling in expectation. He

LET'S TALK

Being whole is different from any of its parts, but also depends on all its parts. Discuss how this truth is found in each of the following symbols of wholeness:

- A loaf of bread
- A green salad
- An automobile
- The human body

---

1 "The Heedless Man at the Gates of Paradise," Quoted in William Bennett, *The Moral Compass* (New York: Simon & Shuster), p. 267.

213

resolved to stay alert. But, unaccustomed to practicing the virtue of mindfulness, he soon found his attention drifting away. After watching for what seemed an eternity, his shoulders slumped and his head began to nod. His eyelids fluttered, sank, and closed for a second in sleep.

At that instant the mighty gates swung open and—before he could open his eyes—crashed shut again with a thunder that tumbled the heedless man from Paradise.

Becoming Holy

For Christians, becoming a whole person—someone who has it all together—is the same as becoming holy. **Holiness** is a state of being perfect, complete, entire, happy. It means integrating and assembling all the virtues into one whole. For this reason, the Israelites revered God as the "Holy One." At every Mass in the preface to the eucharistic prayer, we recognize and praise God's wonderful integrity with the words, "Holy, holy, holy is the Lord of hosts; the whole earth is filled with his glory" (Isaiah 6:3).

Our God is indeed holy. We become holy by having contact with God, by opening ourselves to God's own grace and life. Holiness, however, does not happen automatically. Like all the virtues, it is a habit, a way of life. It "grows" on us as we continue to choose and practice goodness, power, wisdom, love, mercy, and justice. Perfect holiness consists in eternal union, or life, with God.

Christians believe that all humans are called to holiness. (See 2 Timothy 1:9.) As the Second Vatican Council fathers wrote, "The Lord Jesus, the divine Teacher and Model of all perfection, preached holiness of life to each and every one of His disciples, regardless of their situation."[2] We are to be perfect as God is perfect (Matthew 5:48). We are to live "as imitators of God, as beloved children" (Ephesians 5:1).

In this final chapter of the course, you will be learning more about what it means to be whole and holy. As you will see, the quest for wholeness and holiness is what gives life meaning. It is what true life, being fully alive, is all about.

---

2 *Dogmatic Constitution on the Church*, #40.

15. Wholeness and Holiness

CHAPTER GOALS

In this chapter, you will:

◆ See that becoming whole is a life-long process involving human needs, emotional development, moral development, and faith development;

◆ Discover the characteristics of people who are whole and holy;

◆ Learn more about the goal of human life and good character—union with God.

All cultures have stories about the quest for wholeness and holiness. Certain Native Americans tribes have their "vision quest." Australian aborigines have their "walk-about." Spanish literature has its "impossible dream" of Don Quixote.

In the early sixteenth century, the explorer Juan Ponce de León (1460–1521) learned about a fabulous fountain of youth from the natives of Bimini (in the Bahamas). Supposedly, the fountain was a miraculous spring that could keep a person young forever. So anxious was Ponce de León to obtain this treasure, that he set off at once with his men in search of it.

Another quest story that has engaged the imaginations of generations is that of the **Holy Grail**, dating from the times of the legendary King Arthur. According to Celtic legend, the Holy Grail is the cup Jesus used at the Last Supper to change wine into his own blood (the first eucharist). Joseph of Arimathea supposedly used this same cup to catch some of the blood of Jesus after he was crucified. Later, as the story goes, Joseph took the cup to Wales, where it was eventually lost.

Many people have tried to find the Holy Grail because of their literal interpretation of Jesus' own words, "Whoever drinks my blood has life eternal" (John 6:54). The King Arthur legends say that Sir Lancelot was unsuccessful in finding the Grail because of his poor character (his decision to have an adulterous relationship with Queen Guinevere). However Lancelot's son, Sir Perceval, along with Sir Galahad and Sir Bors successfully found the Grail because of their great purity and single-mindedness in the life-long pursuit of **union with God**.

While the Grail is only legend, it has a great deal to tell us about the quest for wholeness and holiness. To find the "Grail" is to have eternal life because of one's union with the Trinity. Indeed, the grail is a symbol of grace, of God's own life, that is bestowed on faithful believers.

Scripture

Read the following passages. Then discuss how each passage relates to the legend of the Holy Grail and to our own quest for wholeness and holiness.

◆ The sacrifices used throughout the Hebrew scriptures (Hebrews 9:13–14)

◆ The blood of the Passover lamb (Exodus 12:1–30)

◆ The buried treasure (Matthew 13:44)
◆ The priceless pearl (Matthew 13:45–46)
◆ The bread of life (John 6:25–58)

F.Y.I.

Ponce de León never found the fountain of youth, but in his travels he did discover Florida (in 1513).

Understanding the Legend

The legend of the Holy Grail provides us with two insights into Jesus' beatitude, "Blessed are the pure in heart, for they will see God" (Matthew 5:8). First, according to the legend, only the single-hearted—those who want the Grail more than anything else—can succeed in finding it. Likewise, in our Christian quest for wholeness and holiness, only the single-hearted can achieve union with God—eternal life and happiness—after death. Second, finding the Grail means that we shall see God, face to face. Unlike many of the Israelites, who believed that anyone who looked upon the face of God would die, Christians believe that seeing God's face leads to life—full life—for all eternity. Let's explore both of these concepts further.

Single-Heartedness

Single-heartedness is the virtue that enables us to envision a goal and keep our attentions and energies focused on reaching it. Sometimes, single-heartedness is described as **purity of heart** because we want something with all our hearts. (See Matthew 6:21.) We are not in any way divided in our thinking, motives, or desires. We are very clear about what our treasure is, and we do everything possible to obtain it.

Likewise, we exert all our efforts to reach our goal. We don't take detours or become easily side-tracked. We make our goal our No. 1 priority, more important than anything else. Like the three knights who made the Grail their No. 1 priority, Jesus tells us to seek first God's kingdom, God's "way of holiness" (Matthew 6:33). Then we will truly live and enjoy life.

Furthermore, single-heartedness implies integrity, the integration of one's thoughts and values with one's actions. People who are single-hearted are morally good people. Because they seek God first, they seek to become like God in all relationships and situations.

Seeing God's Face

According to the Grail legend, three knights found the Grail; but only one of them, Sir Galahad, could look directly into the Grail and behold its mysteries. Looking directly at God (or an **angel** of God) and seeing God's glorious and radiant face, are terms used throughout the Bible to describe **union with God**. To see the face of Yahweh is not only to be received favorably by God; it is also to become one with God. (See Genesis 33:10; Job 33:26.) Likewise, not to see God's face is to experience disgrace, estrangement, and abandonment. (See Psalms 30:7 and 89:46.)

For Your Eyes Only

What, to you, is the greatest treasure you could find? Why?

LET'S TALK

1. What is one way you can make God's way of holiness your No. 1 priority?

2. Give an example from your own life or from the life of someone else that shows a single-hearted endeavor. What was accomplished?

The experience of not being able to look directly at God's face is similar to the experience represented by the modern-day expression of "turning one's back" on another, refusing to aid or acknowledge a person. According to the prophet Ezekiel, God hid his face in anger at the Israelites whenever they sinned against him. "I dealt with them according to their uncleanness (lack of single-heartedness) and their transgressions, and hid my face from them" (Ezekiel 39:24).

Likewise, the experience of being able to look directly at the face of God is similar to the modern-day expression of being "straight" with others, that is, of being honest and upright with them. St. Paul says that complete oneness with God is a sight beyond anything we have yet seen. "When the complete comes, the partial will come to an end. . . . Now we see in a mirror dimly; but then we will see face to face. Now I know only in part; then I will know fully, even as I have been fully known" (1 Corinthians 13: 10–12.) Seeing God's face is indeed a goal worthy of all our hearts and efforts.

Scripture

Read about the following encounters between humans and God (or an angel of God) described in the Old Testament. Then compare these with the encounters with God described in the **New Testament**. How are the encounters similar? What do they tell you about the experience of wholeness and holiness?

Old Testament	New Testament
Judges 6:1–24	Luke 1:5–25
Judges 13	Luke 1:26–38
Genesis 32:23–31	Matthew 3:13–17
Exodus 33:7–23	Matthew 17:1–8
1 Kings 19:1–18	Acts 2:1–12
Exodus 3 and 4	Acts 9: 1-19

For Your Eyes Only

1. Have you ever been angry with someone and refused to acknowledge that person? Has anyone been angry with you and refused to acknowledge you? What happened? How did you feel?

2. What do you think the experience of seeing God face to face would be like? Describe the image you have of God's face.

Full and Abundant Life

To see God's face, to be in God's good graces, is what gives life its sense of fulfillment and vitality. Whenever we are one with God, we have a sense of full and abundant life because God alone is a "living" God. God alone gives life. God gives life without respect to a person's good character and deeds. We receive the happiness and joy of life through obedience to God's commandments. (See Deuteronomy 30:15–20.)

God sent Jesus to save us from death—not only bodily death that occurs at the end of our earthly lives, but also the psychological and spiritual death that occurs from sin and not being fully alive throughout our life on earth. Jesus came so that we might live life fully, embrace it, and savor its every moment. (See John 10:10.) Christians believe that we are given this new spiritual life at baptism. That is why St. Paul tells the Romans, "If we have died with Christ (been baptized), we believe that we will also live with him. So you also must consider yourselves dead to sin and alive for God in Christ Jesus" (Romans 6:8, 11).

To be holy and whole is to live fully. It is also to be one with God, to see God's light. Jesus explained this to his disciples on the night before he died. "In a little while the world will no longer see me, but you will see me; because I live, you also will live. On that day you will know that I am in my Father, and you in me, and I in you" (John 14:19–20).

LET'S TALK

1. Read Genesis 3:22–24 and Revelation 22:12–14. What do you think the tree of life is? How is this symbol similar to the Holy Grail?

2. Discuss each of the following quotes. What do they say to you about full and abundant life? What does being "fully alive" mean to you?

   ◆ "I want to live fully. I want to seize fate by the throat." (Ludwig van Beethoven, 1801)

   ◆ "Life is meant to be lived, and curiosity must be kept alive. One must never, for whatever reason, turn his or her back on life." (Eleanor Roosevelt, *Autobiography*, 1961)

   ◆ "I went to the woods because I wished to live deliberately, face the essential facts of life, and see if I could not learn what it had to teach, and not, when I came to die, discover that I had not lived." (Henry David Thoreau, *Where I Lived and What I Lived For*)

For Your Eyes Only

What is one improvement you can make in your life to live it more fully?

NOTABLE QUOTABLE

"This world is but a canvas to our imaginations. Dreams are the touchstones of our characters."

—Henry David Thoreau, *A Week on the Concord and Merrimack Rivers*

A Life-Long Process

Becoming a whole and holy person takes time. Like good wine, we have to "age" before we can reach our peak potential and become our best selves. To understand the process of becoming whole and holy, it helps to look at the growth process from different aspects—human needs, emotional development, moral development, and spiritual development.

Human Needs

The noted psychologist, Abraham Maslow (1908–1970), said that people cannot be whole unless their human needs are fulfilled or satisfied. In other words, according to Maslow, every person has certain needs that must be met before the person can be happy and whole.

Maslow also said that every person has a hierarchy of needs, arranged in six layers. (See Figure 1.) Basic needs include Level 1 physiological needs (food, water, sleep, warmth), Level 2 physiological needs (safety and security), Level 3 psychological needs (love affection, sense of belonging), and Level 4 psychological needs (sense of value and worth, accomplishment). Level 1 needs must be met before the other levels can be obtained. Likewise, Level 2 needs must be met before Levels 3 and 4 needs can be obtained. These basic human needs are also called *deficiency needs*, because if they are not met, the person lacks something necessary and will seek to make up what is lacking.

Basic needs must be met before a person can concentrate on obtaining the needs in Levels 5 and 6. These levels deal with higher needs or what Maslow called *metaneeds*. Level 5 needs include the qualities of good character we have been discussing throughout this course—justice, goodness, beauty, mercy, wisdom, and so forth. Level 6 needs include the needs of wholeness and holiness we are discussing now. Maslow called this last level **self-actualization**. According to Maslow, relatively few people reach this level of wholeness because it involves the integration and continual practice of all the virtues of good character.

DO THIS!

Study Figure 1. In a small group, discuss examples of each level of needs. Why do you think it is necessary that lower level needs are met before higher level ones can be met? Write a short essay explaining what implications Maslow's hierarchy has on social justice and Christian *agape*.

MASLOW'S HIERARCHY OF NEEDS

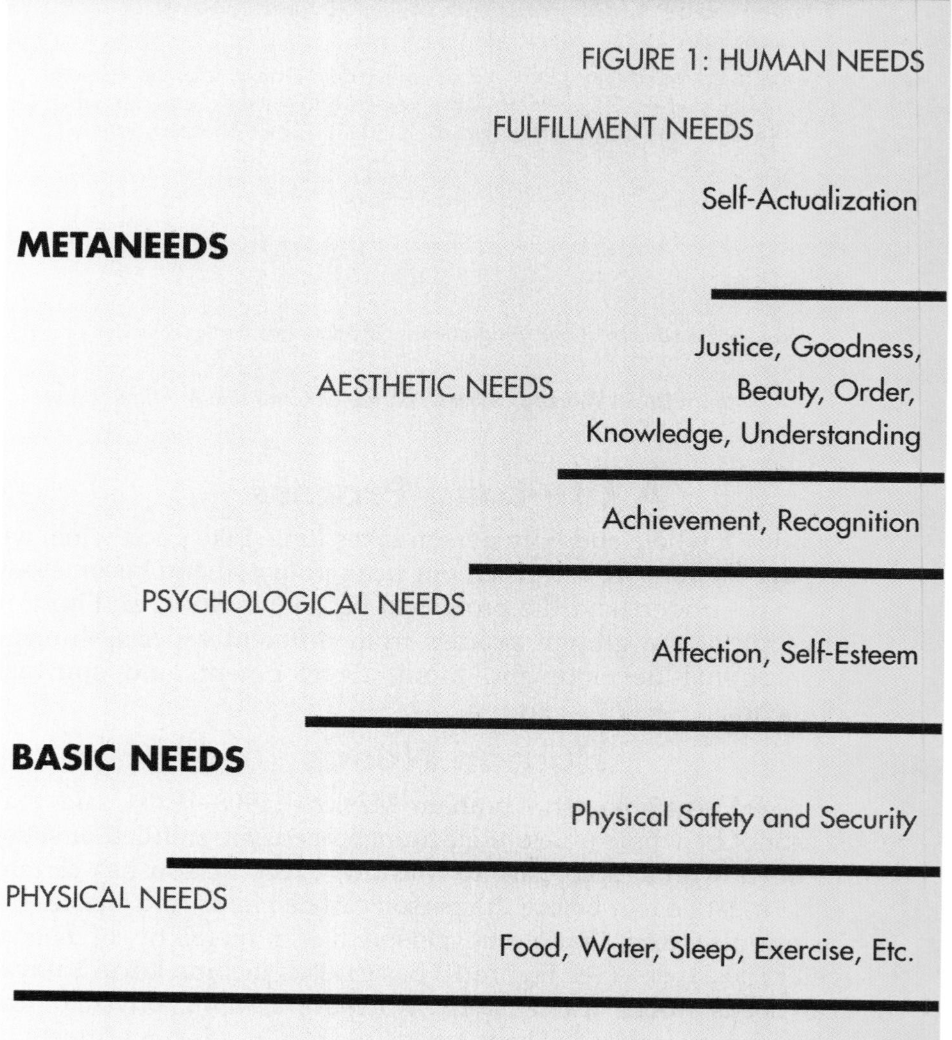

FIGURE 1: HUMAN NEEDS

FULFILLMENT NEEDS

Self-Actualization

METANEEDS

AESTHETIC NEEDS

Justice, Goodness,
Beauty, Order,
Knowledge, Understanding

Achievement, Recognition

PSYCHOLOGICAL NEEDS

Affection, Self-Esteem

BASIC NEEDS

Physical Safety and Security

PHYSICAL NEEDS

Food, Water, Sleep, Exercise, Etc.

Emotional Development

Another psychologist, Erik Erikson, believes that a completely whole person has to have more than an integration of values and virtues. A whole person also has to "have it all together" when it comes to his or her emotions. In his studies, Erikson found that humans develop emotional maturity slowly throughout life. He talked about this process of emotional development in terms of different stages.

The table below describes Erikson's stages of emotional development. At each stage, a person encounters a certain emotional task. (For example, at Stage 1, infants learn to trust or to mistrust the world around them.)

Although Erikson specifies ages at which each emotional task takes place, the ages do not necessarily correspond to each task. Some teenagers, for example, may be at Stage 4; others may be at Stage 6. Likewise, there is no specific age that a person can reach emotional wholeness and maturity. Erikson believes, however, that a person who does reach the final stage will be trusting, independent, able to initiate action, competent, and intimate.

ERIKSON'S STAGES OF EMOTIONAL DEVELOPMENT

STAGE OF DEVELOPMENT (ERIKSON)	MAIN CONFLICT OR TASK	USUAL AGE	CHARACTERISTICS OF STAGE
1: Infancy	Trust vs. Mistrust	Birth to Age 1	Discovering the world as a safe or unsafe place; learning whether people are dependable or not.
2: Early Childhood	Autonomy vs. Shame and Doubt	1–3 years old	Learning to be independent by walking alone, climbing, talking, and controlling toilet functions.
3: Childhood	Initiative vs. Guilt	4–5	Asking questions, playacting, and acting on one's own.
4: Later Childhood	Industry vs. Inferiority	6–11	School learning—both facts and skills. Being creative with arts and crafts.
5: Adolescence	Identity vs. Role Confusion	12–18	Searching for sense of identity. Dealing with peers. Clarifying one's own values.
6: Young Adulthood	Intimacy vs. Isolation	19–40	Ability to cooperate with others and to form affectionate, committed bonds.
7: Middle Age	Generativity vs. Self-Absorption	40–65	Being productive at a job or in a career; helping others.
8: Advanced Age	Integrity vs. Despair	65+	Finding meaning and having a sense of satisfaction and completion about one's life.

Moral Development

While virtuous behavior is essential to wholeness and holiness, it is also important to consider our *motives* for being virtuous. Just as there are stages of needs and emotional maturity, so there are stages of maturity regarding moral motivation. Educator Lawrence Kohlberg has identified six such stages.

Stage 1: According to Kohlberg, a person's motivation for being good in Stage 1 is punishment and reward. The person chooses to do good because he or she wants a reward. The person chooses not to do wrong because of fear of punishment. A teenager, for example, may choose to do household chores because he or she wants a weekly allowance. A teenager may choose not to shoplift for fear that he or she will be caught and punished.

Stage 2: In this stage, the motivation for being good is to build up one's own ego. The person chooses to do good because it is in his or her best self-interest to do so. "I'll do this because it will make me feel good." "I won't do that because then I'll feel guilty."

LET'S TALK

1. Describe a time you were motivated to choose good because of a reward or punishment.

2. Describe a time you were motivated to choose good because you didn't want to feel guilty. How were the results of these two occasions the same? different?

Stage 3: Here, the motivation for being good is what others will think. The person acts from a need for approval—from parents, teachers, or peers. A teenager, for example, may choose to study for a test because he or she wants praise, recognition, or a good grade. A teenager may choose not to smoke because parents or peers consider it "uncool."

Stage 4: In Stage 4, the motivation for being good is righteousness and letter-of-the-law legalism. A teenager chooses not to drink alcohol because it is "against the law." The law, however, does not always determine moral correctness. (Remember, abortion is "legal" in the United States.)

Stage 5: In this stage, the motivation for being good is the "spirit" behind the law. The person may not keep the letter of the law, but instead, obeys the reason, or spirit, behind the law.

Stage 6: Here, a person follows his or her own conscience as well as the external law. The person acts according to universal principles of right and wrong. For example, a teenager chooses not to go with others to vandalize school property because he or she believes it is wrong.

While Kohlberg's stages give us a way to talk about moral maturity, many people believe his stages are inadequate. Often, our motives for being good are mixed. There may be more than one reason, or one stage, that is motivating our decision or behavior. Also, some people believe that a **Stage 7** should be added to the list. In this stage, which is based on grace and faith, a person acts morally as a result of his or her character. Doing good is an expression of who one is—a child of God and a member of the church community. At this stage, the person is whole and holy—someone who has integrated values and virtues with decisions and actions.

LET'S TALK

1. What are some other examples of real-life situations in which a teenager might choose to do good or bad because of the need for peer approval?

2. Besides abortion, what is another example of something that is legal but not moral?

3. Read Matthew 12:1–15. What stage of moral maturity are the Pharisees acting on? What stage is Jesus acting on?

4. How does grace and faith impact decisions you make?

Spiritual Development

A person of good character would not be complete without a mature spirituality—a mature faith in God, self, and others. In the early 1980s, theologian James Fowler described six stages of growth that lead to mature faith. His stages may be described as follows:

Stage 1: Basic Faith. The person has a basic trust in God, others, and self. The person just accepts that everything will turn out for the best. A teenager in this stage doesn't question the meaning of existence or ask why bad things sometimes happen to good people.

Stage 2: Imitation Faith. The person copies, or imitates, the faith he or she sees in the moods, actions, and lives of others. The specifics of a person's faith are strongly influenced by Bible stories and imagination. A teenager in this stage goes to Mass because that is what admired adults or peers do.

Stage 3: Literal-Minded Faith. The person believes everything told him or her about faith, word for word. This includes a **fundamentalist** approach to understanding the Bible. For example, believing that God really created the world in six 24 hour days or that Noah really did save a pair of each animal on earth in the Ark.

Stage 4: Conventional Faith. The person believes certain things about God, Jesus, and morality because that is what the church teaches. A teenager in this stage may believe that all priests and religious should be perfect. If a church leader is found to be imperfect, the teen may have a resulting crisis of faith, thinking that nothing the church teaches is true.

Stage 5: Reflective Faith. The person takes responsibility for his or her own actions, attitudes, beliefs, and sense of meaning. A teenager in this stage chooses to believe in God's love—not only because the church says so, but because that is what he or she truly believes. A teenager in this stage identifies the values he or she considers important and then tries to live by them.

Stage 6: Paradoxical Faith. The person has experienced the world's brokenness, as well as personal imperfections, yet still chooses to believe in God's kingdom of love, peace, and perfection. A teenager in this stage has a greater awareness of the injustice present in the world, but does not give in to discouragement. The teen continues to believe and hope that God's kingdom will one day become a reality.

Stage 7: Incarnational Faith. The person believes because God is a real, felt experience. Because the person's will and God's will are closely aligned, the person is whole, holy, and completely happy.

Union With God

The *Catechism of the Catholic Church* tells us that the reason for our existence is "to know, to love, and to serve God." The goal, or purpose, of our lives is to be happy with God "in Paradise" (1721). There, as St. Augustine writes, "we shall rest and see, we shall see and love, we shall love and praise. Behold what will be at the end without end. For what other end do we have, if not to reach the kingdom which has no end?"

Paradise, heaven, and the kingdom of God are all terms that refer to eternal union with God. In this state of union, God's grace restores in us the integrity, the wholeness, which humans lost through sin. Indeed, it is a perfect state, an experience of everlasting oneness with the divine.

In the twelfth century, St. Bernard of Clairvaux described the process, or states of grace by which humans rise to perfection, to union with God. According to St. Bernard, each state of grace is a degree of love. There are four degrees.

◆ **First Degree of Love:** This type of love consists of self-love and healthy self-esteem.

◆ **Second Degree of Love:** This type of love consists of love for God. We are grateful for all the good we have received—for divine help when facing hardships and for God's forgiveness when we have sinned.

◆ **Third Degree of Love:** In this type of love, we love God for God's own goodness, power, wisdom, love, mercy, and justice. However, God remains outside us. We remain distinct from God.

◆ **Fourth Degree of Love:** In this type of love, God and the person become perfectly one. We become "participants of the divine nature" (2 Peter 1:4). We gaze directly upon God's face and are "transformed into God's image from one degree of glory to another; for this comes from the Lord, the Spirit" (2 Corinthians 3:18). Although no words can adequately describe the experience of wholeness and holiness found in union with the Trinity, it helps to use certain analogies. For example, union with God is like a chemical reaction in which the atoms of hydrogen and oxygen unite to form something entirely new—water. Union with God is like a glass of milk and chocolate, which—once mixed—cannot be separated. Union with God is like the sexual intimacy between a husband and a wife.

For Your Eyes Only

How would you describe your faith at this time in your life?

224

Despite our human inability to describe it, one thing about the fourth degree of love is clear: It can only be attained with God's grace and in a person who has "a pure heart, a good conscience, and sincere faith" (1 Timothy 1:5). We must first be people of good character.

People of Good Character

To be self-fulfilled, people need to integrate all aspects of their character into one, synthetic whole. They need consistency between their values and their actions—what they believe, say, and do.

During his lifetime, Abraham Maslow studied the lives of 49 people he considered to be self-actualized, to have integrated their good character into one, synthetic whole. Among such people were the composer Ludwig van Beethoven (1770–1827), President Abraham Lincoln (1809–1865), naturalist Henry David Thoreau (1817–1862), scientist Albert Einstein (1879–1955), and first lady Eleanor Roosevelt (1884–1962). From his study, Maslow concluded that self-actualized people, people of good character, may be described in the following ways:[3]

1. They are realistically oriented.
2. They accept themselves, other people, and the natural world for what they are.
3. They have a great deal of spontaneity.
4. They are problem-centered, rather than self-centered.
5. They have an air of detachment and a need for privacy.
6. They are autonomous and independent.
7. Their appreciation of people and things is "fresh" rather than stereotyped.
8. Most of them have had profound mystical or spiritual experiences, although not necessarily religious in character.
9. They identify with humanity.
10. Their intimate relationships with a few specially loved people tend to be profound and deeply emotional rather than superficial.
11. Their values and attitudes are democratic.
12. They do not confuse means with ends.
13. Their sense of humor is philosophical rather than hostile or cynical.
14. They have a great fund of creativeness.
15. They resist conformity to the popular culture.
16. They transcend the environment rather than just cope with it.

3 Adapted from *Life and Health,* 2nd ed. (New York: Random House, 1976), pp. 47–49.

Furthermore, self-fulfilled people have an accurate knowledge of their own goals, values, and abilities. They function with integrity and at the peak of their capacity. In other words, they need to be and do all that they are capable of being and doing.

> NOTABLE QUOTABLE
>
> "The most beautiful thing we can experience is the mysterious. It is the source of all true art and science."
>
> —Albert Einstein, *What I Believe* (1930)

For Your Eyes Only

How do you rate yourself according to each characteristic on Maslow's list?

NOTABLE QUOTABLE

"My religion is not just my faith; it is who I am."

—Brie Bamier, Canyon del Oro High School, Tucson, AZ

Wholeness and You

Becoming a whole person and integrating all the virtues discussed in this course may seem like an overwhelming task. The way to perfection, to God's kingdom, is indeed a narrow one. (See Matthew 7:13–14.) Sometimes, it will seem so narrow that it is not a road at all, but a tightrope—like the one discussed periodically throughout this course. True followers of Jesus, however, do not give in to discouragement, nor do they turn back. Instead, they keep in mind two important facts.

First, there is not just one road that leads to perfection and union with God. Instead, there are many different roads. Just as God created each one of us as unique individuals, so there is a unique road that each of us is called to follow. For some people, this road will entail marriage and children. For others, the road will mean ordained priesthood or religious life. For still others, the road will mean being single. No one of these vocations is "better than" or "holier" than the other vocations. All people—in every vocation and in every career path—are called to holiness and wholeness by God.

If you look at the lives of the saints throughout church history, you will find people in all kinds of walks of life—students, housewives, carpenters, artists, soldiers, doctors, lawyers, priests, brothers, sisters, teachers, and so on. All of us have our own road, our own way to oneness with God.

The second fact that Christians remember is that we don't have to travel alone on our road to wholeness. God the Father is always with us. (See Isaiah 43:2–7.) The Holy Spirit, the Sanctifier, is always with us, helping us grow in holiness and wholeness. (See John 16:13–16.) And Jesus himself is always with us (Matthew 28:20).

We remind ourselves of God's continual presence with us whenever we begin Mass with the greeting, "The Lord be with you. And also with you." or the alternative greeting, "The grace of the Lord Jesus Christ, the love of God, and the communion of the Holy Spirit be with you all" (2 Corinthians 12:13). The next time you hear these words, think about what they really mean. You are not alone. The Trinity, present and alive in the church, is here walking with you now—drawing you ever closer to God and to wholeness.

The song "Because You Loved Me," [4] recorded by Celine Dion, was not intended to describe our relationship with God, but in some ways it could. Consider the words from the chorus:

> You were my strength when I was weak,
>
> You were my voice when I couldn't speak.
>
> You were my eyes when I couldn't see,
>
> You saw the best there was in me,
>
> Lifted me up when I couldn't reach.
>
> You gave me faith 'cuz you believed.
>
> I'm everything I am because you loved me.

NOTABLE QUOTABLES

"Sanctify yourself and you will sanctify society."

—St. Francis of Assisi

"Turn yourself around like a piece of clay and say to the Lord: I am clay, and you, Lord, the potter. Make of me what you will."

—St. John of Avila

For Your Eyes Only

What is one lasting memory you will take with you from this course?

Conclusion

This course has given you the knowledge and the skills you need to build good character and to become whole. The next step—applying what you have learned to your own life—is up to you. Good luck, and "may the Lord of peace himself give you peace at all times and in all ways" (2 Thessalonians 3:16).

Prayer

LEADER: May the grace of our Lord Jesus Christ be with you.

ALL: And also with you.

LEADER: Let us pray for a moment in silence, opening ourselves to the God who is with us always.

READER 1: 1 John 1:1–4

READER 2: 1 John 4:7–16

ALL: God of peace and wholeness, make us perfect in holiness. Take away any fear or discouragement we may have and lead us to wholeness and happiness. Fill us with your continual presence so that our entire spirit, soul, and body may one day be united with you. Amen.

For Your Eyes Only

One way I will try to bring fuller life and joy to others in the future is . . .

---

4 By Diane Warren. Recorded by Celine Dion. Copyright ©1996. Realsongs (ASCAP).

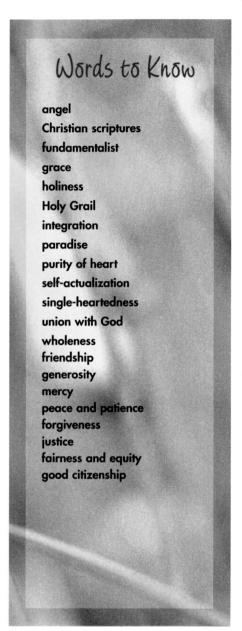

Words to Know

angel
Christian scriptures
fundamentalist
grace
holiness
Holy Grail
integration
paradise
purity of heart
self-actualization
single-heartedness
union with God
wholeness
friendship
generosity
mercy
peace and patience
forgiveness
justice
fairness and equity
good citizenship

Part 8 Test

1. How is human wholeness like a puzzle?

2. What is holiness?

3. What is the legend of the Holy Grail? How does it relate to the Christian quest for wholeness and holiness?

4. What gives Christians a sense of full and abundant life?

5. Explain Maslow's hierarchy of human needs. How do human needs relate to wholeness?

6. Explain Erikson's stages of emotional development. According to Erikson, how do these stages relate to a person who is whole and holy?

7. What are Kohlberg's stages of moral development. Why do some people think a Stage 7 is needed? What would this stage be like?

8. What are Fowler's stages of faith development. How do these stages relate to a person who is whole and holy?

9. What are the four degrees of love according to St. Bernard?

10. What are two reasons Christians do not give in to discouragement or give up on their journey toward wholeness and holiness?

Course Assessment

Part A: Group Work

Work with a small group to complete one of the following projects.

1. Rent and view the movie *Forrest Gump*. Prepare a 10–20 minute oral report for the class that analyzes Forrest's character.

   A) Explain what each of the following virtues is. Then tell how, in the movie, Forrest does or does not show each virtue.

   - goodness
   - self-esteem
   - integrity and honesty
   - respect for others
   - respect for property and nature
   - wisdom
   - good decision-making
   - Christian work ethic
   - love

   B) In the group's opinion, is Forrest a whole and holy person? Why or why not?

2. Research the life of one of the following people. Prepare a 10 to 20 minute creative report for the class about how this person was or was not fully alive, whole, and self-actualized. Specifically, how did this person live the virtues listed in project 1?

   - Ludwig van Beethoven (1770–1827)
   - Abraham Lincoln (1809–1865)
   - Henry David Thoreau (1817–1862)
   - Albert Einstein (1879–1955)
   - Eleanor Roosevelt (1884–1962)

3. Prepare a 10 to 20 minute audio or video reading of the following poem. Include appropriate background music. After the reading, tell which virtues from this course (see the list in project 1) may be found in the poem. Are any virtues missing?

Desiderata [5]

Go placidly amid the noise and the haste, and remember what peace there may be in silence. As far as possible, without surrender, be on good terms with all persons. Speak your truth quietly and clearly; and listen to others, even to the dull and ignorant; they too have their story. Avoid loud and aggressive persons; they are vexations to the spirit. If you compare yourself with others, you may become vain or bitter, for always there will be greater and lesser persons than yourself. Enjoy your achievements as well as your plans. Keep interested in your own career, however humble; it is a real possession in the changing fortunes of time. Exercise caution in your business affairs, for the world is full of trickery. But let this not blind you to what virtue there is; many persons strive for high ideals, and everywhere life is full of heroism. Be yourself.

---

5 By Max Ehrmann (1927). Found in *The Desiderata of Happiness*, ed. Susan Polis Schulz (Boulder, CO: Blue Mountain Arts, 1948), pp. 10–11.

Especially do not feign affection. Neither be cynical about love; for in the face of all aridity and disenchantment, it is as perennial as the grass. Take kindly the counsel of the years, gracefully surrendering the things of youth. Nurture strength of spirit to shield you in sudden misfortune. But do not distress yourself with dark imaginings. Many fears are born of fatigue and loneliness. Beyond a wholesome discipline, be gentle with yourself. You are a child of the universe no less than the trees and the stars; you have a right to be here. And whether or not it is clear to you, no doubt the universe is unfolding as it should. Therefore be at peace with God, whatever you conceive Him to be. And whatever your labors and aspirations, in the noisy confusion of life, keep peace in your soul. With all its sham, drudgery, and broken dreams, it is still a beautiful world. Be cheerful. Strive to be happy.

Part B: Individual Work

Write a 3-page reflection (750 words) that includes these elements:

1. One way during the past year you have lived each virtue.

2. One way you recognize your own developing character.

3. Your vision for the future—the person you hope to be as an adult.

Appendix

Catholic Prayers

Sign of the Cross

In the name of the Father,
and of the Son,
and of the Holy Spirit. Amen.

Lord's Prayer

Our Father, who art in heaven,
hallowed be thy name;
Thy kingdom come,
Thy will be done on earth
as it is in heaven.
Give us this day our daily bread;
and forgive us our trespasses as we
forgive those who trespass against us;
and lead us not into temptation,
but deliver us from evil. Amen.

Hail Mary

Hail Mary, full of grace,
the Lord is with you!
Blessed are you among women,
and blessed is the fruit of your womb,
Jesus.
Holy Mary, mother of God,
pray for us sinners,
now and at the hour of our death.
Amen.

Doxology

Glory be to the Father, and to the Son,
and to the Holy Spirit.
As it was in the beginning, is now, and
ever shall be. Amen.

Act of Faith

Lord God, I believe that you are
one God in three persons. I believe that
you are Father, Son, and Holy Spirit.
I believe that a new life opened for me
through the death and resurrection of your Son
and that your love and guidance continue
through your Holy Spirit.
I believe in the truths taught by
your holy, catholic, and apostolic Church.
By responding in love to your gifts, I believe
that I shall share in eternal joy with you.
This is my belief, Lord God,
and my belief is my joy. Amen.

Act of Hope

Lord God, trusting in your deep love
and goodness, I hope to receive
continued forgiveness for my faults
and your guidance and help in avoiding sin.
My hope for eternal life and joy in you
fills me with joy and love each day I live. Amen.

Act of Love

Lord God, you continually share
your great love with me
through the gifts in my life.
In an attempt to imitate your great goodness
and show my love in return,
I will strive to love you with all my heart,

all my mind, and all my strength,
and I will seek to love my neighbor as myself.
Lord, teach me to love even more. Amen.

Act of Contrition

O my God, I am sorry for my sins.
In choosing to sin and failing to do good,
I have sinned against you and your Church.
I firmly intend, with the help of your Son,
to do penance and to sin no more.

Christian Creeds

The Apostles' Creed

I [we] believe in God, the Father the almighty, creator of heaven and earth

I [we] believe in Jesus Christ, His only Son, our Lord.

He was conceived by the power of the Holy Spirit and born of the Virgin Mary.

He suffered under Pontius Pilate,
was crucified, died, and was buried.
He descended to the dead.

On the third day he arose again.

He ascended into heaven, and is seated at the right hand of the Father. He will come again to judge the living and the dead.

I [we] believe in the Holy Spirit, the holy catholic Church, the communion of saints,the forgiveness of sins, the resurrection of the body, and the life everlasting. Amen.

The Nicene Creed

We believe in one God, the Father, the Almighty, maker of heaven and earth, of all that is seen and unseen.

We believe in one Lord, Jesus Christ, the only Son of God, eternally begotten of the Father, God from God, Light from Light, true God from true God, begotten, not made, one in Being with the Father.

Through him all things were made.

For us men and for our salvation, he came down from heaven: by the power of the Holy Spirit he was born of the Virgin Mary, and became [human].

For our sake he was crucified under Pontius Pilate; he suffered, died, and was buried.

On the third day he rose again in fulfillment of the Scriptures; he ascended into heaven and is seated at the right hand of the Father. He will come again in glory to judge the living and the dead, and his kingdom will have no end.

We believe in the Holy Spirit, the Lord, the giver of life, who proceeds from the Father and the Son. With the Father and the Son he is worshipped and glorified. He has spoken through the Prophets.

We believe in one holy catholic and apostolic Church.

We acknowledge one baptism for the forgiveness of sins.

We look for the resurrection of the dead, and the life of the world to come. Amen.

Glossary

abolitionist A person who opposes the use of capital punishment.

abortion The deliberate termination of a pregnancy, with the resulting death of the embryo or fetus.

abstinence Refraining from sexual intercourse.

accountability Accepting the consequences of and taking responsibility for one's actions and decisions. Not blaming others for one's own problems.

addictive Causing dependence on something or someone. In the case of an addictive drug, the person needs more and more of the drug in order to produce the same high feeling.

adultery Sexual intercourse with someone other than your spouse.

agape A type of love that consists of unselfish, loyal, and benevolent concern for the good of another person. *Agape* refers to love for strangers and enemies. It enables us to extend concern and help to others without any expectation of love or reward in return.

aggravated assault An attack on a person that is more serious than a common attack; it is an assault that is combined with an intent to commit a crime.

AIDS (Auto-Immune Deficiency Syndrome) A fatal condition that prevents the body's immune system from fighting off disease.

Alcoholics Anonymous (AA) A twelve-step program that offers group support to people who want to stop drinking alcohol.

amoral Having nothing to do with moral right and wrong, goodness or evil. Deciding what brand of toothpaste to buy is an example of an amoral decision.

angel A pure spirit created by God; a messenger of God.

anger A strong feeling of displeasure, antagonism, rage, and fury.

anti-Semitism A type of racism that discriminates against people who are Jewish.

arson The deliberate burning of property, with unlawful or fraudulent intent.

attributes of God Characteristics that describe what God is like. The six attributes of God that are the focus of this text are goodness, power, wisdom, love, mercy, and justice.

bagging Deliberate inhalation of household products through a paper bag.

baptism The sacrament whereby a person becomes a member of the Christian community. In the Catholic church, baptism is one of three sacraments of initiation, along with confirmation and eucharist. Baptism celebrates a person's choice to die to evil and to rise to a new life that assumes Christ's own character.

battery The act of beating or using force on a person without the person's consent.

bigot A person who is obstinately or intolerantly devoted to his or her opinions and prejudices.

Bill of Rights The first ten amendments of the U.S. Constitution in which certain rights are guaranteed to all U.S. citizens.

binge drinking Drinking five or more drinks in a short period of time.

biodegradable A substance that is capable of being broken down into harmless products by the action of biological microorganisms.

blasphemy Irreverence toward God or something that is considered sacred.

blunts Marijuana cigars.

burglary Stealing that takes place while breaking and entering a home or building.

capital punishment State-approved killing of a convicted criminal for particular crimes he or she has committed.

capital sins Seven sins that are at the root of all vices. The seven capital sins are pride, greed, lust, anger, gluttony, envy, and sloth (or laziness).

cardinal virtues Fundamental virtues that are the root of all the other moral virtues. The four cardinal virtues are justice, prudence, temperance, and fortitude.

character A distinctive mark, quality, symbol, or trait that marks something permanently. It is the sum of all the attributes or features that make up a human being.

charity Another word for Christian *agape*. Charity is the virtue that enables us to love others as Jesus himself loved the poor, the lepers, the lame, the blind, the grieving, the stranger, and the outcast.

chastity The moral virtue that enables us to express our sexuality in appropriate ways.

cheating Playing unfairly or dishonestly. Examples of cheating include (1) copying someone else's ideas or work and claiming them as your own and (2) obtaining the answers to a test ahead of time.

chrism Blessed oil (olive or vegetable oil mixed with balm) that is used only at baptism, confirmation, and holy orders. The oil is a sign that the person has received a new, "indelible" character—the priesthood of Christ and membership in the people of god, the church.

Christian A follower of Jesus Christ. Someone who lives by gospel values.

Christian work ethic The belief in the dignity of work and the importance of having a positive attitude toward it. The Christian work ethic includes values such as self-discipline, cooperation with others, perseverance, industriousness, creativity, open-mindedness, single-mindedness, service to others, good sportsmanship, honesty, and the appreciation of education and lifelong learning

citizenship A person's membership and participation in a particular social group.

civic responsibility A sense of duty or obligation to take part in the concerns and welfare of a particular community.

clemency Acting mercifully with regard to lessening the severity of a punishment.

common good What is beneficial to everyone or almost everyone in a particular community.

community A group of people linked together by common values and character.

commutative justice The type of justice that calls for fairness and equality in all agreements and exchanges between individuals.

compassion Sympathetic awareness of others' distress, together with a desire to alleviate their suffering.

confession The admitting of one's own faults and sins to another.

confirmation A sacrament of initiation in which the church celebrates the presence and actions of the Holy Spirit in specific individuals and welcomes these people to full church membership.

conscience The mental ability to discern right from wrong.

consumerism Placing undue value on buying things, heedless purchasing of more than one truly needs, just for the sake of buying things.

contributive justice The type of justice that obliges us to participate in society and work for the common good of all people.

conversion A turning away from sin and evil and a turning toward the way of Jesus.

cooperation Working with others to meet a goal.

corporal works of mercy Acts of kindness and compassion by which we help better the physical condition of others. The seven corporal works of mercy are: feed the hungry, give drink to the thirsty, clothe the naked, give shelter to the homeless, take care of the sick, visit those in prison, and bury the dead.

courage One of the cardinal virtues and a gift of the Holy Spirit that enables us to have the moral strength to live by our convictions and values.

covetousness A capital sin that is similar to greed. Covetousness is selfishness "to the max," the self-centered grasping of material possessions. It is concern only about one's own welfare.

diligence The ability to tackle a task with energy and effort, with the attitude of doing one's best.

disciples Students or learners; followers of another person that submit themselves to a certain discipline in order to learn.

discrimination Unfair treatment of others because of their race, ethnic background, age, gender, health status, sexual orientation, or religious beliefs.

domestic violence Any type of violence that occurs between family members or between two people who are involved in a dating relationship.

DUI The crime of driving under the influence of alcohol.

embezzlement Stealing someone else's property or money that has been entrusted to your care.

encyclical A theological letter from the pope to the worldwide church.

endangered species Plants and animals whose populations are dwindling and are in danger of becoming extinct.

environmentalism Concern for the preservation and improvement of the natural world, as well as the control of pollution.

eros A type of love that involves ardent passion and sexual attraction between two people.

eucharist The sacrament of initiation in which members of the church receive Christ's body and blood under the forms of bread and wine.

exorcism A rite in which evil spirits are driven out of a person or place by the authority of God and with the prayer of the church.

extinct No longer in existence. Not to be found anywhere on earth.

faith The theological virtue that allows us to believe in God's existence. It is also the virtue that enables us to trust that God knows us and loves us as a good parent.

First World Industrialized or developed countries with a market economy. The First World includes the United States, Canada, Western Europe, Australia, Japan, South Africa, and Taiwan.

forbearance Patience; refraining from enforcing a debt, right, or obligation that is due.

forgery Stealing that occurs by signing someone else's name to a check or by counterfeiting a document.

forgiveness Pardon; willingness to give up resentment about and payment for a debt, transgression, or offense.

fornication Sexual intercourse between unmarried persons.

fortitude Another word for courage. Fortitude is strength of mind that enables a person to encounter danger or to bear pain or adversity with courage.

fraud Intentional deceit or trickery to get a person to part with something of value.

friendship A non-erotic relationship of mutual care and esteem.

fruits of the Spirit Characteristics that accompany the presence of the Holy Spirit within a person. The fruits of the Spirit are love, joy, peace, patient endurance, kindness, generosity, faith, mildness, and chastity.

fundamentalist A term that describes a Christian who interprets the Bible literally.

generosity The unselfish (liberal or magnanimous) giving of one's time, money, and help without expectation of anything in return.

gifts of the Holy Spirit Gifts from God received at baptism that increase our ability to relate to others with love and with hope. The seven gifts of the Holy Spirit are wisdom, knowledge, understanding, right judgment, courage, reverence, and wonder (awe in God's presence).

global warming The unhealthy increase in temperature of the surface and lower atmosphere of the earth, due in part to human-made pollution.

goodness The quality or state of being morally virtuous, right, commendable, honorable, and reliable.

gossip The sin of revealing private or sensational facts about others.

grace A sharing and participation in the life of God; grace is a gift from God.

grand larceny The unlawful taking of someone else's property over a certain value. (This value varies from state to state.)

greed The capital sin involving excessive desire for money and material possessions.

Hebrew scriptures Another name for the Jewish Bible. The Hebrew scriptures are contained in the Old Testament of the Christian Bible.

hemophilia An inherited blood disease, mostly in males, that prevents blood clotting and causes continual bleeding even after minor injuries.

heresy A religious opinion that differs from approved church teaching.

holiness The perfect state of goodness and righteousness. God alone is perfectly holy, but God calls all people to become holy.

Holocaust Nazi Germany's attempt to kill the entire Jewish race of Europe before and during World War II.

Holy Grail The legendary cup of the Last Supper which contains Christ's blood. According to the legend, anyone who drinks from this cup will live forever.

homophobia Fear of and discrimination against people who are homosexuals.

honesty The refusal to lie, steal, or deceive in any way. Honesty means being sincere and straightforward—both in our words and our behavior.

hope The theological virtue that enables us to trust that God is always working for our good and will someday bring us eternal happiness.

household hazardous waste (HHW) Toxic chemicals whose improper disposal can lead to cancer, respiratory illness, and death, both in humans and in animals. Examples of HHW include used motor oil, antifreeze, house paints, weed killers, insect sprays, pool chemicals, paint strippers, paint thinners, household cleaners, and old car batteries.

huffing Deliberate breathing in of fumes from household products, such as hair spray or lighter fluid, through the mouth.

human A created being with an eternal soul. Humans have the ability to reflect, to reason, and to ask "Why?"

humility The moral virtue that enables us to have healthy self-esteem, to see ourselves as we truly are, and to know our proper place in relation to God and others. Humility is the opposite of pride.

hypocrite An impostor or fake, someone who is not sincere or genuine. Hypocrites tend to say one thing and do another. They do not have integrity.

illiteracy The inability to read or write.

immersion A form of baptism in which the person's whole body or entire head is submerged under water for a brief time.

infusion A form of baptism in which water is poured over the person's head.

integration The blending or uniting of different things into one whole.

integrity Acting according to the values a person holds true. Integrity means being faithful to one's values and beliefs.

intervention A meeting in which friends and family confront a drug user or alcoholic by explaining how they feel and how they are being hurt by the user's behavior. The purpose of an intervention is to get the drug user or alcoholic to face the truth and to seek professional help.

justice A cardinal virtue that is basic to other moral virtues. Justice is the virtue that enables us to know and to do that which is proper, fair, and correct. Justice is a sense of what is right, of what "should" happen.

kindness The gentle, sympathetic, and helpful offering of relief.

kingdom of God A situation of perfect relationships between people. It is the experience of perfect justice, peace, love, joy, and mercy because God is present. Other terms for kingdom of God include "God's reign" and "heaven."

larceny The unlawful taking of personal property that belongs to someone else.

laziness The tendency within a person to be a full-time "couch potato," someone who just wastes time, or takes the easy way out all the time.

love The theological virtue that enables us to worship, praise, and value God above anything or anyone else.

loyalty Faithful allegiance to a person or government.

lust The sin of using another person for our own sexual pleasure.

lying Saying what is false with the intention of deceiving someone who has the right to know the truth.

materialism Placing undue value on having a lot of material possessions; measuring your self-worth by what you possess.

mercy Lenient compassion or forbearance toward an offender. Mercy is an attribute of God. Merciful people are patient with the imperfections and mistakes of others. They forgive and show leniency toward those who hurt them.

moral Involving a choice between ethical goodness and evil. Deciding whether to cheat or study for a test is an example of a moral decision.

moral virtues Virtues that enable us to relate in good ways to other people.

mortal sin A very serious sin that inflicts a "mortal" or deadly wound to one's relationship with God and others. In essence, the relationship is killed.

New Testament The inspired 27 books of the New Covenant, written about Jesus and the faith life of the first Christians.

nonviolence The absence of violence; a peaceful way to deal with conflict.

oil of catechumens Blessed olive or vegetable oil used during baptism as a symbol of the wisdom, strength, and protection from evil that Jesus brings to all Christians.

original sin That which is incomplete and lacking in human nature. The tendency in all humans to be attracted to evil. The church teaches that baptism frees the newly baptized person from original sin.

ozone depletion The unhealthy thinning of the atmospheric layer of ozone needed to protect living creatures from exposure to too much solar ultraviolet radiation.

panhandling Stopping people on the street and begging them for food or money.

paradise Another name for heaven or the kingdom of God. It is the state of being completely in union with God.

pardon Excusing an offense without exacting a penalty.

pastoral letter A letter about theological or moral issues written by a bishop or group of bishops to their church members.

patience A virtue that enables us to be long-suffering and calm in the midst of stress, trials, or provocations.

patriotism Love for and devotion to one's country.

peace Tranquillity; quiet; calm; freedom from disturbance; harmony with others.

penance An action that shows sorrow or repentance for sin.

perseverance A virtue that enables us to keep working toward a goal despite setbacks, mistakes, failures, or discouragement. To persevere means to be persistent and not give up.

phile A type of love in which one person feels a warm, voluntary feeling of attachment, devotion, and tenderness toward another. Examples of *phile* include the love between parents and children, the love between brothers and sisters, and the love between friends.

plagiarism The direct copying of someone else's work and claiming it as your own.

power The ability to act or produce an effect. To have power means to have authority, control, or influence over others—both people and things. Power is force, energy, strength, and might.

premarital sex Sexual intercourse that takes place before the marriage ceremony.

pride The capital sin of valuing oneself too highly and of exaggerating one's own importance. Sinfully proud people are vain, conceited, over-confident, and self-indulgent. People with extreme pride consider themselves to be God's equal.

proactive response Consciously choosing how we will respond to a certain situation or stimulus. We take control of the situation; it does not control us.

procrastination Putting off work until the last possible moment.

prostitution Engaging in sexual intercourse or sex acts in exchange for money.

prudence A cardinal virtue—a virtue that is basic to other moral virtues. Prudence is the ability to be cautious, to weigh the consequences of a decision or action.

public service An action or work that benefits all the people of a particular community.

purity of heart Single-minded focus on goodness and the things of God. Single-heartedness; having motives that are free from moral fault or guilt.

racism Discrimination against others because of their racial identity.

rape Having sexual intercourse with another person without his or her consent.

RCIA The Rite of Christian Initiation of Adults; a process—usually lasting a year or two—in which an adult prepares for the sacraments of initiation and church membership.

reactive response Responding to a certain stimulus without thinking. Reactive responses are like knee-jerk reactions. We don't really think. If we feel anger, we just lash out. The situation or stimulus controls us; we don't control ourselves.

reconciliation The sacrament in which we face ourselves truthfully, express sorrow for any sins we have committed, celebrate God's forgiveness, and are restored to oneness with the Christian community.

responsibility The faithful carrying out of one's obligations and duties. Responsible people can be trusted. They are accountable for their decisions and actions.

retributionist Person who supports the use of capital punishment.

right judgment A gift of the Holy Spirit. Right judgment is the virtue that enables us to make the best choice in a certain situation.

Sabbath The day—from sundown on Friday to sundown on Saturday—when all Jews were required by law to refrain from work and to worship God.

saint A person of good character and holiness who has died and is now with God in heaven.

Satanism Worship of Satan (the devil) and all that is evil.

scrupulous The quality of being painstakingly strict with regard to the law or what is considered right.

Second World Industrialized countries that are presently or were previously under communism (a command economy). The Second World includes China, the Commonwealth of Independent States, and Eastern Europe.

second-hand smoke Smoke from a cigarette or cigar that is inhaled by someone who is not smoking.

self-actualization The state of being fully alive, human, whole, and holy. A state in which all the virtues are integrated into a person's character.

self-discipline Self-control or training. Correction or regulation of oneself for the sake of improvement.

self-esteem A sense of happiness and contentment about who you are as a human being. People with self-esteem consciously appreciate their own worth and importance.

sexism Discrimination against others (usually women) because of their gender.

sexual abuse Unwanted sexual touching or sexual intercourse involving a child. Sexual abuse occurs when someone (usually an adult or someone who is older) kisses, fondles, or has sexual intercourse with a child. Any sexual contact with a child is presumed to be against the child's wishes even if the child does not protest, and is, therefore abusive.

sexuality The way you relate to others as a male or female.

shoplifting Stealing displayed items from a store.

sin An abuse of the freedom God gives to humans so that they are capable of loving. Sin is an offense against God, self, and others.

sin of commission A sinful action; something that is actually done. Lying is an example of a sin of commission.

sin of omission The sinful failure to do something you should have done. Remaining silent instead of telling the truth is an example of a sin of omission.

single-heartedness The virtue that enables us to envision a goal and keep our attentions and energies focused on reaching it. The ability to want just one thing with all our hearts.

slander The sin of deliberately spreading a false story about someone, with the intention of hurting his or her reputation.

sloth A capital sin; the tendency to be lazy.

sniffing Deliberate breathing in of fumes straight from the bottle, from a coated cloth, or by heating them.

solidarity Oneness with others; the recognition that we are all responsible for the welfare of the human family, regardless of national, racial, or economic differences.

spiritual An inner restlessness, searching, and yearning for something more. Usually, spirituality refers to a person's relationship with God.

spiritual works of mercy Acts of kindness and compassion by which we help better the spiritual condition of others. The seven spiritual works of mercy are: counsel the doubtful, instruct the ignorant, admonish the sinner, comfort the sorrowful, forgive injuries, bear wrongs patiently, and pray for the living and the dead.

stealing Taking property that belongs to someone else. Types of stealing include larceny, grand larceny, burglary, forgery, embezzlement, fraud, shoplifting, and swarming.

stewardship The God-given duty to take care of and to protect the earth—all its creatures and natural resources.

swarming Entering a store in a large group and blatantly stealing everything possible.

sweatshop A factory in which workers (in some cases, children) are employed for long hours at low wages and under unhealthy conditions.

synoptic gospels Books in the New Testament that contain a summary, or synopsis, of Jesus' life and that "see with the same eye." The synoptic gospels are Matthew, Mark, and Luke.

terrorism Any act that intends to kill people and destroy property indiscriminately and to create a climate of fear and insecurity.

theological virtues Virtues that enable us to relate to God. The three theological virtues are faith, hope, and love.

Third World Poor, non-industrialized countries, including Southeast Asia, India, most of South America, and most of sub-Saharan Africa.

torture The infliction of great pain or anguish, either physical or psychological.

treason The offense of engaging in acts of war against one's own country, or seeking to give aid to the enemies of one's own country, particularly during time of war.

Trinity The belief that there are three Persons in one God—Father, Son, and Holy Spirit.

union with God A state of eternal happiness, life, and oneness with God.

vandalism The deliberate defacement or destruction of property.

venial sin A less serious sin that hurts or weakens one's relationship with God and others.

vice An habitual and firm disposition to do the morally bad.

virtue An habitual and firm disposition to do the morally good.

war An armed conflict involving one or more governments and causing the death of 1,000 or more people per year.

wholeness The state of being complete and entire. Nothing is lacking.

wisdom A gift of the Holy Spirit. The type of knowing that involves the ability to discern the truth, as well as the best course of action. Other words for wisdom include insight and good sense.

workaholism Addiction to work. Workaholics can't stop working; they feel guilty about resting or taking a vacation. They measure their self-worth in terms of how busy they are or how much they accomplish.

xenophobia Fear and unjust treatment toward newcomers or immigrants.

Index